Greek-Turkish Relations Since 1955

Greek-Turkish Relations Since 1955

Tozun Bahcheli

Westview Press

BOULDER, SAN FRANCISCO, & LONDON

Westview Special Studies in International Relations

Published in 1990 in the United States of America by Westview Press, Inc., 5500 Central Avenue, Boulder, Colorado 80301, and in the United Kingdom by Westview Press, Inc., 13 Brunswick Centre, London WC1N 1AF, England

Library of Congress Cataloging-in-Publication Data
Bahcheli, Tozun.
    Greek-Turkish relations since 1955.
    (Westview special studies in international
relations)
    Includes index.
    1. Greece—Foreign relations—Turkey. 2. Turkey—
Foreign relations—Greece. 3. Greece—Foreign
relations—20th century. 4. Turkey—Foreign
relations—1918–1960. 5. Turkey—Foreign relations—
1960–   . 6. Cyprus—History—20th century.
I. Title. II. Series.
DF787.T8B33 1990   327.4950561   86-32612
ISBN 0-8133-7235-6

Printed and bound in the United States of America

The paper used in this publication meets the requirements of the American National Standard for Permanence of Paper for Printed Library Materials Z39.48-1984.

10   9   8   7   6   5   4   3   2

To Beth, Daniel, and Julia

Contents

Maps

Acknowledgments

This book owes much to the generosity, cheer, and help of many people. I am especially indebted to Professors John Orange, Barry Bartmann, Ozay Mehmet, and Will McKercher as well as John Ibbitson. All of them read the manuscript at least once and made innumerable suggestions for improving it. They are responsible for helping me abide by grammatical rules, fair academic standards, and clarity of expression.

In conducting my research, I have had the pleasure of meeting and obtaining the assistance of many scholars, government officials, and others in Cyprus, Greece, Turkey, the United States, Britain, and Canada. I am very grateful to them all. At the same time, I take full responsibility for the contents of this book.

In northern Cyprus, the late Raif R. Denktash helped make my research more productive and meaningful during the fall of 1985. I have also been assisted by President Rauf R. Denktash, who generously provided documents as well as granted me extended interviews. In addition, I have benefitted in many important respects from the help of the following individuals in northern Cyprus: Oktay Öksüzoglu, Director of Information of the Turkish Republic of Northern Cyprus; The Honourable Necati Ertekün, Legal Adviser to the President; and Saffet Soykal, who readily shared his impressive knowledge of Cypriot affairs.

Among the officials in the south who generously gave of their time as well as provided papers, I want to express my gratitude to the following: the Honourable Glafcos Clerides, the Honourable George Iacovou, the Honourable Andreas Christofides, and Dr. Vassos Lyssarides. I am equally grateful to Drs. Michael Attalides and Kyriacos Markides for sharing their knowledge. As correspondents with long-time familiarity of Cyprus, Tom O'Dwyer and Katherine McIlroy contributed to my appreciation of the Cyprus issue in a special way. Chloe Savvides' help in arranging interviews with a wide range of officials enabled me to use my time efficiently and to meet many responsible and knowledgeable people. Of special note, the hospitality of

Glafcos Constantinides provided a happy reminder of the days before the ravages of communal politics created the present state of affairs in Cyprus.

Also on Cyprus, it was a privilege to meet with James Holger, the Acting Representative of the Secretary-General of the United Nations, as well as with Colonels Dean Wellsman and Robert Mitchell. They contributed substantially to my appreciation of United Nations diplomacy and peace-keeping in Cyprus.

In the course of my research in Greece, I have benefitted from the counsel and expertise of Professors Ted Couloumbis, John Valinakis, Ada Pollis, Paschalis Kitromilides, and in particular, Dr. Thanos Veremis, who worked diligently to ensure that I met everyone with whom I wanted to discuss Greek-Turkish relations. It was thanks to Bruce Clark, the former head of the Reuters Office in Athens, that I acquired a better appreciation of Greek political culture and was able to meet his fellow journalists, including Paul Anastasi, Robert Kaplan, and Haris Bousbourellis.

In Turkey, I was fortunate enough to meet with Ambassadors Riza Türmen and Tugay Ulucevik, who generously gave of their time and provided me with research materials which I needed. I am grateful to Professor Huseyin Pazarci and Dean Mehmet Gönlübol for sharing their expertise on the Aegean issues. I am especially indebted to Professor Mümtaz Soysal for his help in clarifying many issues over a period of several years.

In the course of several visits to Washington, D.C., I met several officials and experts who have substantially contributed to my insight in Greek-Turkish affairs. I am particularly indebted to Dr. Bülent Ali Riza, the Washington Representative of the Turkish Republic of Northern Cyprus, whom I consulted on the chapters dealing with the Cyprus issue. I am also grateful to Dr. Marios Evriviades of the Greek-Cypriot Embassy in Washington, both for providing me with written materials and for enhancing my understanding of the multi-faceted Cyprus dispute. Also in Washington, I have benefitted substantially from discussions of Cyprus and other Greek-Turkish issues with Ellen Laipson, Research Analyst at the Library of Congress. Similarly, I have derived useful insights from discussions of Turkish foreign policy and Turkish-American relations with Dr. George Harris, Director of Analysis for the Near East and South Asia in the Bureau of Intelligence and Research of the Department of State, as well as Alan Makovski, Chief of the Division for Southern Europe, Bureau of Intelligence and Research of the Department of State in Washington, D.C.

My interest in Greek-Turkish affairs took me to some stimulating academic meetings devoted to the subject. The Lehrman Institute's conference on Greek-Turkish relations in May 1986 was especially rewarding because it enabled me to meet some of the foremost authorities on the subject. I gratefully acknowledge the information and insights which the following participants shared with me: Mehmet Ali Birand, Mario Modiano, Alexis Alexandris, Van Coufoudakis, and Ambassador Monteagle Stearns.

In Britain, it has been an asset for me to call upon Dr. Peter Loizos of the London School of Economics for information and ideas. Similarly, I have received much wisdom and information from Professor Paul Rahe of the University of Tulsa, Professor Dimitri Kitsikis of the University of Ottawa, and John Bradbury of the International Civil Aviation Organization in Montreal. For exceptional help with library resources, I am indebted to George Robinson of The University of Western Ontario.

I would like to thank the International Institute of Strategic Studies in London for permission to reproduce Maps 3, 4, and 5 of the Aegean Sea. I have taken the liberty of modifying Map 3 by inserting the "search and rescue" line proposed by the Turkish Foreign Ministry in 1988. I am grateful for the professionalism and meticulous care of Robert Turner, who prepared the maps specially for this publication. In the preparation of this script, I have been very fortunate to count on the diligence and expertise of Jane Pierce and Cathy Mendler.

I am grateful to the Social Science and Research Council of Canada and King's College for providing me with research grants for this book. It is my pleasant duty to thank Barbara Ellington of Westview Press for encouraging the project from the beginning.

Finally, I take this opportunity to thank my wife Beth for her patience, forbearance, and her many sacrifices while I laboured to prepare this book.

Tozun Bahcheli

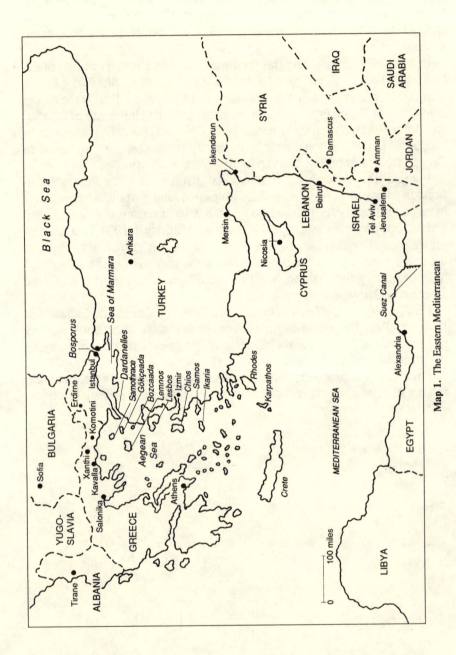

Map 1. The Eastern Mediterranean

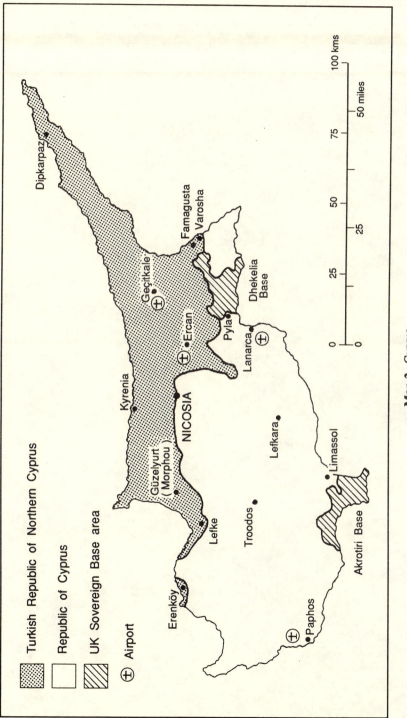

Map 2. Cyprus

Turkish Republic of Northern Cyprus

Republic of Cyprus

UK Sovereign Base area

⊕ Airport

Dipkarpaz

Kyrenia

Güzelyurt (Morphou)

Geçitkale

Famagusta

Varosha

Erenköy

Lefke

NICOSIA

Ercan

Dhekelia Base

Troodos

Lefkara

Lanarca

Pyla

Limassol

Akrotiri Base

Paphos

0   25   50   75   100 kms

0   25   50 miles

Introduction

The unhappy historical memories that have influenced the relationship of contemporary Greeks and Turks owe an obvious debt to their Ottoman past, as well to more recent conflicts. Past memories of injustices, grievances, and mistrust have provided a crucial context for modern Greek-Turkish disputes.

The troubled history of the two nations is consequently reflected at the popular level in the stereotyping one can find in contemporary literature and history books, as well as in popular aphorisms. Greeks tend to view Turks as crude and barbaric, and Greek history books recall the suffering of their people under the oppressive Turks during Ottoman rule. Whereas Turks and Turkey feature quite prominently in Greek public life, Greeks are usually of only marginal concern for Turks. Nonetheless, popular Turkish images of Greeks reflect past resentments and bitterness. Greeks are not considered trustworthy and are accused of bearing an ancient enmity toward the Turks and, thus are seen to be liable to hit Turkey at any moment of weakness. Further, Turks think of Greeks as being petulant, liable to run for help from others whenever their follies get them in trouble with the Turks.

As much as earlier conflicts always cast a shadow on contemporary relationships, Greeks and Turks have shown that they are not entirely prisoners of past memories. A history of conflict has not ruled out periods of peace and reconciliation, nor even of fairly close and interdependent relations. After all, it was only eight years after their last war, fought with great ferocity and bitterness, that Greece and Turkey began a period of détente.

Greek-Turkish reconciliation was introduced in 1930 by their famous leaders, Atatürk of Turkey, and Venizelos of Greece, much before their own people were ready to bury the hatchet. Both Venizelos and Atatürk had come to the conclusion that a policy based on confrontation and indefinite enmity would not advance their respective national interests. At the same time, both countries viewed the ambitions of neighbouring Bulgaria and the more distant Italy as posing more immediate threats to their security interests.

The Greek-Turkish détente of Atatürk and Venizelos yielded agreements in the political, economic, and security spheres and weathered occasional irritants. In the post-Second World War era, the prospects for closer relations between the two neighbours were further enhanced when they opted to join the Western alliance system and simultaneously became NATO members in 1952.

It was in the midst of these auspicious developments that Cyprus became an arena where Greek and Turkish interests clashed, beginning in the mid-1950s. As the dispute over the island persisted and intensified, previous suspicions were reawakened and old wounds inflamed. Before long, détente gave way to tension and conflict. Relations between the two countries seriously deteriorated in the aftermath of the collapse of the partnership government of the Greek and Turkish communities in Cyprus in 1963. In particular, Turkey's military intervention in Cyprus, in response to the Ioannidis junta's coup in July 1974, brought the two states' relations to their lowest ebb. In the meantime, additional disputes over the continental shelf and related issues of jurisdiction in the Aegean, as well as other long-standing problems over the treatment of each other's minorities, caused further strains in Greek-Turkish relations.

This book examines the unravelling of the Greek-Turkish détente and subsequent three decades of strained relations that followed the Cyprus conflict emerging in 1955. The Cyprus issue was pivotal in the deterioration of contemporary Greek-Turkish relations. Greece's policy of support for Enosis and Turkey's policy of preventing that goal laid the basis for the Greek-Turkish conflict. The issue has dominated and damaged Greek-Turkish relations more than any other since the post-Second World War era. Thus, I have devoted more than one-half of this book to the study of the Cyprus issue.

The existence of the Greek and Turkish communities on the island has made Greece and Turkey view their own interests in Cyprus as a national imperative; hence, the strong motivation for their support of their island kinsmen. At the same time, the national interests of Athens and Ankara have not always coincided with those of their respective communities.

Both Greece and Turkey have been capable of bringing substantial influence to bear on their respective communities and of shaping the destiny of Cyprus, as witnessed by the Ioannidis regime's coup and Turkey's military intervention of 1974. However, it is erroneous to conclude, as some writers have done, that Greece or Turkey or other external powers such as the United States have been wholly or even largely responsible for far-reaching developments in Cyprus.

In his study of the Cyprus dispute, Kyriacos Markides has advanced the thesis that "no significant change occurred in Cypriot society that was not the result of external impacts from the beginning of the Mycenian migrations in 1400 B.C. to the 1974 coup and Turkish invasion."[1] Similarly, Christopher Hitchens has argued that "the Turkish invasion of 1974 was not the climax of the struggle for the union of Cyprus by Greece, but the outcome of a careless and arrogant series of policies over which Cypriots had little or no control."[2]

This book challenges the validity of this prevalent thesis by arguing that the Cypriot communities often took initiatives and determined the course of events on the island and that their role has been underestimated. For example, the responsibility for the failure of the partnership government of the Cyprus Republic during the crucial period 1960-1963 does not rest on Greece and Turkey. Rather, it can be explained by the inability of the two communities to reach a consensus on fundamental matters and the desire of the Greek-Cypriot leadership to revive the Enosis policy. Greek and Turkish governments have often reacted to Cyprus developments rather than initiated them.

In examining Greek-Turkish disputes, I use a historical approach. The brief summary offered in Chapter One is intended to familiarize the reader with the antecedents of contemporary Greek-Turkish disputes and the provisions of the Treaty of Lausanne (1923), which established a balance of power between the two states after their last war.

Chapter Two focuses on Cyprus and examines two major levels of relationships during the colonial era: that between the island communities, thus furnishing the reader with background information on the domestic aspects of the Cyprus dispute, and that of Greece and Turkey and their policies and involvement in Cyprus before the emergence of the EOKA movement in the mid-1950s.

The next two chapters on Cyprus trace the post-war development of Greek and Turkish policies and involvement in the island during the various stages of the dispute, from the beginning of the Enosis struggle to the Greek coup and Turkish intervention of 1974 and beyond. This survey analyzes the interaction between Ankara and Athens and their respective communities in the island and how these interactions influenced the conduct of the mainland governments. It also examines other inputs on Greece and Turkey's Cyprus policies by considering the role of actors with important interests in Cyprus, such as NATO, the United States, Britain, the Soviet Union, and the United Nations.

Greece and Turkey's relations with one another, including their disputes, contain elements of the old and the new. This is true not only for Cyprus but also for their Aegean disputes, the subject of Chapter Five. For, although the basis of some of the major disagreements in the Aegean are found in relatively new concepts such as sovereign rights over the continental shelf and conflicting interpretations of recently developed international laws, a student of Greek-Turkish history will recognize that at the heart of many of these issues is the perennial problem of mistrust: fear that one would alter the strategic balance or gain vital resources at the other's expense.

In dealing with the Aegean issue, I compare the Greek and Turkish cases on the various issue areas. Principally, these involve sovereign rights in the continental shelf, limits of the territorial sea, sovereignty over air-space and air traffic control zones in the Aegean, and the question of the remilitarization of the eastern Aegean islands. In the issues that involve the drawing of maritime boundaries, Greece has adopted a legalistic position in the belief that her case will be vindicated by international law and practice. Turkey, on the other hand, has viewed the Aegean issues in a wider political context and advocated the principle of equity.

As long as Greece and Turkey's relations with one another were reasonably harmonious, the treatment of their respective minorities was relatively benign. However, once the Cyprus issue aroused passions and each sought ways and means of pressuring the other, repressive measures on the minorities were sanctioned, forcing many to emigrate. Chapter 6 considers the Greek and Turkish grievances concerning the treatment of their respective communities in each other's country (and the Greek Orthodox Patriarchate in Istanbul) in order to ascertain the bases of these complaints. As occasional irritants, the minority issues have contributed to the Greek-Turkish estrangement. However, they have been of secondary importance when viewed in the context of the totality of Greek-Turkish disputes.

Since the mid-1950s, the Cyprus issue has been instrumental in undoing the gains of the previous one-quarter century of détente between Greece and Turkey and reviving past suspicions and resentments. Although the detailed examination of the Cyprus and the Aegean disputes indicates fundamental differences of approach to issues involving vital interests, the future prospects of Greek-Turkish relations need not be discouraging. This will be addressed in the short concluding section of the book, which will contain an appreciation of opportunities for the recovery of détente between the two neighbours.

While many books (which also consider the role of Greece and Turkey) have appeared on the Cyprus conflict, there has been a lack of comprehensive studies in English of the full range of contemporary Greek-Turkish disputes. This study aspires to fill that gap.

Notes

1. Kyriacos Markides, *The Rise and Fall of the Cyprus Republic*, New Haven: Yale University Press, 1977, p. 177.

2. Christopher Hitchens, *Cyprus*, London: Quartet Books, 1984, p. 10.

Burying the Hatchet:
The Lausanne Settlement
and Greek-Turkish Détente to 1950

The troubled relations of Greece and Turkey in recent decades are the legacy of their historical conflicts dating from Byzantine and Ottoman times. Some writers trace the historical rivalry of Greeks and Turks as far back as 1071 when Selçuk Sultan Alparslan defeated Byzantine Emperor Diogenes' soldiers in the battle of Malazgirt, thus starting the Turkish conquest of Asia Minor. However, it was the Ottoman Turks' capture of the Byzantine capital of Constantinople in 1453, which ushered in four centuries of Ottoman Turkish rule over Greeks, that is more commonly cited as an historical turning point.

The Making of Modern Greece

While the Turkish victory made Greeks the subject peoples of the Ottoman Empire, they enjoyed a considerable measure of autonomy in the prerogatives and obligations of the *millet* system. This system was a form of communal self-government which helped the Ottoman rulers to govern and to retain the loyalty of their subjects in a multi-ethnic, non-national state.

In this context, the Greek Orthodox Patriarch of Istanbul was granted special privileges and served both as the spiritual and temporal ruler of the empire's Greek Orthodox subjects. By the end of the eighteenth century, the Patriarch exercised his authority over 13,000,000 Christians, who comprised one-quarter of all the Ottoman Empire's subjects.[1] In his duties, the head of the Greek Orthodox Church was assisted by many educated and wealthy Greeks who, in many instances, also attained positions of high office in the Ottoman bureaucracy as ambassadors and administrators. Some among this administrative aristocracy, known as the *Phanariots*, rose to the highest ranks of Ottoman government to become *Dragoman* (chief interpreter) or *Vezir* (chief minister). According to Kitsikis, a Greek historian of the Ottoman Empire, the *millet* system of self-rule elevated Greeks to the status of "partners" of the Ottoman Empire.[2]

After the French Revolution, however, the religious and cultural autonomy exercised by the individual *millets* created the basis of separatist ethnonationalism. Though the Greeks enjoyed cultural and civil autonomy comparable to other ethnic communities in the empire, this did little to assuage their sense of subjugation and alienation, especially after the advent of nationalism in Ottoman lands. Indeed, these very distinctions of status promoted sensibilities of separateness and victimization. The Greeks became the first of the Ottoman Empire's European peoples to achieve national independence.

With considerable external help, the Greeks succeeded in establishing an independent state in 1830 after an eight-year struggle. However, the settlement that defined the boundaries of the new state left most Greeks still living under Ottoman rule. Consequently, from the earliest days of independence, Greek nationalists dreamt of the eventual liberation of the Greeks who remained under the Ottomans. But Greek interests were not confined to rescuing their kith and kin. Far more exciting was the prospect of recreating the Byzantine Empire under Greek sovereignty. These two ambitions constituted the *Megali Idea* (Great Idea). In his perceptive analysis, Michael L. Smith described Greece's national aspiration in these terms:

> The Great Idea ... in the mid-nineteenth century came to contain at least three different strands. Strictly interpreted, it was the romantic dream of revival of the Byzantine-Greek Empire centred on Constantinople. Less strictly it was the aspiration for Greek cultural and economic dominance within the Ottoman Empire, leading to its gradual subversion from within by a natural process which need not entail a violent clash between the rival Greek and Turkish nations. Thirdly, the Idea could be interpreted in terms of the modern nation state, as the progressive redemption of the Greek irredenta by their incorporation in the Greek kingdom, which entailed a head-on clash with the Ottoman Empire. Though all these conceptions survived into the twentieth century, it was the third which prevailed.[3]

In spite of the Ottoman Empire's declining fortunes during the nineteenth century, a process that had started more than a century earlier, the resources and armies of the small Greek state were hardly a match for those of the Ottoman government. This is why, despite periodic agitation by Greek nationalists in Thessaly and Crete aimed at severing Ottoman rule, Greece did not make war against the Turks for several decades. Notwithstanding their desire to expand, the realities of power during the nineteenth century obliged the leaders of Greece to accept piecemeal additions to the territories under their control. However, the ambitions of the Great Powers to diminish Ottoman power, and the agitation of neighbouring Balkan nationalities for independence, created other possibilities.

The first addition of territory to the Greek state occurred not by taking up arms against the Turks but by persuading Britain to cede the Ionian islands in 1864. The next addition of territory occurred in 1881 when Greece was rewarded for her neutrality during the Russo-Turkish War of 1877-1878. The Great Powers gave her much of fertile Thessaly and the district of Arta in Epirus.

Of the remaining "unredeemed" territories with Greek majorities, Crete was almost regularly in turmoil, with the majority of its population aspiring to join Greece. The Greek government helped the Cretans with arms and volunteers, and in 1897 sought to force the Sultan's hand by declaring war. This first major war by the Greek state against the Ottomans ended in total victory for the Sultan's forces. But the Great Powers intervened to spare Greece any loss of territory; indeed, Greece became a beneficiary so far as Crete was concerned because the Powers forced the Ottoman government to give the island an autonomous status, with Prince George of the Greek royal family as its governor.

Greece had to wait for several more years before exercising sovereignty over Crete. However, the prospects for the *Megali Idea* were enhanced with the rise to power of Eleftherios Venizelos, a gifted politician from Crete. After assuming power in 1910, Venizelos set out in earnest to realize the vision of creating a Greater Greece. He forged an alliance with neighbouring Bulgaria, Serbia, and Montenegro as a prelude to joint military action against the Ottoman Turks in 1912. The timing of the war coincided with the weakening of the Turks during the 1911-1912 war with Italy over Libya, and the Albanian revolt. The defeat of the Turkish forces in what has been called the first Balkan War paved the way for Greece to extend her control over substantial territories, namely southern Macedonia (which contained the coveted port city of Salonika), southern Epirus, and virtually all of the Aegean islands.

According to Stephens, Turkish resentment against Greek territorial gains

> was [the] strongest over Greece's formal annexation of Crete and occupation of the Aegean islands, especially Chios and Mitylene. These two large islands lie only a few miles off the coast of Western Anatolia and cover the approaches to the port of Smyrna (Izmir). The Turks feared they might be used as a base to attack Asia Minor as indeed happened six years later.[4]

For the Turks, the humiliation felt over the territorial losses to the Greeks was compounded by the problem of waves of Muslim-Turkish refugees from the captured territories who poured into Istanbul and the surrounding area. It is worth noting that the dislocation and forced movement of entire communities of Turks and Greeks started well before the better-known larger exodus that occurred during and after the Greek invasion of Anatolia and the Turkish War of Independence (1919-1922). According to figures of the Ottoman Ministry of Refugees, as cited by Arnold Toynbee, 297,918 Muslims became refugees as a result of the loss of Turkish territories during the Balkan Wars[5]; of these refugees, 122,655 came from the territories captured by Greece. This upheaval prompted the Turkish authorities to persecute and expel several Greek communities in western Anatolia.[6] According to Stephens "some 30,000 Greeks were deported or driven from their homes on the coasts of Thrace and Anatolia. The Turkish authorities claimed that their jobs and homes were needed for the Moslem refugees who were pouring from Macedonia." [7]

Even before the outbreak of the Balkan Wars and the accompanying refugee issues, the forces of change in the Ottoman Empire brought about by the Young Turk Revolution accentuated Greek-Turkish differences and increased animosities. "The Young Turk revolution by its introduction of parliament and constitution awoke feelings and hopes among the Christians — visions of becoming 'co-governors' of the Empire, in Ion Dragoumis's phrase — which were soon dangerously frustrated by the Young Turks' policy of 'Ottomanization' of the minorities."[8]

As the fortunes of the Ottoman Empire waned at the dawn of the First World War, Greece appeared resurgent and the fulfillment of the *Megali Idea* looked to be within its grasp. Anatolian Greeks identified with the grand aspiration of their brethren in Greece to control western Anatolia. Consequently, they were viewed as a disloyal element by the Turks who believed that they would act as a "fifth column" for Greece — as indeed they did during the Greek invasion of 1919-1922.

It is worth noting that Greeks were the majority in all the territories that Greece incorporated during the period of its expansion from the beginning of Greek independence to the conclusion of the Balkan Wars (1912-1913). But in the Anatolian territories and Istanbul which the Greek nationalists coveted, the Greeks were a minority. According to the Ottoman census of 1911-1912 as presented by Justin McCarthy, there were 1,254,333 Greeks in Anatolia as compared with over 14,000,000 Muslims, the great majority of whom were Turks.[9] Even in areas of their greatest concentration in Anatolia, Greeks were heavily outnumbered by Turks and others. According to the Ottoman census figures for 1895 provided by Stanford Shaw, for example, there were 161,867 Greeks in Istanbul which represented 18 percent of the population; according to the same source, there were 229,598 Greeks in Aydin province (15.5 percent) and 288,968 in Edirne (29.3 percent).[10]

These demographic realities were downplayed by the Greek leaders who were seized by the mission of reviving Hellenism in Asia Minor. It is worth recalling that its victories during the Balkan Wars had enabled Greece to double its territory to 550,000 square miles, and to increase its population from 2,600,000 to 4,363,000. Referring to the Greek gains, Kenneth Young stated that "all of these were to stimulate future appetites, just as the comparatively easy regaining of Macedonia and Epirus encouraged elated expectations of a return to western Anatolia and Constantinople itself."[11]

Venizelos, the architect of the Balkan victories, "was gripped by a false but seductive determinist theory of the rising power of Greece and the declining power of Turkey, a process which must end with the total dissolution of the Ottoman state."[12] He hoped to dislodge the Turks from western Anatolia and Istanbul by striking them at a time of weakness, as he had done in 1912, and was confident that he could secure the help of the European powers in realizing his mission. Greece's opportunity arrived in 1914, when the Young Turk Government committed the Ottoman Empire to war on Germany's side. With the exception of a few victories such as at Gallipoli where the Turks were led by their future leader Mustafa Kemal (later named Atatürk), Turkish armies were forced to retreat on all fronts and the Sultan's government sued for peace. Heavy Turkish losses and war-weariness in what remained of the Sultan's Empire had created a yearning for peace. But the terms of the Sèvres Treaty of 1920 (which incorporated provisions of four secret agreements concluded among the Allies during the war) were so severe and humiliating for the Turks as to provoke an angry nationalist reaction, and yet another war to redress its terms.

Under the terms of the Sèvres Treaty, the Ottoman Empire was to be reduced to a small state in central Anatolia. The Greeks were to be one of the major beneficiaries of the carving up of Anatolia. Venizelos' vigorous diplomatic efforts and service to the Allied war effort yielded rich rewards. The Treaty allocated to Greece eastern Thrace, as well as the strategically important islands of Gökçeada (Imbros) and Bozcaada (Tenedos), which together command the entrance to the Dardanelles. This was unpalatable enough for the Turks, but even more damnable to them was the Allied decision to let Greece administer Izmir, together with a substantial hinterland in western Anatolia, for five years; at the end of the five-year period, the people of the area would decide in a plebiscite whether or not to join with Greece.

Other terms of the Treaty of Sèvres were equally severe for the Turks. Under American mandate, an independent Armenian Republic and an autonomous Kurdistan were to be set up in the east and southern Anatolia. In addition, the special concessions to European traders called *Capitulations*, which were a source of bitter resentment for the Turks for many decades, were to be further extended. Furthermore, France and Italy were allocated large zones of influence in Anatolia.

There was, however, one crucial omission in the Treaty of Sèvres: "how it was to be enforced."[13] In fact, the treaty was never ratified. "The Turks had resigned themselves to accept a period of stringent allied controls and the loss of the non-Turkish portions of their empire. They were not prepared to tolerate the loss of parts of the Anatolian heartlands."[14] They were especially outraged when the Greek army landed in Izmir, in 1919, under the escort of British, French, and American naval vessels. By provoking the nationalist feelings of the Turks, the landing of Greek troops "gave a new and decisive impetus to the still uncertain movement of national resistance led by Kemal which other factors also encouraged: the growing disunity of the allies, their inability effectively to disarm Turkish forces in central Anatolia, and the support of Bolshevik Russia."[15]

While Turkish diplomacy capitalized on the divisions within Allied ranks, and negotiated French and Italian withdrawals from Anatolia, Kemal's troops prepared to check the Greek forces. In the ensuing fierce and bitter battles, the Greek armies were repulsed and decisively defeated. This defeat during the Turkish War of Independence (1919-1922) put the *Megali Idea* to rest until the 1950s when it was revived (at least, in Turkish eyes) through the quest for the union of Cyprus with Greece. Turkish nationalists re-asserted their control over Anatolia and eastern Thrace, and established a Turkish Republic in 1923 after abolishing the Sultanate.

The Lausanne Settlement (1923)

Greece's European Allies were unable or unwilling to save her from disaster during the invasion of Anatolia. However, at the peace conference in Lausanne, which began in November 1922, they stood by Greece and sought to mitigate her defeat by Turkey. For example, the Allies spared Greece from paying war reparations by rejecting Turkish demands for such compensation. British representative Lord Curzon, in particular, played an active role in resisting Turkish demands and scaling down Turkish gains. Nonetheless, Ismet Inönü, Turkey's representative at Lausanne and Kemal's future successor, proved a tough negotiator and realized most of his government's objectives. As for the Greeks, they were represented by Eleftherios Venizelos, the old protagonist of *Megali Idea*, who displayed considerable diplomatic skill and realism at the conference.

In Lausanne, Turkey's boundary with Greece was set at the Maritsa River which separates western and eastern Thrace. Greece retained her sovereignty over the Aegean islands except for Gökçeada and Bozcaada; these islands, which guard the entrance to the Straits, were restored to Turkey. Turkish security concerns were also a factor in the decision to demilitarize the islands of Mytilene, Chios, Samos, and Ikaria. Turkey also tried but failed to regain the Dodecanese islands, located off her southwestern coast, which Italy had seized from the Ottoman Empire during its 1911-1912 war. The conference turned down both Turkish and Greek claims, and instead consented to continued Italian control over the islands. Inönü also tried unsuccessfully to secure an Italian commitment not to relinquish the islands to Greece in the future.[16]

While the Italians retained their hold of the Dodecanese, the British held on to Cyprus. Britain had been granted the administration of the island in 1878 by the Sultan's government in return for helping check Russia's expansionist ambitions. Britain annexed the island in 1914 upon the Ottoman Empire's entry into the war on Germany's side. While it was clear that Turkey would resist any Greek claims on the island, Ankara agreed to renounce its sovereign rights in favour of Britain. Turkish leaders were prepared to do so in spite of Turkish-Cypriot petitions to Ankara to press for the island's return to Turkey.

Given Britain's wish to continue to rule Cyprus, Greece was not well placed to mount a serious claim. For the Greeks, "on Cyprus the only satisfaction was that the Turks formally renounced their sovereignty to Britain."[17] Any revival of Greek claims to Cyprus could wait for the future, especially since other issues, primarily the resettlement of refugees, demanded more immediate attention.

Aside from the task of determining issues of sovereign control over disputed territories, the most difficult issue that the Lausanne conference addressed was that of the Greek and Turkish minorities and their exchange. Greece's irredentist claims to Thrace and western Anatolia had been based, at least partly, on the existence of substantial Greek communities there. The bulk of the Greeks of Anatolia had shared the aspiration of their brethren on the mainland for Greece to extend control into Anatolia and welcomed the Greek army as liberators; many of them collaborated with the Greek occupation forces against the Turks. When Greek forces retreated in defeat, so did most of the Anatolian Greeks. In order to eliminate future irredentist Greek claims on Turkish territory, the Kemalist government resolved not to allow the departed Greeks to return. Greek proposals for a voluntary exchange of minority populations were rejected by the Turks. Ultimately, the agreement reached by both sides at Lausanne provided for the compulsory exchange of the Greeks of Anatolia and the Turks of Greece, with two exceptions — the Greeks of Istanbul who numbered about 100,000, and the Turks of Western Thrace in Greece who numbered about 124,000.[18] Since most Greeks had already left before or with the evacuated Greek troops in 1922, the number of Greeks who were transferred to Greece from Turkey after 1923, in accordance with the Lausanne agreement, amounted to

188,000. During the period of the formal exchange, 388,000 Turks left Greece for Turkey.[19] The Lausanne Treaty included several clauses concerning the rights and protection of these "non-exchangeable" minorities.[20]

The compulsory exchange of minority populations, which was unprecedented in its scale, was a radical and painful solution for those involved; entire communities were uprooted from the environment in which their forebears had lived for centuries. On the other hand, the exchange removed what historically had been an important source of friction, even though the treatment of the small unexchanged minorities in Istanbul and Western Thrace did cause irritations in the future. In addition, the exchange of minorities helped to create more homogeneous national populations in Greece and Turkey. This was particularly important for Atatürk, keen as he was to create a united Turkish nation-state in Anatolia to replace the destroyed multinational Ottoman Empire. Furthermore, Atatürk's government actually encouraged Turks from other territories (including Cyprus) to settle in Turkey to help repopulate Anatolia and to relieve manpower shortages. Greece's settlement of the majority of refugees in Macedonia ensured a substantial Greek majority there for the first time in many decades.

One of the issues over which the Greek and Turkish representatives clashed at Lausanne was over the institution of the Patriarchate. During the period of Turkish defeat and despair, the Patriarchate and Istanbul's Greek community had supported the Athens government in the cause of the *Megali Idea*. In 1919, even when the Sultan's government was still in office, Greek Orthodox churches issued a declaration calling for "union with Greece." The Patriarch petitioned the Allied powers to support the Greek cause. Money and volunteers were sent to aid the Greek army fighting Turkish forces in central Anatolia. He "assumed unilaterally complete sovereignty over the (Greek) community. From March 1919 onwards, the Phanar (Patriarchate) refused to communicate directly with the Sublime Porte and the Greeks were urged to abstain from municipal, communal, or general elections."[21] The idea of tolerating such a disloyal and compromised institution was unpalatable to the new Turkish leaders. In any case, they had decided to remove the Caliphate, the Patriarchate's Islamic counterpart.

At Lausanne, however, the Allies (except for Italy) pressured Turkey to allow the Greek-Orthodox Patriarchate to stay. Curzon argued that if the Patriarchate was removed from Istanbul "a shock would be delivered to the conscience of the whole civilized world."[22] Others among the Allies were concerned that the Russian Orthodox Church might assume greater influence if the Istanbul Patriarchate were to be expelled. Venizelos tried to win Turkish agreement by offering to help retire Patriarch Meletios IV, whose anti-Turkish activities had been a source of great aggravation for Turkey's leadership. Ultimately, the Turks consented to the Patriarch's continued presence in Istanbul provided that he would confine himself to purely religious matters.

Post-Lausanne Relations
and Developing Greek-Turkish Détente, 1924-1954

The settlement reached at Lausanne laid the foundations for peaceful relations between Greece and Turkey for many years to come. Exhausted by many years of war, both countries faced enormous problems of domestic reconstruction. However, the memories of their bitter struggle did not recede quickly. A number of irritants emerged to sour relations in the years immediately after Lausanne. For example, each routinely accused the other of maltreating its minorities during the mid-1920s. Relations became dangerously tense when, during his brief dictatorship, General Pangalos of Greece threatened war and contemplated an attack on Turkish Thrace. As well, there was a bitter quarrel over the election of Constantine Araboglu as Patriarch in December 1924. Turkey disqualified the Patriarch-elect on the grounds that he was an "exchangeable" Greek. Greece's appeal to the League of Nations in 1925 did not resolve the issue, but subsequent conciliatory gestures by the Turkish government toward the Patriarchate, and the election of a new Patriarch, facilitated a *modus vivendi*. A major factor in the development of eventual détente between Greece and Turkey, which gained ground in the late 1920s, was a growing perception of common defense interests. While Greece and Turkey eyed each other warily after 1923, each also had serious concerns about Bulgaria's ambitions to gain access to the Aegean, as well as about Mussolini's intentions in the region.

Moreover, in spite of continuing popular xenophobia in both countries, Venizelos and Atatürk were committed to reconciliation. Atatürk had predicted the re-establishment of friendly relations between Greece and Turkey at the end of the Turkish-Greek War in Anatolia when he stated: "I could never myself keep on hating a nation for the mistakes of their government... and toward the Greeks I feel the same. I am confident that we shall soon be great friends."[23]

Venizelos' authority and commitment were as significant. As Psomiades noted:

the immense popularity of Venizelos, especially among the refugees, enabled the Greek statesman to impose his will on the nation and to conclude an unpopular understanding with Turkey... The refugees whose interests were to be sacrificed to the détente, supported Venizelos only because he was their idol. Possibly, no other man in Greece at the time could have prevented them from opposing and destroying such an agreement.[24]

In 1930, Greece and Turkey signed an agreement that settled all remaining disputes arising from the exchange of populations and the value of properties left behind. Although the terms of the agreement were criticized in Greece as too favourable to Turkey, Venizelos attached a high priority to a policy of reconciliation with the Turks. Earlier in the year, Venizelos had resisted arguments for increasing the defence budget to match the naval superiority that Turkey attained with her modernization of the reconstructed famous battleship *Yavuz*. He justified his decision not only by citing the need for austerity in view of the adverse economic conditions in Greece but by stressing the importance of developing a relationship of trust with Turkey.

Following these positive developments, Greek and Turkish leaders paid visits to each other's countries and provided momentum to the process of détente. During his visit to Turkey, Venizelos signed a Treaty of Neutrality, Conciliation, and Arbitration, as well as a protocol providing for parity of naval armaments. While in Ankara, Venizelos reportedly declared that his presence there "signified the end of a conflict between Greece and Turkey which had lasted for ten centuries."[25] Atatürk responded with a symbolic gesture by ordering that Ayasofya (Santa Sofia) be converted into a museum. This great Byzantine cathedral had been turned into a mosque after the Ottoman Turks had captured Istanbul in 1453. Both leaders went so far as to discuss, in general terms, the possibility of some form of union between Greece and Turkey.[26]

Greece and Turkey reached a number of additional agreements in the aftermath of Venizelos' visit and Turkish Premier Inönü's return trip to Athens during 1931. In September 1933, the two countries signed a Friendship Pact guaranteeing the inviolability of their borders and committing them to consult each other on matters of common interest. In an effusive statement made during a brief visit to Athens in November 1933, Turkish Foreign Minister Aras declared that Greece and Turkey "have almost become one country."[27] During the following year, the two countries took another step in collaboration when they joined the Balkan Entente in 1934 with Yugoslavia and Rumania.

By joining the Balkan Entente, the Greeks and Turks hoped to discourage anticipated pressures from Italy and Germany. However, neither this nor subsequent bilateral Greek-Turkish agreements deterred Italy and Germany from pursuing their ambitions to penetrate and control the Balkans. In any case, Greece and Turkey were unprepared to undertake obligations that might involve them in war with a great power. Accordingly, when German troops occupied Greece in 1941 (following the unsuccessful Italian invasion in October 1940), Turkey remained neutral.

Turkey's decision to stay neutral during the Second World War was a source of aggravation to Greece. Greek leaders felt that Turkey was under an obligation to come to Greece's aid under the terms of the Balkan Entente and subsequent Turkish assurances to help Greece.[28]

Other irritants clouded the Greek-Turkish entente during the war years. The Ankara Government did not appoint an ambassador to the Greek government established in Crete in 1941 and waited until the summer to appoint an ambassador to the Greek government-in-exile based in Cairo. However, much more worrisome for the Greeks was the possibility that Turkey might take over the Dodecanese islands as a reward for entering the war either on the side of Germany or the Allies.

In fact, the British had offered the Italian-ruled Dodecanese as a reward to Turkey in October 1940 if she declared war on Italy in the event of an Italian attack on Greece.[29] Similarly, the German Ambassador Papen advised his government to offer some of the Dodecanese as an inducement for Ankara to sign an alliance with his government.[30] Turkey, however, was determined to remain neutral through the war and declined all offers. Nonetheless, Greece remained suspicious that the Turks harboured designs over these primarily Greek-inhabited islands. Accordingly, the Turkish government sought to allay the Greek government's concerns by informing it on two occasions during 1943 that it would not object to the annexation of the Dodecanese by Greece "so long as the Greek government remained on friendly terms with Turkey."[31] Turkey, in fact, did not oppose Greece's incorporation of the Dodecanese in 1947, although in subsequent years when Greek-Turkish relations deteriorated over the Cyprus issue, many Turks regretted their government's failure to lay claim to these islands.

One other issue strained Greek-Turkish relations during the Second World War: Turkey's imposition of an emergency capital levy, called *varlık vergisi*, in November 1942. The Turkish government justified the tax on the grounds that it needed to raise revenue to finance Turkey's growing military expenditures. "Concurrently, it was expected to tax the abnormally high profits amassed by a portion of the business community in Turkey since the outbreak of the Second World War and to help curb the galloping infla-tion."[32] However, Greeks and members of other minorities bitterly com-plained that they were assessed higher levies than Turks, and the Greek government lodged protests to Ankara. In view of the adverse reaction to the tax, the Turkish government removed it a year after its imposition.

Greek resentment caused by the *varlık* tax and Turkish neutrality were mitigated, to some extent, by several acts of Turkish friendship and support in the course of the Second World War. When Greece was attacked by Italy in 1940, hundreds of volunteers were organized from among the Greek community of Istanbul and sent to fight in Greece's defence, with the approval of the Turkish authorities. During 1941-1942, when Greece was under German occupation and experienced widespread starvation, Turkey dispatched food across the Aegean, earning the gratitude of the Greek public. Furthermore, the Turkish Government allowed Allied support of Greek guerillas from her territory,[33] and permitted "escapees from Greece, including military personnel, to pass through Turkish territory and reach the Allied forces in Egypt. Thus, soon after the German occupation of Greece, for example, the Greek warship *Adrias* found refuge in Turkish territorial waters before reaching the Allied-held North Africa."[34]

Not only did the détente launched by Atatürk and Venizelos in the aftermath of Lausanne survive the suspicions and irritants experienced during the Second World War; in its aftermath, identical Greek and Turkish security concerns vis-a-vis the Soviet Union prompted them to establish closer ties with the West. Both states became beneficiaries of the Truman Doctrine of 1947, and both sent contingents to fight in Korea. Subsequently, when they simultaneously became member states of NATO in 1952, Greek and Turkish political and military collaboration became routine and institutionalized. In 1953, the two neighbours joined Yugoslavia to sign a Treaty of Friendship and Assistance, and all three formed the short-lived Balkan Pact a year later.

The warming trend in Greek-Turkish relations was reflected in the statement by Turkish President Celal Bayar during a state visit to Greece in January 1954, when he described Greek-Turkish co-operation as "the best example of how two countries who mistakenly mistrusted each other for centuries have agreed upon a close and loyal collaboration as a result of recognition of the realities of life."[35]

As long as Greek and Turkish interests coincided, as they did for nearly a decade after the Second World War, there was no reason why their warming relationship could not have made further progress. This is what could reasonably have been expected in the early 1950s given their fear of the Soviet Union and commitment to the Western Alliance. However, when the vital interests of one was seen to be threatened by the other, as happened with the Cyprus issue during 1954-1955, the progress attained in Greek-Turkish reconciliation and collaboration was threatened and, ultimately, undone.

Notes

1. Brian Dicks, *Greece*, London: David & Charles, 1980, p. 102.

2. Dimitri Kitsikis, *Sugkritiki Istoria Ellados Kai Turkias ston 20 Aiona (A Comparative History of Grece and Turkey in the 20th Century)*, Athens: Estia Publishers, 1978, p. 53.

Kitsikis has noted that with the advent of independence in Greece, Ottoman history was re-interpreted by Greek nationalists so as to portray the Turks as the exclusive rulers of the Ottoman Empire and to deny the "partnership" status of the Greek community. (Interview with the author on February 11, 1988).

3. Michael L. Smith, *Ionian Vision: Greece in Asia Minor, 1919-1922*, London: Allen Lane, 1973, p. 4.

4. Robert H. Stephens, *Cyprus: A Place of Arms*, London: Pall Mall Press, 1966, p. 89.

5. As reported in Smith, *Ionian Vision*, pp. 30-1.

6. *Ibid.*

7. Stephens, *Place of Arms*, p. 90.

8. Smith, *Ionian Vision*, p. 30.

9. Justin McCarthy, *Muslims and Minorities: The Population of Ottoman Anatolia and the End of the Empire*, New York: New York University Press, 1983, p. 110.

10. Stanford Shaw and Ezel Kural Shaw, *History of the Ottoman Empire and Modern Turkey*, Vol. II, Cambridge: Cambridge University Press, 1977, p. 268.

11. Kenneth Young, *The Greek Passion: A Study in People and Politics*, London: J.M. Dent & Sons, 1969, p. 184.

12. Smith, *Ionian Vision*, p. 53.

13. Stephens, *Place of Arms*, p. 97.

14. Smith, *Ionian Vision*, p. 102.

15. John Campbell and Philip Sherrard, *Modern Greece*, London: Ernest Benn, 1968, pp. 123-4.

16. Harry J. Psomiades, *The Eastern Question: The Last Phase - A Study in Greek-Turkish Diplomacy*, Salonika: Institute for Balkan Studies, 1968, p. 55.

17. C.M. Woodhouse, "Diplomatic Developments: Nineteenth and Twentieth Century" in J.T.A. Koumoulides (ed.), *Greece in Transition: Essays in the History of Modern Greece, 1821-1974*, London: Zeno Publishers, 1977, p. 120.

18. Figures from Stephens, *Place of Arms*, p. 103.

19. Campbell & Sherrard, *Modern Greece*, p. 129.

20. For the text of the Lausanne Treaty, see Fred Israel (ed.), *Major Peace Treaties of Modern History, 1648-1967*, Vol. IV, New York: Chelsea House, 1967, pp. 2301-68.

21. Alexis Alexandris, *The Greek Minority of Istanbul and Greek-Turkish Relations, 1918-1974*, Athens: Centre for Asia Minor Studies, 1983, p. 57.

22. Psomiades, *Eastern Question*, p. 89.

23. Ferenc A. Vali, *Bridge Across the Bosporus: The Foreign Policy of Turkey*, Baltimore: The John Hopkins Press, 1971, p. 225.

24. Psomiades, *Eastern Question*, p. 109.

25. Stephens, *Place of Arms*, p. 114.

26. Alexis Alexandris, "Turkish Policy Towards Greece During the Second World War and Its Impact on Greek-Turkish Detente," *Balkan Studies*, 1982, Vol. 23, No. 1, p. 160.

27. *Ibid.*, p. 161.

28. *Ibid.*, p. 182.

29. *Ibid.*, p. 184.

30. *Ibid.*, p. 185.

31. *Ibid.*, p. 186.

32. *Ibid.*, p. 189.

33. Vali, *Bridge Across*, p. 226.

34. Alexandris, "Turkish Policy," p. 197.

35. *New York Times*, January 30, 1954, as quoted in Vali, *Bridge Across*, p. 228.

Political Dynamics in Divided Cyprus and Greek-Turkish Involvement Before Independence

Of the various issues over which Greece and Turkey have quarrelled during the last half century, none has had as profound, damaging, and prolonged an impact as Cyprus. Since the start of the post-war Enosis struggle in the 1950s, Cyprus has been a major, if not the overriding, concern of Greece and Turkey. The stake of each country in the island has been so high that both countries have periodically threatened to use force to protect their individual interests. Indeed, both resorted to arms in Cyprus in 1974, though not simultaneously. Greece initiated a coup against the Makarios regime, and Turkey, in reaction, intervened to keep the island from being controlled from Athens.

With an area of 3,572 square miles, Cyprus is the third largest island in the Mediterranean, comparable in size to neighbouring Lebanon. It is more than five hundred miles east of the Greek mainland but only about forty miles from Turkey's southern coast. Largely because of its strategic location, Cyprus has been an attractive prize for successive empires. Settled by Greek and Phoenician colonizers in its earliest recorded history, the island was later ruled successively by the Assyrians, Egyptians, Romans, Arabs, Byzantines, Lusignans, Venetians, Ottoman Turks and, lastly, the British, who ruled the island until it became an independent Republic in 1960.

Before analysing the interests and involvement of Greece and Turkey during the various stages of the island's discord, it will be useful to examine the conflict at another level of paramount importance: that of the Greek and Turkish-Cypriot communities. Indeed, an appreciation of the communal politics in Cyprus is necessary in order to evaluate the relative importance of local and external forces in the development of the Cyprus dispute.

Cultural Cleavages and Historical Legacies

Since 1571, when Cyprus came under Turkish rule, the Cypriot population has been comprised of two main ethnic groups: Greeks and Turks.

According to a recent estimate, out of a total population of 650,000, Greek-Cypriots comprise roughly 80 percent and Turkish-Cypriots account for about 20 percent.[1]

Greek-Cypriots are Orthodox Christians who speak Greek. Turkish-Cypriots, on the other hand, are Turkish-speaking Muslims. Although many educated Cypriots have some knowledge of English, only a small minority of the Cypriot population has a working knowledge of both Greek and Turkish, and their numbers have declined in recent years. This, combined with their different religious affiliation, has contributed to a low level of interaction between the two communities and has helped reinforce ethnic separateness. Although communal conflict in Cyprus has not found expression in serious sectarian antagonisms, as is the case in Northern Ireland, religious division has been nevertheless responsible for separate educational systems and a relative lack of social interaction.

Such separation has also been reinforced by the traditional tendency of the Greek and Turkish communities to identify with Greece and Turkey; this has meant that the two communities' perceptions of each other and their relations with each other have been, to some degree, influenced by the historically adversarial relations between the Greek and Turkish nations. During colonial rule, for example, Greek-Cypriot volunteers went to fight for "mother Greece" in every conflict with Ottoman Turkey. Although Greek-Turkish disputes were not replicated in intercommunal violence in Cyprus, they had the impact of perpetuating separate self-views and inhibiting any disposition to Cypriot national identity.

Even more importantly, exclusive political socialization of the two communities over a long period of time caused them to develop their own separate national aspirations. In terms of administration and self-rule, the communities exercised rights and privileges granted under the *millet* system, electing their own judicial and administrative officials such as *muhktars* (village headmen). Under the *millet* system, the two communities were institutionalized as distinct *cemaats* (communities).

The major vehicle for this process has probably been the separate educational systems maintained by the two communities. For centuries, Greek and Turkish-Cypriot children have attended separate schools. The curricula and standards of Greek and Turkish-Cypriot schools (at both the elementary and the secondary levels) have been tailored to correspond respectively to the Greek and Turkish educational school systems. Teachers from the mainland usually infused a strong sense of patriotism in the schools where they taught.

Since there is no intercommunal university in Cyprus, the great majority of Cypriot students attend Greek or Turkish universities. The Greek and Turkish governments have provided these students with more generous scholarships and facilities than those made available to mainland students. Greek and Turkish graduates returning to Cyprus have been socialized into the historical self-images of the mainland communities, which has hardly encouraged cultural bridge-building between the Greek and Turkish-Cypriot youth.

In addressing the role of education in developing a sense of separate Greek and Turkish nationalism in Cyprus, a Greek-Cypriot scholar wrote:

> The importance of this cultural aspect of ethnic differentiation cannot be adequately emphasized. It provided the context within which the two Cypriot communities became conscious of their primordial attachments and the basis of their socialization into Greek and Turkish nationalism respectively. As a result, a commonly shared system of social communication that could conceivably form the basis of an integrated Cypriot society was precluded from developing.[2]

The cultural separateness of the two communities has determined, in large measure, the pattern of their settlement on the island. During most of the colonial period, Greek and Turkish-Cypriots lived interspersed throughout the island. Nevertheless, Greeks and Turks lived mostly in separate quarters in towns and mixed villages, and most villages were either Greek or Turkish.

This pattern of segregation gradually became more pronounced even before the communal clashes of the 1950s. In his valuable study of the political geography of the Cyprus conflict, Richard Patrick has provided statistical evidence indicating a substantial decline in the number of mixed Greek-Turkish villages from 1891 to 1931.[3] After 1931, the decrease of mixed settlements became even more pronounced, reflecting at the very least the preference of people of both communities to live in areas of their co-religionists. Concerns about personal safety, especially for the Turkish minority, account for the evacuations from mixed settlements from the late 1950s to the early 1970s. According to the 1960 census, there were 114 mixed villages out of a total of 634 (395 were entirely Greek and 121 Turkish).[4] However, these mixed villages were then composed predominantly of one community or the other; the minority group was represented by a handful of people.[5] Even at that, by 1970 the number of mixed villages decreased to 48 as a result of the Turkish-Cypriot exodus following the communal strife which began in December 1963.[6] Ultimately, as a result of the 1974 war, total segregation of the two communities came into effect. Except for a handful of people from both sides, there have been no contacts between Greek-Cypriots who live in the south and Turkish-Cypriots who have gathered in the northern third of the island.

Much before the total physical segregation of the two communities occurred, the economy of Cyprus reflected the ethnic dichotomy and separation on the island. Although under ordinary circumstances Greek and Turkish-Cypriots bought from and sold to each other, the ethnic factor intruded into the economic life of the island. Greek-Cypriot businesses controlled most of the island's manufacturing and import-export trade which rarely employed Turkish-Cypriots except as labourers and then only when Greek-Cypriots were unavailable. The same was true on a much smaller scale for Turkish-Cypriot enterprises. Also, on the whole, Greek-Cypriot incomes and living standards have been substantially higher than those of Turkish-Cypriots. This differential assumed considerable political salience in the course of the troubled communal relations after the mid-1950s, and especially after 1963 when Greek-Cypriots alone controlled the Cypriot state.

In spite of these long-established, fundamental, and obvious differences between the two communities, and in spite of their vivid images of separate destinies, they did not share a history of recurring violence. Several authors who have surveyed the history of Cyprus have reported on the near-total lack of communal violence between the Greek and Turkish-Cypriots during almost four centuries of living side by side. Until the mid-1950s, there were relatively few events of communal violence on the island. However, this shows only one side of the coin. A brief survey of the relations between Greek and Turkish-Cypriots during colonial rule will also reveal the historical antecedents of the more contemporary communal politics in Cyprus.

Communal Relations During Ottoman and British Rule

Progressive reform marked the start of the Ottoman rule in 1571. The Ottomans abolished feudalism and serfdom. They granted freedom of religion, and they officially recognized the Greek Orthodox Church as an autonomous, self-governing Archbishopric. The Archbishop was also elevated to the rank of *Ethnarch* (political leader) of the Greek-Cypriot *millet*. These changes were welcomed by the Greek-Cypriots who had suffered under the oppression and intolerance of the Catholic Venetians, the previous rulers. It was in these auspicious circumstances that the Ottoman Turks brought in settlers from Anatolia, thus establishing a Turkish community in Cyprus. In time, this new community grew in numbers and in proportion to the total population of the island. During some periods of Turkish rule, the number of Turks on the island was estimated to be about the same as that of the Greeks.[7] However, by the end of Ottoman rule, the Turks' share of the total population had dropped to about one-quarter, and eventually to the current ratio of 20 percent.

As Muslim subjects in an Islamic state, the Turks of the island had some legal privileges. They paid lower taxes than the Christian subjects. Also, Christians were legally obliged to show deference to Muslims and were not allowed to possess arms. On the other hand, Greeks were exempt from military service, and this prompted them to turn to commerce and business. Under the *millet* system, Greek-Cypriots enjoyed self-government. The church was the real ruler of the Greek community, regulating social, educational, and religious affairs of the Greek-Cypriots. In practice, most Turkish peasants were no better off than their Greek counterparts. According to one historian,

> the Turkish peasant of Cyprus was subject to the same trials and tribulations at the hands of the government as was his Christian neighbour; and when the power of the Archbishops was at its height, he felt the effects of their supremacy no less than the Orthodox peasant.[8]

Another historian pointed out that,

> by the middle of the nineteenth century Greek-Cypriots had made advances in education, trade and finance over Turkish-Cypriots, taking advantage of new liberal constitutions by the Ottoman Empire.[9]

Most historical accounts indicate that the Greeks and Turks of Cyprus coexisted relatively peacefully during three centuries of Turkish rule. Indeed, in several instances they collaborated to help oust governors or other high officials who were accused of excessive taxation. Sir George Hill, whose authoritative history of the island has been widely quoted, has shown that in a number of popular revolts which took place during Turkish rule, poor Turks and Greeks joined forces against the authorities, usually protesting heavy taxes and the harshness of some governors.[10]

There were other manifestations of the peaceful coexistence and interaction among members of the two communities. Although Greeks and Turks tended to live in separate villages and in separate quarters in towns, some lived side by side in mixed communities. One traveller, writing in 1837, was quoted as saying that "it was far from unusual, before the Greek revolution, for a Mohammedan to stand as godfather to the child of his Christian friend."[11] Intermarriage, though a rare occurrence, was not unheard of. Both communities also borrowed from each other's customs. In spite of the considerable interaction and record of peaceful relations between the Greeks and Turks of Cyprus, their sense of separateness remained and sometimes became even more pronounced.

The event with the greatest consequence for both communities was the Greek War of Independence. The emergence of an independent Greece in

1830 heightened the national feelings of the Greeks of Cyprus and widened the gap between the national feelings of the Greek and Turkish-Cypriots.

Greek-Cypriots sympathized with the Greek War of Independence, which started in the Greek mainland in 1821. Some volunteers participated in the mainland revolution; others donated money and provisions. Evidence of links between Greek-Cypriots and the mainland insurgents, although tenuous, prompted the Ottoman Governor to execute the Archbishop, other clergy, and various leading members of the Greek community in 1832. Although there were reports of some Turks intervening to save the lives of Greek friends, these events had negative consequences for the relations between the two communities. Violence between Turks and Greeks flared periodically. Thousands of Greeks emigrated in the ensuing years.

The replacement of Ottoman with British rule in 1878 encouraged those Greek-Cypriots who looked to Greece as the motherland. In welcoming the first British High Commissioner, the Archbishop of Cyprus declared: "...we trust that Great Britain will help Cyprus, as it did the Ionian islands, to be united with Mother Greece, to which it is naturally connected."[12]

British rule did more than encourage Greek-Cypriot aspirations for Enosis; i.e., the island's union with Greece. It created opportunities in education, finance, and commerce that Greek-Cypriots exploited more successfully than Turkish-Cypriots. Under British rule, Turkish-Cypriots not only lost their Ottoman legal privileges, they also faced for the first time the possibility of real domination by the Greek-Cypriots, even Enosis with Greece. Consequently, they sought parity in whatever constitutional arrangements the British introduced. Furthermore, on every occasion that the Greek-Cypriots petitioned Britain for Enosis, Turkish-Cypriots sent counter-petitions to London against union and (usually) pleas to the Ottoman Government for support.

It is striking that since the beginning of British rule in 1878 to our day — over a century — the paramount political aim of the Turkish-Cypriots has remained constant: no to Enosis and simple majority rule (which to them means domination by the Greek majority). This is the defensive position of a threatened community which, having been overtaken by a more activist and affluent community, fears a worse fate if they became the subject peoples of the majority nation. At no time in their history have Turkish-Cypriots ever considered the possibility that they would be treated fairly by the more numerous Greek-Cypriots or under a Greek administration in the event of Enosis.

In view of the continuing strategic value of Cyprus, the British too opposed Enosis, although they did offer the island to Greece in 1915 in an unsuccessful bid for its support in the war. On Cyprus, the British authorities and the Turkish-Cypriot representatives effected an alliance against the

Enotist claims of the Greek-Cypriots led by the Greek Orthodox Church. This inevitably caused Greek-Cypriot resentment.

Much before the intensification of the Enosis struggle in Cyprus in the mid-1950s, Greek-Cypriot agitation for union, and Turkish-Cypriot opposition to it, created periods of tension and occasional violence under British rule. Some writers have argued that the dispute of Greeks and Turks in Cyprus over Enosis did not affect the harmonious everyday relations of the two communities.[13] This contention is only partially valid. It is true that the bulk of ordinary Greek and Turkish-Cypriots went about their ways peacefully and continued to interact with one another as they had done in the past. It is also true that periods of tension and violence were occasional, and usually stimulated by external events; namely, Greek-Turkish quarrels and wars. (During British rule alone, mainland Greeks and Turks fought each other in four full-fledged wars: 1880, 1897, 1912, and 1919-1922.)

Nevertheless, the pattern of confrontation that emerged over Enosis, and the increasing alienation of the Turkish community, caused both peoples to grow further apart. Hundreds, and sometimes thousands, of Cypriots demonstrated for or against Enosis.[14] In one of the worst communal clashes in 1912, five people died and 134 were injured.[15] Accordingly, much before EOKA began its violent campaign for union with Greece in 1955, it was evident that Greek and Turkish-Cypriots were on a collision course.

Greece and Turkey's Interest in Cyprus: From Lausanne to the Early 1950s

In the aftermath of the Lausanne Treaty of 1923, Greece and Turkey sought to develop close relations with Britain. Consequently, they refrained from causing Britain any offence in or over Cyprus. Notwithstanding the persistence of the Enosis movement in Cyprus, Greece did not challenge British rule for more than three decades after Lausanne. Turkey viewed continued British rule to be compatible with her security interests and, later, as a bulwark against Enosis.

At the same time, the developing cultural and political ties of Greece and Turkey with their respective communities on Cyprus enhanced the interest of the mainland governments in the island. These links played a major role in the subsequent reappraisal of policy by the two countries towards Cyprus and provided the bases of their deeper involvement in the island from the 1950s onwards.

In the aftermath of the Greek-Turkish war of 1919-1922, and for several years thereafter, Turkey (like Greece) had other, much more pressing issues to contend with than Cyprus. In the course of the First World War and the Turkish War of Independence, millions of people perished in Anatolia. In addition, the exodus of more than 1,500,000 Greek and Armenian refugees had further depleted Turkey's population. In order to help alleviate manpower shortages, Turkish leader Atatürk and his associates tried to encourage those Turks who had remained outside the boundaries of the new Republic to emigrate there.

During the Lausanne negotiations Turkey sought, and received, the right for the Turks of Cyprus to opt for Turkish nationality and emigrate to Turkey. In order to give adequate information to Turkish-Cypriots and assist in their passage, the Turkish Government opened a consulate in Nicosia in 1925.[16] So keen was the Turkish government to have a substantial number of Turkish-Cypriots settle in Turkey that it pressed Britain to extend the time permitted those who wished to take Turkish nationality from three to twelve months, so that they could wind up their affairs and emigrate.[17] Indeed, the Ankara government lodged several complaints to the British Foreign Office; it believed the British administration on the island created difficulties intended to discourage those Turkish-Cypriots who wanted to emigrate.[18]

Ultimately, in spite of Ankara's hopes, only about 9,000 Turkish-Cypriots opted for Turkish nationality, and of these, about one-half are estimated to have actually emigrated to Turkey.[19] It is worth pondering briefly what would have happened had the bulk of the Turkish-Cypriots departed to the mainland. Clearly, Turkey would have been hard pressed to justify having a say over the future destiny of its former possession when its sovereignty became an issue. Yet Turkish policy on Cyprus, for many years after Lausanne, showed how little Ankara was concerned with her stake on the island just forty miles from her southern coast.

Atatürk's primary concern was domestic national reconstruction. His foreign policy was based on the motto "Peace at home, peace abroad." Consequently, Ankara was careful to avoid any interference in Cyprus under British rule. Nevertheless, Turkey's relations with the Turkish-Cypriot community had far-reaching consequences, both for that community and, ultimately, for Cyprus as a whole. For the Turkish-Cypriots, the new Turkish Republic replaced the world of Islam as a source of their collective identity. By identifying with Atatürk's vision of Turkish nationalism, the Turks of Cyprus were also asserting their sense of separate identity from their Greek-Cypriot neighbours who, in turn, looked to the people of Greece as their national brethren. Admittedly, there were religious groups or individuals in the Turkish community who did not favour the secular orientation of Kemalist[20] Turkey; however, their influence in the community declined as reforms inspired and encouraged by Turkey gained growing acceptance. Moreover, Turkish-Cypriots viewed Turkey as a bulwark against Enosis. After all, Atatürk's Turkey had dealt Greece's irredentist ambitions a heavy blow by defeating it on the battlefield.

Although it was a gradual process, the spread of secularism and nationalism among the Turkish-Cypriots was nevertheless remarkable. For example, Turkish-Cypriots voluntarily accepted many of the reforms introduced by the sanction of the state in Turkey. When Atatürk replaced the Arabic script with the Latin alphabet for the Turkish language in 1928, the new alphabet was speedily adopted by Turkish-Cypriots. Likewise, European dress was adopted voluntarily. Soon after the creation of the Turkish Republic, Turkish-Cypriots celebrated the same national holidays as the new state, including those that recalled Turkish victories against the Greek invasion. Turkey started to extend assistance to Turkish-Cypriot education, albeit on a modest scale.[21] Ankara sent teachers and provided easy access to Turkish universities for Turkish-Cypriots. All this helped inculcate Turkish nationalist ideas among Turkish youth.

Although younger elements were the most receptive to Atatürk's ideas, Turkey's cultural and political influence was soon felt by a wide cross-section of the Turkish-Cypriot population. Turkish-Cypriot newspapers reported widely on developments on Turkey; some of these began to subscribe to a Turkish press service as far back as the early 1920s.[22]

Even though religious groups among Turkish-Cypriots resisted Atatürk's secular reforms for several years, the growing cultural and political influence of Republican Turkey strengthened the hand of the Kemalist Turkish-Cypriots, who ultimately prevailed over the anti-secular elements. By the late 1930s, "Kemalism had taken firm root on the island, and its influence could be felt in virtually every aspect of life within the Turkish Cypriot community."[23]

British rule on the island unwittingly encouraged Turkish-Cypriot identification with Turkey. Most studies of recent Cypriot history and politics have emphasized the alliance between Turkish-Cypriots and Britain against Greek-Cypriot nationalism. To be sure, the Turks of Cyprus and Britain were allied against Enosis. However, most accounts have overlooked the divergent positions of the British rulers and the Turkish-Cypriots on other important issues, and the political strains this created.[24] For instance, Turkish-Cypriots sought to gain greater control over their communal institutions, including their schools and the *evkaf*, the Islamic endowments. They resisted restrictions on their assertions of Turkish national allegiance, such as flying the Turkish flag. British resistance to their efforts stimulated Turkish nationalism and greater allegiance to Turkey within the community.

Not only did this situation create growing estrangement between Turkish-Cypriots and the British colonial administration, it also created possibilities for friction between Britain and Turkey. The British supported conservative pro-British individuals for leadership positions and sought to weaken the appeal of nationalist leaders and organizations in the Turkish community. On the other hand, in keeping with its ideological orientation, Kemalist Turkey favoured the very secular and reformist factions the British feared.

Ankara monitored developments on the island through its consulate and gave discreet support to the Kemalist elements in the community. However, it was anxious not to be seen as interfering in the affairs of the community or challenging British sovereignty. British officials on the island, however, believed that at least some Turkish consuls were active in sponsoring nationalist causes and individuals, and that they did so under instructions from Ankara. They were particularly concerned about the activism of Assaf Güvenir, who served as Consul from 1925 to 1931.[25] Allegations of his interference in Turkish-Cypriot affairs prompted a request from the Foreign Office to Ankara to give its Consul a warning to stay clear of political activity. Ankara responded by recalling its Consul and appointing successors who did not ruffle British feathers. As McHenry aptly wrote:

> The fact that the Turkish Government transferred him with so little prompting is illustrative of the importance which Atatürk attached to friendly relations with Great Britain. He appeared eager to avoid even the slightest suggestion that Turkey intended to pursue a policy of extending its influence in the Turkish Cypriot community with the aim of intervening in the island's internal affairs.[26]

The concerns which the British had regarding the growth of Kemalism and Turkey's stake in Cyprus were mild compared with the challenge posed to their rule by the Enosis movement on the island and the prospects of Greece's involvement in the struggle for union.

While Turkey accepted British rule as a reality, Greek policy was aimed at eventual Enosis. On the one hand, Hellenic nationalism was spread through education. Diplomatically, Greece adopted a

> low-keyed campaign aimed at persuading the British to surrender their predominant position on the island in exchange for strategic guarantees and base rights. The strategy was to keep Cyprus alive as a diplomatic issue without needlessly antagonizing the British.[27]

But Greek policy was not entirely risk-free. It could spill into open violence. For example, anti-British riots by Greek-Cypriots took place throughout the island in 1931. The British authorities accused Greek Consul Kyrou (who was Cypriot by birth) of inciting Greek-Cypriots to rebel against British rule. Athens promptly complied when Britain demanded his recall from the island.

The British were becoming increasingly alarmed by the growth of

Hellenic nationalism and the continuing appeal of Enosis among Greek-Cypriots. They reacted to the 1931 riots by adopting a variety of harsh measures designed both to strengthen British control and curb Greek nationalism among Greek-Cypriots: the elected Legislative Council and local councils were abolished, political parties were banned, and press censorship introduced. Also, the teaching of Greek (as well as Turkish) history was forbidden; the flying of the Greek flag was prohibited; in fact, to advocate orally or in writing any change in the sovereignty of the island became a criminal offence.[28]

One of the primary targets of the British administration was the Greek-Cypriot school system, which was blamed for spreading Greek nationalism. In 1933, primary education was put under the control of the island's government. Secondary Greek-Cypriot schools were not as rigidly controlled, however, perhaps because they were not as dependent on government funding. In any case, the British authorities failed in their attempts to undercut the appeal of Greek nationalism and Enosis.

Although political activity was severely restricted by the post-1931 measures on the island, Enotist activity and propaganda flourished in Greece. In Athens, former President Admiral Koundouritis founded the Cyprus Central Committee, "whose motto was 'Long Live Greek Cyprus', (and) had most of the prominent Greek politicians and academics as members."[29] Also active were the Cypriot Students Brotherhood, the Society of Friends of Cyprus, and the Cyprus National Bureau.[30] These groups kept Cyprus alive as an issue in Greece and garnered growing popular support for Enosis.

The British Foreign Office generally had few complaints about the official conduct of the Athens governments before the 1950s, but the British authorities in Cyprus saw Greece's influence in a different light. They believed that Athens deliberately fanned the flames of Greek nationalism and Enosis. This subject has been well-documented in a study of the Enosis movement by Richard Barham.[31] To cite from one of his examples, "in 1935 Governor Palmer again raised the issue of pro-Greek propaganda in Cyprus terming the influence of the Greek press 'enormous' and propaganda from Greece by newspaper or wireless 'a real danger'."[32]

Another illustration of the Colonial Office's perception of Greece's role in Cyprus is contained in a statement made by Sir William Battershill, a former Governor of Cyprus, during a discussion of political affairs in Cyprus in 1942:

> ...the attitude of the Greek Government has in fact been far from helpful on more than one occasion. The Greek Consuls, with the exception of the present one, have consistently fostered Enosis agitation and the anti-Government manifestations. In fact, Consul Kyrou

took such an active part in the political intrigues and movements which led to the 1931 disturbances that he was recalled by his government — but only after very strong representations by H.M.G. There can be no doubt that these Consuls were acting on instructions. Recent wishful thinking and public statements on the part of some of the members of the Greek Government regarding the cession of Cyprus to Greece after the war has given a considerable impetus to the Enosis cause in Cyprus.[33]

There was not much that the British authorities could do other than register their displeasure. Further examples of Greek support for Enosis are contained in the following passage from Barham's study, which also provide a glimpse of the traffic between Greece and Cyprus:

The Cyprus Government's report to the Colonial Office on the political situation in July 1947 described visits to Cyprus of Greek athletes, a Greek member of Parliament, and a theatrical troupe from the Greek National Theatre. The leaders of the theatrical company 'openly made speeches in favour of Enosis' and the Greek Government through the Greek Consul was viewed as 'taking active steps for union'.[34]

At the governmental level in Greece, in spite of a desire not to offend Britain, some of the highest officials nevertheless periodically made statements calling for the union of Cyprus with Greece. In a luncheon address in London on November 15, 1941, Greek Prime Minister Tsouderos stated, "I visualize a Great Greece including North Epirus, the Dodecanese, Macedonia, and Cyprus,"[35] which provoked a protest from Foreign Secretary Eden. Some years later, in 1948, King Paul of Greece provoked further British protests, as well as excitement in Cyprus and Greece, by stating that "Greece certainly desires and will continue to desire the union of Cyprus with Greece. It is difficult to understand why this has not been effected."[36]

The post-war Greek demand for Enosis was endorsed by one faction of the British opinion. Numerous British politicians (usually of the Labour Party) encouraged the Greek-Cypriots and Greece about the future prospects of Enosis. Admittedly, the British government itself repeatedly turned down Enosis, but neither the leaders of Greece nor of Greek-Cypriots took the British 'no' for an answer.

Three decades of involvement by Greece and Turkey in Cyprus after Lausanne may be summed up in the following terms: Greece strengthened its existing ties with the Greek-Cypriot community and, encouraged by the persistence of the Enosis movement, increasingly viewed Cyprus' ultimate union with Greece as a realizable national goal. Although Turkey renounced its sovereignty over Cyprus at Lausanne, and even sought to encourage the bulk of Turkish-Cypriots to emigrate to the mainland, its interest in the island's affairs and future destiny grew as it developed closer ties with an increasingly secular and nationalist Turkish community on the island.

Greece and Turkey's Involvement in the Cyprus Struggle of the 1950s

With the benefit of hindsight, several writers have remarked that the diplomats at the Lausanne Conference who separated Greek and Turkish peoples and territories failed to anticipate the political future of Cyprus.[37] At the time, Greece and Turkey had issues of greater magnitude to worry about than that of the long-term future of the island. As well, the British were not in any mood to give away their security interests. On the other hand, the overall settlement agreed upon at Lausanne did feature prominently in the minds of Greek and Turkish leaders as they reacted to the emergence of the Cyprus issue in the 1950s.

In Turkish leaders' eyes, the settlement at Lausanne had created a strategic balance between Greece and Turkey. Even though Lausanne merely formalized the losses of the First World War, Turks regarded this acknowledgement as tantamount to territorial sacrifice. Many Turks believed that, in spite of their nation's victory over the invading Greeks, Turkey had made substantial territorial sacrifices by consenting to Greek sovereignty over Western Thrace (with its Turkish majority) and, especially, the islands that ring her Aegean coast.

In the case of Cyprus, the Turks were content for the British to rule the island indefinitely, particularly after ties between Britain and Turkey were cemented through their alliances within NATO and the Baghdad Pact. However, in Turkish eyes the prospect of Greek annexation of Cyprus would substantially tilt the bilateral strategic balance at Turkey's expense. The Lausanne balance had already been modified in Greece's favour when the Italian-ruled Dodecanese islands were granted to it in 1947 as part of the post-war settlement. Turkey was unable to oppose the cession of the Dodecanese to Greece even if it had wanted to because of its weak bargaining position as a result of its neutrality during the Second World War. By the early 1950s, however, Turkey's status in the West had improved substantially. Turkish troops had served with distinction in Korea, and Turkey emerged as a central actor in Western strategic designs in the Middle East.

To the Greeks, Lausanne meant Turkey's formal abdication of its sovereign rights on Cyprus in favour of Britain. Consequently, Turkey had forfeited any claim as a party in determining the status of the island in the future. In 1922, Greece had suffered a great national defeat. It had been obliged to accept Turkey's expulsion of virtually the entire Greek community from Anatolia. It also abandoned the long-cherished claim to lands where Greeks had lived continuously for a long time. As Psomiades wrote, "By one stroke of the pen, the 2,600-year history of the Greek communities in Asia Minor came to an end, the victims of modern nationalism."[38] In the post-Lausanne agreements which Venizelos signed with Turkey, the Greeks had made further sacrifices in Turkey's favour by agreeing to forfeit their claim to Greek properties left behind by the refugees.[39]

Notwithstanding periodic statements of support for Enosis by Greek leaders, however, Greek governments were content to wait for more favourable conditions before pressing for the island's union. This worked until 1950. The Greek-Cypriot nationalist leaders, on the other hand, were impatient and decided to take the initiative in the early 1950s.

The Greek-Cypriots' campaign for Enosis coincided with the period of accelerating decolonization. They argued that Cyprus deserved her freedom as much as any other Afro-Asian colony attaining its independence from British rule. Yet, as Turkish and British opponents of Enosis asserted, the Greek-Cypriot aspirations differed from that of other colonial peoples: rather than independence as such, Greek-Cypriots envisaged the transfer of sovereignty from one state to another — from Britain to Greece. In any case, British governments believed that their possession of Cyprus served important strategic interests and were unwilling to yield. For the Greek-Cypriot leaders this meant organizing a struggle like that of other colonial peoples seeking their liberation.

The intensification of the Enosis campaign came in the wake of the election of Makarios as Archbishop. "I shall not rest for a moment in my efforts to see union with Greece achieved,"[40] he declared on the occasion of his enthronement on October 18, 1950, voicing the traditional aspiration of the Greek-Orthodox Church in Cyprus. Because of his charismatic appeal and dedication, Makarios was able to go much further than his predecessors in mobilizing mass opinion to the cause of Enosis. It is likely that his energetic Enotist activity was a factor in Makarios' election as Archbishop at the relatively young age of thirty-seven. After all, the Church had traditionally regarded itself as the repository of Hellenic nationalist aspirations.

In 1949, while still Bishop, Makarios had declared publicly that he did not believe

> as some traitors and friends of England do, that our ideal will be realized within the framework of Anglo-Greek amity. Enosis will not be granted. It can only be won by a continuous struggle.[41]

In January 1950, a few months before he became Archbishop, Makarios organized an island-wide plebiscite in Greek-Cypriot churches in January 1950. The results of this plebiscite in which 96 percent of eligible Greek-Cypriots voted for Enosis were highly publicized; a deputation of Greek-Cypriot spokesmen visited Greece, Britain, and the United Nations. Turkish-Cypriots protested against the plebiscite, and students and youth organizations demonstrated against it in Cyprus as well as in Istanbul and Ankara.

In concurrence with their publicity thrust, Makarios and his fellow Greek-Cypriot nationalists made preparations for an armed insurrection against the British on the island. Such action would serve two purposes: it would harass British personnel and undermine Britain's hold on the island, and it would help publicize the Greek-Cypriot case to the world.

The Greek-Cypriot underground organization, EOKA, started its campaign of violence on April 1, 1955. But plans for this campaign had been made several years earlier in Cyprus and Greece. Among the many contacts that Makarios made in Cyprus and Greece was Colonel George Grivas, whom he had met in 1951 while the latter was in Cyprus studying the prospects for armed insurgency against the British. Grivas was born in Cyprus, but since the age of seventeen he had lived most of his life in Greece where he became a successful career soldier. Both men were independent and proud individuals who did not defer to others. In an uneasy alliance, Makarios assumed the political leadership of the Enosis movement while Grivas organized EOKA as an operational secret force.

Although the impetus for armed insurgency came from Grivas and Makarios, as well as their co-nationalists in Cyprus, they turned to Greece for help and sponsorship. These Greek-Cypriot nationalists assumed that their aspirations for Cyprus and Greece were one and the same. Greece had long viewed Cyprus as unredeemed Greek territory; Enosis "re-kindled the remaining embers of the 'Great Idea'."[42]

The *Megali Idea* had failed to recover Istanbul and western Anatolia. But it did not necessarily die with the Anatolian defeat. It continued to stir Greek passions, and at least some Greeks saw the prospect of Cyprus' union with Greece as partial fulfilment of the national dream. As Christos Doumas put it:

> ... no self-respecting Greek politician could afford to show scorn or even neglect [for Megali Idea]... the union of Cyprus with Greece appeared to the masses to be a step toward the realisation of Megali Idea. To be against it was tantamount to being against the idea of Greece itself, and could spell one's extinction.[43]

While Greece's support for Enosis could be expected, Greek leaders were initially reticent to confront the British by supporting an armed insurgency. Britain, after all, had come to Greece's aid during the Greek War of Independence, and several times of national emergency since then, and most recently had helped the anti-Communist factions prevail in the bitter civil war that had ended only in 1949. Most Greek leaders expected or hoped that Britain would eventually give up the island and allow Enosis to be realized. Accordingly, in the early 1950s, they did not wish to risk Greece's alliance with Britain by confronting her in international forums or by supporting the armed insurgency against British rule on the island. However, as a result of pressure from Greek-Cypriot Enotist leaders, and the growing public interest and pressures in Greece, governments in Athens began to lay aside their reservations.

In 1950, following the Enosis plebiscite on the island, 200 deputies in the Greek parliament signed a petition expressing support for the island's union with Greece. Enotist campaigns in the country made Cyprus a national issue. A Pan-Hellenic Committee for the Cyprus Struggle formed under the chairmanship of the Archbishop of Greece. Makarios spoke over Athens Radio urging more active participation in the Enosis struggle.

On occasion, the Greek government was at pains to cool the ardour of Cypriot Enotists. The Greek-Cypriot delegation that visited Athens following the 1950 Enosis plebiscite was told by Premier Plastiras that all Greek people favoured the union, but that his government wished to deal with the issue "within the framework of friendly relations with our great ally (Britain) at the opportune time."[44] Along with Plastiras, Premier Venizelos and also Papagos at the beginning of his ministry, turned down Makarios' requests to raise the Cyprus issue at the United Nations. The Archbishop even threatened that he might ask another state, Syria, to sponsor the Greek-Cypriot cause at the United Nations.[45] According to Sophocles Venizelos (then Foreign Minister), Makarios added the following warning to him if the Greek government did not comply: "I shall denounce you to the Greek people. I shall tell them that you refuse to appeal to the United Nations."[46] Venizelos retorted: "You can do what you like, denounce me to anyone you like, but I am not going to have you dictate the foreign policy of Greece."[47]

Makarios, however, was determined to increase pressure on the Greek government. In an address on Athens Radio during 1952, he condemned the Greek government in the following terms:

I am obliged to speak to you in the language of truth and to denounce both the government and the opposition. They have not risen to the occasion. They have shown neither courage nor spirit. In response to the Nation's call for an appeal (to the United Nations), they replied hesitantly and sleepily that they were keeping the matter under vigilant observation. The political leaders are deceiving themselves and, worse still, they are deceiving the Greek people and the unfortunate Cypriots.[48]

The pressures brought to bear by the Greek-Cypriot Enotists and their Greek allies ultimately won over the Greek government. Discreet approaches to Britain to give up her sovereignty on the island proved fruitless.

British leaders countered demands for Enosis by arguing that the strategic location of Cyprus necessitated their presence on the island for the fulfilment of their defence obligations in the Middle East. Eden, who was Prime Minister during the intensification of the Enotist campaign until January 1957, justified his government's reluctance to relinquish sovereignty over Cyprus in these terms:

> Our military advisers regarded it [Cyprus] as an essential staging point for the maintenance of our position in the Middle East, including the Persian Gulf. There must be security of tenure. It was not thought enough to lease certain sites on the island from some future administration on whose policies we could not depend.[49]

The proximity of Cyprus to British oil interests in the Persian Gulf, and her strategic location on the sea routes of the eastern Mediterranean and air routes from Europe to Asia, were key considerations for Britain. However, there was an important political element too. Eden had been under fire by old guard Tories for agreeing to quit Suez, and he did not want to be seen to be retreating again.

Thus, in the face of British inflexibility, the Greek government began to yield to Makarios. The Greek Prime Minister Papagos sponsored the question of Cyprus at the United Nations in August 1954. Having abandoned hopes for a change in British policy, he then gave the green light for EOKA to start its operations in Cyprus, which began on April 1, 1955.

In retrospect, it seems that the Greek government ignored the Turkish reaction to such a drastic change in its Cyprus policy. Did Greek leaders think at this time that Turkey would remain indifferent to the prospect of Cyprus' union with Greece? As the former Greek Foreign Minister Dimitri Bitsios stated:

> Up to the middle of 1955, the Turkish factor was conspicuously absent from the planning of our Cyprus policy. Since Turkey had, by the Treaty of Lausanne, relinquished her rights on the island, it was considered in Athens that she had no role to play in our quarrel with Britain. The argument was legally irreproachable, but politically questionable.[50]

It is possible that in the early 1950s, the mild reactions of Turkish leaders to renewed Greek-Cypriot calls for Enosis led the Greeks to believe, or hope, that Turkey would remain aloof. Moreover, it suited Greek policy to proceed on the assumption that Turkey had no legitimate grounds to become engaged in the Enosis dispute. Any recognition of Turkey as a party would invite a

Turkish veto.

Initially, Turkey expected that the new Enosis campaign of the 1950s would fizzle in the manner of previous attempts. Given Britain's determination to hold on to Cyprus, Turkey did not expect the island's sovereignty to change hands. However, although initial official Turkish reaction to Enosis was restrained, the Turkish public was clearly concerned with the island's fate. The demonstrations in Ankara and Istanbul in 1950, in response to the Church-organized Enosis plebiscite in Cyprus, and subsequent anti-Enosis activities by student groups during the succeeding years, showed the depth of Turkish domestic interest in the future of their compatriots there.

Even though Turkish public opinion was more concerned about the growing Enosis campaign than were Turkish officials before 1954-1955, the government did convey its position in 1951 when Foreign Minister Köprülü made the following statement to a Turkish newspaper:

> It is only natural that we are closely concerned with Cyprus, considering its geographical proximity and importance, and the presence of our compatriots who constitute an important community with whom we have maintained historical ties. We do not see any reason for a change in the legal status of the island. Should any changes in the existing arrangements be seriously considered, we shall not permit such changes to take place without our participation and due regard for our rights.[51]

The Turkish Foreign Minister went on to say that the activation of the Cyprus issue was harmful "especially at a time when serious threats to the very existence of the free world makes it imperative for all free and friendly nations to stand together unreservedly."[52] Köprülü's reference to the prevailing cold war reflected the major preoccupation of his government (one year before Turkey and Greece became NATO members) with the problem of security in the face of perceived threats from the Soviet Union. Of course, Greece, too, shared these concerns regarding the Soviet Union, as was demonstrated by her eager membership of the Western Alliance and the short-lived Balkan Pact.

In spite of the post-war improvements in Greek-Turkish relations, Turkish leaders' strategic concerns vis-a-vis Greece remained. Already feeling hemmed in by Greek islands in the Aegean, the Turks felt that Greece's sovereignty over Cyprus would enable it to control access to its southern ports of Mersin and Iskenderun thereby completing Turkey's encirclement. These concerns were at the heart of Turkey's objection to Enosis then and later.

There were other reasons for Turkey's unwillingness to let Greece gain a strategic advantage. The Greek civil war during 1945-1949 demonstrated the power of the communist elements in Greece; despite their defeat, the possibility of the Communist Party gaining power in the future remained. This, and the substantial following of AKEL, the Communist Party in Cyprus, increased Turkish misgivings.

Turkey was also concerned that, under Greek rule, the Turkish community would be treated poorly, much as the Thrace Turks had been in Greece since Greece's formal incorporation of Western Thrace in 1923. Concern for the fate of the Turkish-Cypriots featured prominently in newspaper articles and organized meetings, where the government was urged to press Turkey's case on Cyprus more vigorously. The *New York Times* reported on June 28, 1954:

> Turkish public opinion led by the mass-circulation Istanbul newspapers, such as *Hürriyet* and *Yeni Sabah*, is bitterly opposed to putting the Turkish minority of 90,000 persons on Cyprus under Greek rule. Many Turks believe Greece mistreats the Turkish population of Western Thrace and would discriminate in equal measure against the Moslem minority in Cyprus once the British had left the island.

Although their initial reactions to renewed calls for Enosis had been guarded, Turkish leaders began to express themselves in stronger terms, particularly after EOKA began its violent campaign on the island, and Greece put Cyprus on the agenda of the United Nations. Also, in an effort to neutralize the Greek case for Enosis, British Prime Minister Eden encouraged Turkish leaders to express their opposition more forcefully. As he wrote in his memoirs:

> The Turkish newspapers had hitherto been more outspoken than the Turkish Government, which had behaved with restraint. It was as well, I wrote on a telegram at that time, that they should speak out, because it was the truth that the Turks would never let the Greeks have Cyprus.[53]

Eden's strategy of emphasizing Greek-Turkish differences on Cyprus (which was a blatant case of divide and rule) worked in the short term, although in the long run it failed to save the island for Britain. Turkey's support for the continuation of British rule in Cyprus suited British purposes. But the policy of relying on Turkish support subsequently enabled the Turks to exercise a virtual veto on British policy; Britain now needed their co-operation for a settlement.

Some observers of the question have argued that Turkey's policy was shaped in response to British prodding on the question of Enosis.[54] Is this a persuasive hypothesis? Would Turkey have become directly involved in the dispute had the British not encouraged her? Most writers have argued that Turkey would not have consented to Enosis regardless of British policy. On the other hand, it was not inconceivable that Greece could have won Turkish consent if Turkey had been offered facilities on the island (such as a military base) to satisfy her security concerns and special safeguards to ensure that the Turkish community would be well treated.

At Eden's invitation, Greek and Turkish representatives, but not Cypriots, attended a conference in London during August 1955. Eden's invitation to Turkey caused great anger among Greek-Cypriot leaders and the Greek government, since it acknowledged Turkey's right to have a say in the future of Cyprus. Makarios tried but failed to dissuade the Greek government from attending. The Greeks accepted the invitation with reluctance, for not to accept would support Turkish charges of intransigence. Nonetheless, Greek policy was determined to increase pressures on the British government (at the United Nations and on the island) to yield and to exclude Turkey as a party to a Cyprus settlement.

Although the Enosis policy united them, Greek governments and Greek-Cypriot leaders regularly disagreed on the handling of the issue. The Greeks were aggravated by Makarios' periodic accusations of weakness and by his interference in Greek government. During 1956, for example, the Ethnarchy of Cyprus demanded, and secured, the resignation of Greek Foreign Minister Theotokis on the grounds that he was too moderate in his pursuit of the Enosis issue.[55] Later, during 1958, when the Enosis struggle was faring poorly, Makarios asked that Greece threaten to leave NATO to improve her leverage over Cyprus; Karamanlis rejected such a course.[56]

The London Conference achieved nothing. Greece and Turkey's positions seemed more irreconcilable than ever. While Turkish Foreign Minister Zorlu did not question Britain's right to continue ruling Cyprus, he demanded that the island be returned to Turkish rule in the event that the British withdrew. Further, he threatened to repudiate the entire Lausanne Treaty if the status of Cyprus, set by the treaty, was altered.[57] The Greek representatives, on the other hand, argued for self-determination based on the wishes of the island's majority. This prompted Zorlu to remind the Conference that at Lausanne, Greek leader Venizelos had argued against self-determination for Western Thrace, which had a Turkish majority.

The Conference came to an inconclusive end at the heels of the anti-Greek riots in Istanbul and Izmir. Turkish leaders had encouraged demonstrations as an expression of public support for Turkish-Cypriots and Turkish interest in Cyprus, but the demonstrators became unexpectedly violent. The riots caused enormous damage to Greek property and churches.

Undaunted, Eden's government tried to settle the issue by offering Cypriots a wide measure of self-government while keeping the door open to self-determination at some unspecified date in the future. The terms which British Governor Harding offered Makarios during their talks on the island in February 1956 were good enough for the Greek government, who urged Makarios to accept.[58] However, the Archbishop rejected them. Soon afterwards, citing evidence of Makarios' complicity with EOKA, the British government sent him into exile on the Seychelles in the Indian Ocean.

In Makarios' absence, however, the British soon discovered that no Greek-Cypriot leader would dare enter into negotiations with them. Thus, the Radcliffe proposals of December 1956, which offered to give more power to the Greek-Cypriot majority than had earlier proposals,[59] and which recognized the principle of self-determination after an unspecified period of self-rule, came to nothing. At this time, Greek and Greek-Cypriot leaders would settle for nothing less than Enosis, although they would agree to a period of self-rule before Enosis was allowed.

Greek-Cypriot and Greek leaders hoped to increase the pressures on Britain by means of an armed insurgency on the island. EOKA's campaign of violence was directed, in the first instance, against British officials, security forces, government buildings, and property. However, EOKA also struck "enemies" within the Greek community: the chief targets were Greek-Cypriots who collaborated with the British administration, as well as members of the Communist Party AKEL, which supported the end of colonial rule but did not share the Greek nationalist vision of uniting the island with right-winged NATO-allied Greece.

Before long, Grivas and his fighters were successful in harassing the British administration and popularizing Enosis among the masses of the Greek-Cypriot population. They were so effective that Britain was forced to commit tens of thousands of troops to the island, thus increasing the cost of continued British presence.

The British administration made extensive use of Turkish-Cypriot recruits against EOKA. A new auxiliary police force created by the colonial authorities was almost entirely Turkish. Such extensive use of Turkish-Cypriot police to control Greek-Cypriot and EOKA disturbances exacerbated tensions between the two communities.

Initially, Turkish-Cypriots reacted to the new Enosis campaign with anti-union pronouncements and demonstrations. They lodged the usual appeals to Britain and Turkey to stand firm against Enosis. Turkish-Cypriots and the Turkish government expressed support for the continuation of British rule in the expectation that the Enosis campaign would run its course. However, by the end of 1956, when intercommunal killings began and the Greek international campaign to present the issue as a colonial struggle for liberation registered some successes, they changed their position and began to advocate partition.

The idea of partition had been put forth initially by the British government in order to deflect the campaign for Enosis. It was first suggested by the British Colonial Secretary in 1956, when he announced the Radcliffe proposals to the House of Commons. In one respect, Turkey's adoption of the partition idea represented an admission of failure over its previous policy of support for Britain's continued colonial rule, a position which had fared poorly at the United Nations. On the other hand, Turkey's advocacy of partition proved effective in combating Enosis.

The Turks argued that since Cyprus was made up of two national groups, each with its distinct language, religion, and national identification, the Turkish community was entitled to exercise the right of self-determination as much as the Greek community. This was countered by a number of Greek arguments stressing the practical difficulties involved in dividing a mixed population, and the dangers of creating precedents that would sanction minority secession, thus violating the territorial integrity of new states. However, the fundamental objection to partition by the Greeks (and Greek-Cypriots) rested on their view of Cyprus as an indivisible Greek island.

Turkey's adoption of partition as a solution coincided with its decision to pursue a tougher policy over Cyprus. The basic aim of Turkish policy remained the same as before: to ensure that Britain would not make a deal with Greece or the Greek-Cypriots without Turkey's full participation. A number of developments during 1957 led the Turks to believe that British resolve to retain sovereign control over Cyprus was weakening. In March 1957, the new British Prime Minister, Harold Macmillan, decided to release Makarios from exile in the Seychelles. He also replaced Sir John Harding, the military Governor of Cyprus with Sir Hugh Foot, a high-ranking colonial administrator with a liberal reputation. Turkish worries were further increased when Britain's Labour Party adopted a resolution calling for self-determination for Cyprus after an interim period of self-government.[60]

The anti-colonial campaign conducted by the Greeks at the United Nations garnered increasing support and this had an impact on Britain. [61] It was obvious to the Turks now that Britain was increasingly vulnerable to pressures on two fronts. At the United Nations, Greek charges of anti-colonialism were winning increasing support. And in Cyprus itself, the cost of countering terrorism was mounting daily.

At the same time, the Turkish-Cypriots clamoured for help to combat EOKA's threat and to be recognized as a party on the same level as the Greek-Cypriots. It was during this period that Ankara increased its aid to enable the Turkish-Cypriot leadership to replace the underground organization called VOLKAN (volcano) with the better-led TMT (Türk Mukavemet Teskilatı — Turkish Defence Organisation).

As Greece and Turkey solicited support internationally, EOKA and TMT jockeyed for position on the island. The escalation of violence between Greek and Turkish-Cypriots increased and reached its climax during 1958 "with large-scale rioting, terror killings and the evacuation of ethnic minorities from several villages."[62] During the worst eight-week span of violence, 120 people were killed and over 300 were injured.[63]

The impact of the communal violence was not just limited to the island. In Turkey and Greece, public opinion was further roused and, in turn, kept the pressure on their governments not to retreat from their declared policy. The Turkish government and the Turkish-Cypriot leaders argued that the mounting communal violence proved the case for partition. Turkish Premier Menderes declared in a speech that "the utmost sacrifice we can make consists of the partition of Cyprus."[64]

But the Turks were not in a position to dictate partition, and the British had not become despondent enough to give up on other avenues of settlement which could obtain Greek consent. A new set of proposals to resolve the dispute, known as the Macmillan Plan, were unveiled in June 1958. In summary, the plan provided for the appointment of one representative each by Greece and Turkey whom the British Governor would consult. The island as a whole would be run by a Council consisting of the British Governor, the representatives of Greece and Turkey, four Greek-Cypriot and two Turkish-Cypriot ministers. The island's international status would be unchanged for seven years, at the end of which Britain would consent to share its sovereignty with Greece and Turkey.

The Turkish government gave the plan conditional approval by saying that it was not incompatible with partition. However, the Greek government and Makarios rejected the plan outright.[65] From their point of view, the most objectionable feature of the proposals was Turkey's participation in the island's administration, thereby effecting a permanent veto over Enosis. Also, unlike earlier proposals providing for an effective Greek majority in the legislature (as was the case with the Radcliffe Proposals of 1956), this plan introduced fundamental constraints on the will of the Greek-Cypriot majority.

The introduction of the Macmillan Plan coincided with some of the worst communal fighting on the island, and the British government sought to convey its exasperation by threatening to implement it without Greek and Greek-Cypriot support. In fact, however, the British had already made a fundamentally important decision that introduced needed flexibility into what appeared to be an intractable situation: a review ordered by Prime Minister Macmillan had concluded that Britain's strategic needs could be met by having bases on the island rather than exercising sovereign control. This opened the doors for the settlement later negotiated by Greece and

Turkey. Thus, the Cyprus dispute inched toward a new turning point, leading to independence.

What prompted Greece and Turkey to alter their course and negotiate independence? By 1958, it was clear to both countries that neither could succeed in achieving its preferred goal; a standstill had been reached. Enosis was not feasible given the determination of Turkish opposition. Furthermore, both Greek and Greek-Cypriot leaders feared that further escalation in Cyprus would prompt an exasperated Britain to divide the island between Greeks and Turks. Makarios publicly declared his willingness to accept independence in an Athens interview with Barbara Castle, a prominent British Labour Party member, on September 20, 1958. Although Karamanlis and his ministers had considered pursuing the option of independence during 1958, the Archbishop had failed to consult them before announcing his new position.[66] Karamanlis followed suit by telling Mrs. Castle that Greece would accept Greek-Cypriots' choice of solution for Cyprus.[67] However, the Greek-Cypriot leader's upstaging of the Athens government caused considerable aggravation. As Foreign Minister Averoff later wrote:

> Not only was the Greek government, which was chiefly responsible for dealing with foreign governments over the Cyprus question, taken by surprise and made to look foolish. Above all, the handling of the new initiative — which, after all, represented a fundamental shift of position — was wrong because we could have prepared the ground for it through diplomatic channels...[68]

In their turn, the Turks doubted that Britain would allow partition in the face of adamant Greek opposition. Admittedly, Turkish leaders had pursued partition with such vigour during 1957-1958 as to raise questions whether they could reverse themselves and settle on another form of settlement. The *Observer* wrote on June 15, 1958, that "the Turkish Government indeed has nailed its colours so firmly to the mast of partition in recent months, that to unstick them now might well involve its fall. In fact, it shows no sign whatever of doing so."[74]

In reality, as later events demonstrated, partition had been a maximalist position and Ankara was prepared to settle for less. The Turks worried that a new British government might yield to Greek pressures and grant self-determination for all Cypriots (rather than for each of the two communities), and thus pave the way for Enosis. It was unlikely that the Conservatives would do so given their earlier commitments to the Turks, but Ankara was concerned about the Labour Party assuming power, since many Labour spokesmen had supported the Greek-Cypriot case for self-determination and had criticized the Conservative Government for allowing Turkey to dictate British policy on Cyprus.

Ultimately then, Greek and Turkish concerns about the dangers of further escalation, coupled with Britain's decision that sovereign bases rather than sovereignty over the entire island would be adequate for British strategic interests, paved the way for the compromise settlement of 1959 and the creation of an independent Cyprus Republic in 1960. There were other incentives, as well, which played a role in encouraging Greek and Turkish movement towards a compromise settlement. As Stephens explained:

> The outlook was black not only on the island but internationally. Khrushchev, flushed with the success of Russia's first sputnik, was putting pressure on the Western powers over Berlin. There was a call from Washington for a closing of the ranks in NATO to meet the new Soviet threat. Cyprus was drifting into a civil war which threatened to involve Britain, Greece and Turkey — all NATO members — in deepening conflict. All of the parties concerned found they had reasons for considering a compromise.[69]

A meeting between the Greek and Turkish Foreign Ministers in December 1958 started a series of talks that took place during January and culminated in a summit meeting in Zurich on February 6, 1959, led by Prime Ministers Menderes of Turkey and Karamanlis of Greece. The negotiators apparently kept no official minutes[70] and bargained for five days before reaching a comprehensive settlement. On February 11, 1959, the Prime Ministers of Greece and Turkey signed an agreement for the establishment of the Republic of Cyprus. The outline of the settlement was then taken to London for final ratification. On February 19, 1959, the Prime Ministers of Britain, Greece, and Turkey, together with the representatives of Greek and Turkish-Cypriots (Archbishop Makarios and Dr. Küchük respectively), signed the Cyprus agreements.

The settlement to the Cyprus issue was negotiated with minimal involvement by Greek and Turkish-Cypriot leaders. Neither Greek nor Turkish-Cypriot representatives were present during the crucial Zurich talks which finalized the Cyprus settlement. Turkish leaders had consulted with Turkish-Cypriot leaders Küchük and Denktash. Both the Turkish-Cypriots and the Turkish government decided to abandon partition. Once this decision was made, their diplomatic objectives were confined to securing the most favourable terms within the framework of independence. By all accounts, the Turkish-Cypriot leaders were amply satisfied with the terms of the Zurich accords, although they were sceptical over the prospects of co-operation with the Greek-Cypriot leadership in a communal partnership government.

By contrast with their Turkish counterparts, the leaders of Greece faced a difficult task in dealing with the Greek-Cypriot leadership, although during the initial negotiations they did not anticipate the extent of Greek-Cypriot bitterness. The position of the Karamanlis Government of that time period has been fairly described in the following terms:

> The Greek Government had been much exhausted by the Cyprus campaign, and it had no real desire to become responsible for the island. It consulted Makarios as far as it thought necessary over the Turkish proposals, but Karamanlis was determined to get rid of the problem so long as he could avoid partition.[77]

Precisely how much Karamanlis and Averoff consulted with Makarios on the terms agreed to at Zurich has been hotly debated, particularly by Greek-Cypriots. There was some agreement between the Greek and Greek-Cypriot leadership on various major issues that were being discussed with the Turkish government. Makarios was kept informed of the negotiations that were conducted by the Greek Foreign Minister with his Turkish counterpart. He also had a meeting with Prime Minister Karamanlis on 29 January 1959, during which a Greek-Cypriot notable, the Bishop of Kition, and Greek Foreign Minister Averoff were present. The discussions at this meeting helped in reaching a common ground on key issues. For example, both Makarios and Karamanlis agreed to resist Turkey's demand for a federation for Cyprus, which they viewed as a partitionist solution.

In addition, according to Mayes, during their January 29 meeting,

> Karamanlis reported that Turkey still insisted on having a military base in Cyprus which, he said, Greece had just as vigorously opposed. Makarios signified his approval of the Greek stand but raised no objection to Zorlu's idea of a Greek-Turkish headquarters on the island, which Karamanlis thought was worth considering.[72]

The two leaders also reached an identity of views on the adoption of a presidential system of government for the envisaged Republic of Cyprus with a Greek-Cypriot President and Turkish-Cypriot Vice-President, and a 70:30 ratio of Greek-Cypriots to Turkish-Cypriots in the legislature.

> Karamanlis said that Greece had raised no basic objection to Turkey's demand that the Vice-President should have the right of veto on matters of foreign policy and defence. Makarios accepted this but argued that there must be other well-defined areas in which there would be no Turkish-Cypriot veto.[73]

One issue which was later to create so much friction — the question of separate Greek and Turkish Cypriot municipalities — caused no trouble at this stage. Averoff said that he had always opposed this idea as a divisive element in any constitution. However, Makarios and the

Bishop of Kitium both thought that, if the spectre of partition had disappeared, separate municipalities might not be a bad thing. The Greek Cypriots would then be relieved of responsibility for improving conditions in the Turkish quarters of the towns, which lacked many of the amenities of the Greek side.[74]

Following the Zurich agreement, Karamanlis returned to Athens and showed Makarios the full Zurich text and asked for his support. Initially, Makarios expressed his support with the minor qualification that he wanted to negotiate with Turkish-Cypriot leaders for changes by mutual consent. The following day, however, he expressed more fundamental reservations, drawing particular attention to the Treaty of Guarantee which conferred on Turkey, as well as Greece and Britain, the right to intervene in Cyprus in the event of a breach of the agreements. Karamanlis "replied (prophetically) that only through fault of the *Ethnarch* himself could a situation arise in Cyprus that would allow the intervention of the guarantor states."[75] Finally, Makarios told Karamanlis that he would bring a delegation of representative Greek-Cypriots to the London Conference for consultations.[76]

In London where the various parties gathered to sign the Zurich accords, Makarios caused further aggravation for Karamanlis and Averoff by demanding the right to renegotiate unsatisfactory terms. All the other leaders, including the Turkish-Cypriot leader Küchük who had met separately with Makarios, refused the Archbishop's request. The Greek Premier and Foreign Minister were in a particularly awkward position. They urged Makarios to accept the agreements and threatened that, if he refused to ratify them, Greece would abandon Cyprus.[77] During their argument over the settlement, Greek Prime Minister Karamanlis reportedly shouted to Makarios impatiently, "I give you Cyprus on a plate, and you refuse to take it. It's monstrous!"[78]

Makarios himself described the deliberations at the London Conference in the following terms:

In London, I tried hard to get some changes made but there was not enough time to study the agreement. But at the very first reading I singled out thirteen points which were the thirteen points which I raised again in 1963. I tried hard and I failed... I am sure that if I did not sign the agreement, there might be partition. Cyprus would be divided as a colony and we should not be able to raise the question again. The less bad thing was to sign.[79]

In subsequent years, Makarios argued that the Zurich-London agreements were imposed on the Greek-Cypriots and that, therefore, he did not feel morally bound by them.[80] The thesis that the Accords were imposed on the Cypriots was the basis of Makarios' later attempts to abrogate the treaties of Guarantee and Alliance (to which references are made later) on the grounds that they infringed on the sovereignty of the Cypriot state.

Had the Greek-Cypriot leadership participated fully in the negotiation of the agreements, the 1959 settlement would certainly have acquired greater legitimacy. On the other hand, it is a matter of historical conjecture whether an agreed settlement freely negotiated by Turkish and Greek-Cypriots, and acceptable to Turkey, Greece, and Britain, would have been possible or more favourable from the Greek-Cypriot perspective.

Many writers of the Cyprus issue have described the 1959 Accords as a victory for Turkey and the Turkish-Cypriots. That is how the Menderes government characterized the settlement in Parliament in justifying Turkish abandonment of the partition policy. In fact, the Menderes government was spared any damaging criticism by the opposition.[81]

Admittedly, Turkish leaders could not prevail on Greece to accept the creation of a Turkish military base (along with a Greek base) on the island. Nor were they able to win Greek acceptance of a federation that would provide separate governing authorities for Greek and Turkish-Cypriots. Nonetheless, Turkish diplomacy succeeded in winning a veto for Turkey over Cyprus' future through the Treaty of Guarantee and Greece's formal acknowledgement of Turkey's rights on the island. This treaty declared that any activity aimed at Enosis or partition was prohibited.

As "guarantors", Turkey, Greece, and Britain undertook to safeguard the independence of the island. It was upon Turkey's insistence that the controversial Article IV was adopted, which reads as follows:

> In the event of any breach of the provisions of the present Treaty, Greece, the United Kingdom, and Turkey undertake to consult together, with a view to making representations, or taking the necessary steps to ensure observance of these provisions.

> In so far as common or concerted action may prove impossible, each of the three guaranteeing Powers reserves the right to take action with the sole aim of re-establishing the state of affairs established by the present Treaty.[82]

Thus, Turkey secured legal sanction for the use of force, if it became "necessary" and the right to act unilaterally in the event that acting in unison with the other two guarantors could not be arranged. (Following the Greek coup on the island on July 1974, Turkey cited this authority to justify her military intervention). Also, in accordance with the Treaty of Alliance, Turkey was authorized to station 650 troops on the island (as was Greece with 950 troops), providing both an additional recognition of Turkey's rights and further support for the state of affairs established by the Constitution.

In the Independence agreements that it negotiated with Greece, Turkey also secured substantial veto powers and other rights for the Turkish community. The basic structure of the Cyprus Republic provided for a Turkish-Cypriot Vice-President who, either separately or together with the Greek-Cypriot President, could veto any decision of the Council of Ministers (which consisted of seven Greek and three Turkish-Cypriot ministers) or any law or decision of the legislature concerning foreign affairs, defence, and security.

The 70:30 ratio of the Council of Ministers was to be applied in the legislature (House of Representatives) and the civil service. In the 2,000-men Cyprus army, however, it was agreed that the ratio of Greek to Turkish-Cypriot representation would be 60:40.

The 1960 Constitution provided that separate majorities among the Greek and Turkish-Cypriot legislators were needed for laws imposing duties or taxes. This was one of the several safeguards the Turks obtained in the constitutional negotiations in order to assuage Turkish-Cypriot fears of domination by the Greek-Cypriot majority.

In Greek-Cypriot eyes, however, this and other safeguards constituted excessive privileges for the Turkish-Cypriots and were a source of resentment. But the fundamental flaw of the Zurich accords for the Greeks and Greek-Cypriots was that they ruled out Enosis. This is why the Karamanlis government was accused by the Greek Opposition for having committed a "betrayal" Sophocles Venizelos, the leader of the Liberal Party described the Zurich accords as a "national humiliation" and pledged that his party would not be bound by them.[83] "The Liberal and Communist Opposition attacked the agreements for sounding the death-knell of Enosis, leaving Cyprus neither free nor independent but instead putting it under a triple occupation and, worst of all, bringing Turkey back to the island."[84] Nonetheless, the Karamanlis government survived a motion of non-confidence in the Greek parliament.

The manner in which the Zurich-London accords were negotiated, and the terms which were agreed upon, demonstrated that what had begun as a campaign upon Greek-Cypriot leaders' initiative to unite the island with Greece became a much larger issue embracing important interests beyond Cyprus. From the beginning of the EOKA insurgency, Greece and Turkey became central parties in the dispute; without them, no settlement could be reached. The Zurich-London agreements conferring the role of guarantors to these two countries demonstrated their paramount importance in the destiny of the island.

Notes

1. United Kingdom (House of Commons), *Foreign Affairs Committee Report on Cyprus*, London: HMSO, May 1987, p. x.

2. Paschalis M. Kitromilides, "From Co-Existence to Confrontation: The Dynamics of Ethnic Conflict in Cyprus," in Michael A. Attalides (ed.), *Cyprus Reviewed*, Nicosia: Zavallis Press, 1977, p. 44.

3. Richard A. Patrick, *Political Geography and the Cyprus Conflict: 1963-1971*, Waterloo: Department of Geography Publication Series, No. 4, University of Waterloo, 1976, pp. 8, 12.

4. Republic of Cyprus, *Census of Population and Agriculture*, Vol. I, 1960, p. 58.

5. T.W. Adams, *U.S. Army Area Handbook for Cyprus*, Washington: U.S. Government Printing Office, 1964, p. 64.

6. Patrick, *Political Geography*, p. 12.

7. Sir Harry Luke, *Cyprus Under the Turks, 1571-1878*, London: Oxford University Press, 1921, pp. 14-15.

8. *Ibid.*

9. Stepan D. Wosgian, *Turks and British Rule In Cyprus*, Ph.D. dissertation, New York University, 1962, p. 8.

10. Sir George Hill, *A History of Cyprus*, Vol. IV, Cambridge: Cambridge University Press, 1952, p. 39.

11. James A. McHenry, Jr., *The Uneasy Partnerhship on Cyprus, 1919-1939: The Political and Diplomatic Interaction Between Great Britain, Turkey, and the Turkish-Cypriot Community*, Ph.D. dissertation, University of Kansas, 1981, p. 24.

12. C.W.J. Orr, *Cyprus Under British Rule*, London: Robert Scott, 1918, p. 160.

13. For example, see Kitromilides "Co-Existence to Confrontation," pp. 46-7.

14. McHenry, *Uneasy Partnership*, pp. 28-9.

15. *Ibid.*, p. 29.

16. *Ibid.*, p. 134.

17. *Ibid.*, p. 46.

18. *Ibid.*, p. 166.

19. *Ibid.*, p. 161.

20. Kemalism refers to the principles of nationalism and extensive reforms which Kemal Atatürk and his successors have implemented in Turkey.

21. McHenry, *Uneasy Partnership*, pp. 152-3, 188-9.

22. *Ibid.*, p. 140.

23. *Ibid.*, p. 153.

24. A notable exception is the excellent study by James McHenry Jr. which has been amply utilized in this chapter.

25. *Ibid.*, pp. 175-8.

26. *Ibid.*, p 178.

27. *Ibid.*, p. 51.

28. Hill, *History of Cyprus*, p. 553.

29. Stavros Panteli, *A New History of Cyprus*, London: East-West Publications, 1984, pp. 156-7.

30. *Ibid.*, p. 157.

31. Richard Wendell Barham, *Enosis: From Ethnic Communalism to Greek Nationalism in Cyprus, 1878-1955*, Ph.D. dissertation, Columbia University, 1982.

32. *Ibid.*, p. 174.

33. *Ibid.*, p. 175.

34. *Ibid.*, p. 178.

35. Quoted in Barham, *Enosis: Ethnic Communalism*, p. 176.

36. *New York Times*, July 28, 1948.

37. For example, see Stephens, *Place of Arms*, p. 104.

38. Harry Psomiades, "The Consequences of the Lausanne Settlement" in Couloumbis, Petropoulos, Psomiades (eds.), *Foreign Interference in Greek Politics*, New York : Pella, 1976, p. 78.

39. Van Coufoudakis, "Greek-Turkish Relations, 1973-1983: The View from Athens," *International Security*, Vol. 9, No. 4, Spring 1985, p. 186.

40. *Manchester Guardian*, October 20, 1950.

41. Quoted in Stephen Xydis, *Cyprus: Conflict and Conciliation, 1954-1958*, Columbus: Ohio State University Press, 1967, p. 132.

42. David Holden, *Greece Without Columns: The Making of Modern Greeks*, New York: J.B. Lippincott Co., 1972, p. 202.

43. C.L. Doumas, *The Question of Cyprus*, Ph.D. dissertation, University of California at Los Angeles, 1963, p. 109.

44. *New York Times*, May 27, 1950.

45. *Ibid.*

46. Evangelos Averoff-Tossizza, *Lost Opportunities: The Cyprus Question, 1950-1963*, New York: Aristide D. Caratzas, 1986, p. 18.

47. *Ibid.*

48. *Ibid.*, p. 19.

49. Anthony Eden, *Full Circle*, London: Cassell, 1960, p. 396.

50. Dimitri Bitsios, *Cyprus: The Vulnerable Republic*, Salonika: The Institute of Balkan Studies, 1975, p. 26.

51. Mehmet Gönlübol, Cem Sar, et al., *Olaylarla Turk Dıs Politikası, 1919-1965 (A Survey of Turkish Foreign Policy)*, Ankara: Turkish Foreign Ministry Press, 1968, pp. 294-5.

52. *Ibid.*

53. Eden, *Full Circle*, p. 400.

54. See Stephens, *Place of Arms*, p. 54. See also *The Economist*, October 13, 1955.

55. *The Times*, March 6, 1956 and May 29, 1956.

56. Woodhouse, *Karamanlis*, p. 80. See also Bitsios, *Vulnerable Republic*, p. 85.

57. Fahir Armaoglu, *Kıbrıs Meselesi, 1954-1959- Türk Hükümeti ve Kamuoyunun Davranısları(The Reaction of the Turkish Government and Public Opinion in the Cyprus Dispute)*, Ankara: Sevinc Matbaası, 1963, pp. 145-6.

58. Stephens, *Place of Arms*, p. 145.

59. Radcliffe proposed an elected legislative assembly of thirty-six members with a Greek-Cypriot majority of twenty-four and six Turkish-Cypriot members elected through a separate electoral roll. In most matters of internal self-government, legislation would be passed by simple majority. See United Kingdom, *Constitutional Proposals for Cyprus: Report Submitted to the Secretary of State for the Colonies by the Right Hon. Lord Radcliffe, C.B.E.*, London: HMSO, Cmnd. 42, 1956.

60. Stephens, *Place of Arms*, p. 151.

61. For a concise and highly informative discussion of this subject, see Chapter 2 in Thomas Ehrlich, *Cyprus, 1958-1967: International Crises and the Role of Law*,

London: Oxford University Press, 1974.

62. Patrick, *Political Geography*, p. 7.

63. Markides, *Rise and Fall*, p. 25.

64. Quoted in Armaoglu, *Kıbrıs Meselesi*, p. 365.

65. *New York Times*, August 11, 1958.

66. Bitsios, *Vulnerable Republic*, pp. 78-9.

67. *Ibid.*

68. Averoff, *Lost Opportunities*, p. 254.

69. Stephens, *Place Of Arms*, p. 157.

70. Mayes, *Makarios*, London: Putnam Press, 1981, p. 128.

71. *Ibid.*, p. 124.

72. *Ibid.*, p. 127.

73. *Ibid.*, p. 127.

74. *Ibid.*, p. 128.

75. John Reddaway, *Burdened With Cyprus: The British Connection*, London: Weidenfeld & Nicholson, 1986, p. 123.

76. *Ibid.*

77. Stephens, *Place of Arms*, p. 175.

78. Halil Ibrahim Salih, *Cyprus: The Impact of Diverse Nationalism on a State*, Alabama: The University of Alabama Press, 1978, p. 15.

79. This statement is part of an interview given to Robert Stephens, *Place of Arms*, pp. 165-6.

80. Keith Kyle, *Cyprus*, London: Minority Rights Group Report No. 30, 1984, p. 8.

81. Armaoglu, *Kıbrıs Meselesi*. See pages 519-45 for a survey of reactions by the Turkish political parties and press to the Zurich-London Accords.

82. United Kingdom, *Conference on Cyprus: Documents Signed and Initialled at Lancaster House on February 19, 1959*, London: HMSO, 1964, p. 11.

83. Nancy Crawshaw, *The Cyprus Revolt: An Account of the Struggle for Union with Greece*, London: George Allen & Unwin, 1978, p. 345.

84. Mayes, *Makarios*, p. 136.

3

Reacting to Cyprus Developments: Short-lived Communal Partnership, Civil Strife, and Further Mainland Involvement

The Zurich-London Agreements in Application and Greek-Turkish Cooperation, 1960-1963

Having settled the Cyprus issue at Zurich, both the Greek and Turkish governments turned their attention to other areas of concern. Admittedly, the acceptance of the Agreements posed greater difficulties and risks for the Greek than for the Turkish government. After all, Greeks in Greece and Cyprus had to come to terms with abandoning the old national dream of Enosis. The Zurich Accords may have settled the Cyprus dispute, but the desire for Enosis did not wane in Cyprus or Greece. Thus, in due course, Makarios, Grivas, and Greek politicians in Athens were able to exploit widespread national disenchantment in their renewed bid to pursue union.

Forsaking Enosis was not easy even for a statesman like Karamanlis who well understood the limitations of Greece's power. According to C.M. Woodhouse, Karamanlis' biographer, the Greek Premier believed in the historical inevitability of Enosis. But he also believed in the need for avoiding a confrontation with Turkey. As Woodhouse stated:

> His advice had been that Makarios should seek to assuage the suspicions of the Turks, to co-ordinate his policy with the Greek government, and to join NATO as an independent state. Thus the Greek nation would have two voices in all international bodies. In more than one later letter Karamanlis argued that if Makarios had followed his advice, we should easily arrive one day at Enosis.[1]

What Karamanlis envisaged was the increasing dominance of the economically advanced Greek majority in Cyprus to the point where they would ultimately become full masters on the island. Enosis would be attained in practice if not in title.

Long-term hopes aside, however, Karamanlis believed that the agreements were not without major benefits for Greeks and the Greek-Cypriots.

In his book dealing with the 1959 Cyprus agreements, Greek Foreign Minister Averoff expressed these advantages in the following terms:

> First, the Agreements preserved the unity of Cyprus and backed it with watertight safeguards. Second, they made it possible for all the inhabitants to live in peace, in whichever part of the island they wished. Third, they created the right conditions for the Greek-Cypriot community to prosper, despite the special privileges granted to the Turkish-Cypriots. Fourth, they ensured that the Greek imprint on Cyprus would remain and grow progressively more marked, since the Greek-Cypriots were more advanced culturally and better businessmen than the Turkish-Cypriots, as well as being four times as numerous. Lastly, as many people pointed out at the time (and were subsequently proved right), the Agreements paved the way for the creation of 'a second smaller Greece' which would win international recognition as such.[2]

Thus, there was much to be gained from making the agreements work, and Karamanlis encouraged the Greek-Cypriot leadership accordingly. At the London meeting convened to ratify the Accords, he gave this advice to Makarios: "Father, take the agreements into thy hands and work patiently upon them. We shall all help."[3]

In Turkey, the Menderes government, which had negotiated the Cyprus agreements, was overthrown in a military coup in May 1960, before the Cyprus Republic was proclaimed. However, one day after their takeover on May 27, 1960, the military rulers "went on record in support of the Zurich and London agreements."[4] The new military leaders channelled their energies into introducing a new Constitution and civil administration. After the elections of October 1961, a civilian government took office from the military.

In the course of the long and highly publicized Yassiada trials of the overthrown government leaders during 1960-1961, former Prime Minister Menderes, Foreign Minister Zorlu, and Hadimli, the former Governor of Izmir, were convicted of organizing the anti-Greek riots of 1955. According to Alexandris, "the willingness of the military government to bring up the issue of the anti-Greek riots during the Yassiada trials was interpreted as a guarantee of the future well-being of the Greek minority in Turkey by Athens."[5]

Other gestures of goodwill helped ease the strains the Cyprus confrontation had brought about. For instance, on December 25, 1960, President Gürsel appointed an Istanbul Greek, Kaloudis Laskaridis, to the newly created Turkish Senate.[6] In March 1961, at a meeting between Turkish and Greek editors and publishers, an understanding was reached "aimed at improving and increasing the flow of reliable news and views between Greece and Turkey."[7]

It was during this period of improved Greek and Turkish bilateral relations that the partnership government of the Cypriot communities began. For the first time in the history of Cyprus, the two communities were political masters of the island. Obviously, the bitterness and mistrust had to be overcome to make collaboration work. Nonetheless, given the supportive policies of the mainland governments, the Cypriot communities had a unique opportunity to embark on a partnership government.

In the presidential elections of December 1959, Archbishop Makarios was challenged over his abandonment of Enosis. Among the critics of the settlement was EOKA leader Grivas, who had returned to Greece to a hero's welcome. Nevertheless, Makarios defeated John Clerides, the rival candidate for the presidency, winning two-thirds of the votes. He proceeded to win every subsequent Greek-Cypriot election with huge mandates. The Archbishop's political acumen and charismatic personality enabled him to exercise enormous authority in the Greek-Cypriot community. Andreas Papandreou, the future Greek Prime Minister, said of him that "he was not just a president, not just an archbishop; he was a chief in the tribal sense."[8] His political skills were such that he won electoral support "from all the diverse social and political forces, from the extreme Left to the conservative Right."[9]

On the Turkish-Cypriot side, Dr. Fazıl Küchük was acclaimed as Vice-President. Another Turkish-Cypriot leader of considerable stature was Rauf Denktash, a brilliant lawyer and rousing speaker, who became President of the Turkish Communal Chamber and who exercised an influential role in his community's politics.

Cypriot leaders saw themselves as guardians of their respective communities' interests. This approach, as well as the absence of a consensus on how to cope with the major aspects of government, led to constitutional disputes within less than a year. One of the contested provisions stated that civil service jobs were to be allocated between Greek and Turkish-Cypriots in the ratio of 70:30. Since the Turkish share of the population was 20 percent, Greek-Cypriots argued that this was discriminatory to them. Turkish-Cypriots, on the other hand, whose job prospects in the private sector were less favourable than Greek-Cypriots, were eager to have their allocation of public service jobs without delay. According to Nancy Crawshaw, "Turks were not always available to take up specific posts but in some cases the Greeks obstructed their appointment to posts which they were qualified to fill."[10] The issue provoked considerable discord and ultimately weakened the prospects for a successful partnership government.

Another controversial issue that seriously damaged intercommunal relations concerned the division of municipalities in the five major towns. The Constitution provided for the establishment of separate Greek and Turkish municipalities. Ironically, as stated in the previous chapter, it was Makarios (and another senior Greek-Cypriot cleric, Bishop Anthimos of Kition) who had asked Greek Foreign Minister Averoff in 1959 to secure separate municipalities on the grounds that "the Turkish quarters of the towns were squalid and beset with problems and so it would be necessary to spend considerable sums of the Greek-Cypriot taxpayers' money to improve them."[11] However, after independence Greek-Cypriot leaders wanted to defer separation, claiming it could be used as a basis for partition in the future. On the other hand, Turkish-Cypriots pressed for implementation because they feared that Turkish neighbourhoods would be poorly served by unified municipal authorities controlled by the Greek majority. The issue was referred to the Supreme Constitutional Court of the Republic, which ruled in favour of separate municipalities in April 1963.

Yet another disagreement arose over the organization of the Cyprus army. The Constitution provided for an army of 2,000 men, to be recruited after independence: its composition was to be 60 percent Greek-Cypriot and 40 percent Turkish-Cypriot. The Constitution did not specify whether Cyprus army contingents were to be integrated or formed as separate units. Both Vice-President Küchük and Defence Minister Örek (a Turkish-Cypriot) favoured separate units, pointing out that integrated contingents would face great difficulties due to linguistic and religious differences of Greek and Turkish-Cypriot soldiers. Makarios opposed separate units. Consequently, the Greek-Cypriot majority in the Council of Ministers decided on unified contingents. Upon Küchük's use of his veto, Makarios decided not to have an army at all.

These, and other lesser issues, caused deadlock and immobilized the partnership government. To make matters worse, Greek-Cypriot leaders began to advocate Enosis in speeches and statements, even though the island's union had been ruled out by the London-Zurich accords. In a speech he made to mark the anniversary of the start of EOKA's struggle, Makarios declared that the Cyprus state created by the Zurich and London agreements of 1959 was not the object of EOKA's struggle "in any shape and form." The agreements, he stated, were "a landmark and a start for the march forward and the conquest of the future."[12] Even more provocative were the Arch-bishop's statements during a speech in his native village of Panayia on September 4, 1962:

> Until this small Turkish community that forms part of the Turkish race
> which has been the terrible enemy of Hellenism is expelled, the duty
> of the heroes of EOKA cannot be considered as terminated.[13]

Some Greek-Cypriot ministers, especially those who were former members of EOKA, openly advocated Enosis. Statements by Interior Minister

Yorgadjis that "Cyprus has always been Greek" and "Our dream for which EOKA began its campaign will be realised"[14] infuriated Turkish-Cypriots and evoked protests from them and the Ankara government. Such statements strained communal relations and also strengthened the hand of those Turkish-Cypriots who advocated partition.

Since Turkish-Cypriots felt they were not getting the rights granted to them by the constitution, they sought the use of their separate majority and veto rights. In March, 1961, for example, at the height of the 70:30 controversy, the Turkish-Cypriot members used their separate majority right and refused to support two new tax laws in the House of Representatives. This move was intended to put pressure on the Greek-Cypriot leadership to allocate the Turkish-Cypriot share of positions in the civil service. The Greek-Cypriots accused the Turkish-Cypriots of obstruction.

Fundamentally, "Greek-Cypriot objections to the Constitution were political rather than practical."[15] As Reddaway observed in his recent study on Cyprus:

The Greek Cypriots simply did accept bi-communalism in the form and to the extent that it informed the 1960 settlement and from the outset were determined to resist and frustrate it as far as lay in their power. They did not disguise their intention and from their standpoint the position they took was logical, even if questionable on the grounds that it involved dishonouring commitments solemnly entered into at London. The settlement did involve an equality of partnership between Greeks and Turks in Cyprus which seemed to them unjust and which was anathema to them as a denial of their national aspirations and rights as a majority.[16]

This is why the Greek-Cypriot leaders were uninterested in making piecemeal improvements to what they considered to be a fundamentally flawed constitution. Instead, they planned on replacing it altogether with one that would permit the expression of their national aspirations; i.e., realize Enosis. Since they had no illusions that force would have to be used, as in the EOKA days, they began preparing for armed confrontation. As Patrick reported:

The clandestine recruiting, training and organizing of the Greek-Cypriot 'secret army' began early in 1961. Although the EOKA organization of the 1955-1959 campaign had been disbanded, many of its weapons had never been handed over to the Cyprus police and the loyalties and obligations of its cells remained intact. These cells became the cadres of the new force. In 1962, weapons training for company-sized units was being conducted in the Troodos Mountains under the guidance of the Greek-Cypriot officer-cadets of the Cyprus

Army and using arms 'borrowed' from government armories. By December 1963, there were up to 10,000 Greek Cypriots who had been recruited and trained to some extent.[17]

Makarios himself had authorized the drawing up of a blueprint for action, entitled the Akritas Plan. This confidential plan, the contents of which were later published by an anti-Makarios paper,[17] outlined the Greek-Cypriot leaders' strategy: to emphasize the "negative elements" of the constitution while vigorously stressing the principles of "self-determination" and "minority rights" in order to elicit maximum international support.[18] Once self-determination was realized, the Treaty of Guarantee would then be declared redundant and Enosis realized through a plebiscite.

While preparations for the use of force in an anticipated confrontation continued, Makarios sought to turn the impasse to his community's advantage by claiming that Turkish obstructionism made necessary basic Constitutional revisions. As far back as January 4, 1962, he alleged that the Zurich-London agreements conferred rights on Turkish-Cypriots "beyond what is just" and that

> since the Turkish minority abuses these constitutional rights and creates obstacles to the smooth functioning of the state, I am obliged to disregard, or seek revision of, those provisions which obstruct the state machinery and which, if abused, endanger the very existence of the state.[19]

Greek-Cypriot pressures on the constitution led the Turkish-Cypriots to seek Turkey's help and to engage in contingency planning of their own. According to Patrick:

> TMT planning was based on the assumption that a constitutional deadlock would probably lead to inter-communal fighting in 1964. It was thought that the fighting would take the form of the inter-communal riots, kidnappings, and terror killings of 1958. Turk-Cypriot military planning therefore concentrated on preparations for sealing off Turk-Cypriot quarters in the larger towns from Greek-Cypriot mobs and snipers, fortifying Turk-Cypriot villages against Greek-Cypriot police patrols, and by being prepared to counter abductions and assassinations by reprisals in kind.[20]

Both the Turkish and the Greek government of Karamanlis supported the constitutional framework of 1960 and encouraged accommodation. According to Mayes, "the first Turkish ambassador to Nicosia, Emin Dırvana, was instructed to encourage the moderation of Dr. Küchük rather than the more militant attitude of Mr. Denktash."[21] Turkish-Cypriot leaders were discouraged from expecting Turkey's support for the settlement of disputes outside the framework of the Republic's constitution.[22] In short, Turkish-Cypriots were told not to seek a separatist solution as a way out of the constitutional impasse. In his book dealing with the disputes of the 1960-1963 era in Cyprus, Turkish-Cypriot leader Denktash complained bitterly that Dırvana (Turkey's ambassador in Cyprus) kept on counselling moderation in the face of what most Turkish-Cypriots viewed as Greek-Cypriot attempts to usurp Turkish rights. Dırvana continually expressed his confidence that the Cyprus Republic would survive.[23]

As far as amendments to make the constitution more workable were concerned, Ankara's position was based on its belief that Greek-Cypriot leaders were not applying the Constitution in good faith, and that not enough time had passed to justify their allegations that the Constitution was unworkable. Accordingly, the Turkish government asked the Greek-Cypriot leadership to seek solutions to the political crises by working within the framework of the 1960 Constitution.

In an address to the Turkish parliament on March 4, 1964, following the breakdown of intercommunal government in Cyprus, Turkish Premier Inönü disclosed that Turkey made a total of fourteen representations to the Greek-Cypriot leaders between February and December of 1962, warning them to heed the Constitution. In the same speech, responding to Opposition charges of government inaction in the face of Makarios' attempts to alter established constitutional order, Inönü stated that he had warned against unilateral attempts to change the Constitution when the Greek-Cypriot leader paid a state visit to Turkey in November 1962.[24]

At the same time, according to Averoff, who was Greek Foreign Minister at the time, Turkey's policy on the issue of constitutional revision was flexible. Averoff's account of the discussions between the Greek and Turkish governments, and between the Greek-Cypriot leadership and Turkey, is the fullest that has been published so far. In August 1962, during an official visit to Turkey, Averoff sought the Turkish government's support for the amendment of the Constitutional clause requiring separate majorities for the passage of financial legislation. (The Turkish-Cypriot deputies had used this clause to pressure Greek-Cypriots into applying the disputed laws.) Inönü responded favourably and promised to help, once the municipalities issue was resolved fairly.[25]

On the subject of municipalities, Turkey supported the application of the Constitutional provision for separate authorities; however, Ankara suggested that joint coordinating committees be established in each town. Ankara hoped that the committees could evolve into the united municipal councils the Greek-Cypriot leaders favoured.[26]

Three months later, when Makarios went to Ankara, Averoff wrote the following account of the Greek-Cypriot leader's talks with Inönü:

> In general, whenever Makarios based a point on the sound argument that 'certain provisions of the Constitution and of the Agreements present serious difficulties in practice', the Turkish side appeared willing to make concessions. What they did ask was that 'practical ways should be found to implement the controversial provisions' and that 'a climate of mutual trust should be created'. The Archbishop too was prepared to make concessions. He gave convincing explanations for his actions and assured the Turks that the Agreements would be put into practice and that the harmonious co-existence of the two communities was essential.[27]

However, upon the Archbishop's return to the island, the constitutional crisis continued unabated. One month after Makarios' state visit, in response to the Greek-Cypriot decision to abolish separate municipal councils, the Turkish government called upon him to "rectify this decision" and insisted that the Constitution "necessitates the separation of the municipalities."[28]

The Turkish government also sought to enlist the support of the other two guarantors, especially Greece, to help preserve the terms of the Zurich-London Accords. According to Inönü's tally, Ankara made representations to the Greek government on eleven occasions between 1960 and 1963, regarding the Greek-Cypriot leaders' challenge to the legitimacy of the Constitution.[29]

Available evidence indicates that the Karamanlis government declined to become involved in the bid to bring about major changes to the Constitution.[30] Indeed, Karamanlis cautioned Makarios against provoking the Turks.[31] Whether Karamanlis could have dissuaded the Archbishop more forcefully before 1963 is an open question. What is clear is that, fearing Turkey's reaction, he did not encourage Makarios on his chosen course in 1963. In a letter he wrote to the Greek-Cypriot leader on April 19, 1963, Foreign Minister Averoff warned him "...we are determined to dissociate ourselves publicly from your policy if any move should be made towards unilateral denunciation of the Agreements or any part thereof."[32]

Makarios, however, was not daunted by the lack of support from the Karamanlis government or the opposition from Turkey and the Turkish-Cypriots. In any case, in November 1963, elections in Greece resulted in Karamanlis' defeat and the accession to power of George Papandreou, initially at the head of a minority government before winning a substantial majority in the elections in February 1964. This encouraged Makarios because Papandreou not only approved of the revamping of the Constitutional order, but he also promised further support for a policy of Enosis. There was also political change in Turkey. In the following month, Inönü's second coalition government failed to win parliamentary support to continue in power.

It was in the midst of these developments that Makarios decided to act. In a memorandum to Dr. Kuchuk, the Turkish-Cypriot Vice-President, he proposed thirteen changes in the Constitution. Copies of the memorandum were sent to the governments of Greece, Turkey, and Britain. The "thirteen points" amounted to a wholesale revision. If accepted, they would have created an integrated, unitary state, where Turkish-Cypriots would have no veto rights. They would reduce Turkish-Cypriot representation in the civil service and the police force from 30 to 20 percent. Furthermore, they would do away with separate municipalities and unify the administration of justice.

The Turkish government rejected the proposals, and before the reply of the Turkish-Cypriot Vice-President could be given, hostilities broke out. Full-fledged communal warfare began on December 23, 1963. Within days, the partnership government of Greek and Turkish-Cypriots collapsed.

During the three years of intercommunal government, Greek-Cypriots claimed that the Constitution was unfair and unworkable. In their turn, Turkish-Cypriots blamed Greek-Cypriot leaders and Enosis militants for showing bad faith and not working within the spirit of the Constitution. Basically, notwithstanding its complexity and its limited amending power, the Constitution was as workable as Greek and Turkish-Cypriots wanted it to be. This has been retrospectively appreciated by many Greek-Cypriots,[33] but only because the Turkish intervention of 1974 brought about the island's division and cost them dearly; some Greek-Cypriot leaders have publicly acknowledged that the Accords could have been made to work.[34]

The Zurich-London order failed primarily because the Greek-Cypriots viewed it as dishonorable and unjust; their leaders set out to remove it before the ink was dry. This was their agenda and not that of the Greek government in power at the time. Indeed, Makarios and other Greek-Cypriot leaders acted in defiance of the warnings from the Karamanlis government.

During 1958-1959, it was the mainland governments that seized the initiative in the Cyprus dispute by reaching an agreement for the island's government at Zurich. After independence, however, it was the Cypriot communities who determined the course of events. This was a period of relative mainland disengagement which the two communities could have exploited for successful partnership government. Throughout the 1960-1963 period, the thrust for altering the *status quo* came from the Greek-Cypriot leadership, with Ankara and Athens reacting to the Greek-Cypriot leaders' initiatives: Turkey in a bid to save the 1960 Constitution and hence preserve Turkish-Cypriot and Turkish gains, and Greece in an attempt to dissuade the Greek-Cypriot leaders from provoking Turkey's intervention.

Changing Course: Civil Strife, Greek Support for the Renunciation of the Zurich Accords and Turkish Reactions

The Greek-Cypriot decision to remove the Zurich-London Accords was a calculated risk given the anticipated reaction of the Turkish-Cypriots and Turkey. Makarios and his associates had to take into consideration the ability of Turkey to respond militarily.

On the other hand, the Greek-Cypriots had the advantage of considerable local military superiority. Former EOKA leaders directing Greek-Cypriot armed forces felt confident of their ability to crush Turkish-Cypriot resistance before Turkey had a chance to intervene; after all, these were the fighters who believed that they had defeated the professionally trained British forces during the EOKA insurgency. In addition, Makarios expected the new Greek Prime Minister, George Papandreou, to help deter a Turkish intervention by threatening Greek retaliation. Furthermore, Makarios felt assured that his international stature as a prominent member of the non-aligned group of states would enable him to mobilize support among the anti-colonial bloc within the United Nations, particularly since he had sought from the beginning to win condemnation of the 1960 Accords from the world body as having been imposed on the Cypriots. Lastly, since he presented the Greek-Cypriot initiative as a bid to bring about internal changes to the Constitution and to check the guarantor powers' intervention (all of them NATO members), rather than as an attempt to realize Enosis, the Soviet Union could be expected to warn against NATO meddling in the island's affairs.

Within days of the start of hostilities, Greek-Cypriot policemen and irregulars led by several prominent ex-EOKA men, some of whom served as ministers in the Republic's cabinet, launched a major attack on the Turkish areas of Nicosia. Among the militia commanders was Nicos Sampson, a notorious former EOKA gunman who led the attack on the Turkish suburb of Küchük Kaymakli, who was briefly installed as President of Cyprus following the Greek junta's coup in 1974.

As the author of a major work on the Cyprus disturbances stated, "the Greeks aimed at the subjugation of the Nicosia Turks by a swift knockout blow and, in consequence, the automatic surrender of the smaller Turkish communities in the rest of the island."[35] The scale of the fighting in December 1963 in Cyprus surpassed all previous experiences of intercommunal violence. During the most intense period of fighting, between December 21 and 25, hundreds of people were killed, wounded, or taken as hostages. Turkish-Cypriots, outnumbered and outgunned, suffered heavier losses. However, the defence of their positions in Nicosia and several other settlements was effective enough to frustrate the Greek-Cypriot strategy of a quick military victory before Turkey had a chance to intervene with its troops from the mainland. The success in retaining control of the Turkish quarters of major towns, especially Nicosia, made the Turkish military intervention of 1974 possible more than a decade later.

Ultimately, however, it was the threat of Turkey's military intervention that checked the Greek-Cypriot offensive. Two days after the civil strife started on December 23, 1963, Turkish fighter jets were sent on flights over Nicosia as a warning to Greek-Cypriot leaders. In addition, the Turkish army contingent, stationed under the Treaty of Alliance, was ordered to leave its barracks and take up a strategic position controlling the road to Kyrenia. The Turkish government also warned that it would intervene unless Greek-Cypriot attacks on Turkish-Cypriots ceased. In turn, the threat of Turkish action on the island brought the Athens government deeper into the dispute with the warning that Greece would follow suit if Turkish troops intervened.[36]

In the meantime, all the parties agreed to a ceasefire and to let 2,000 British peace-keeping troops patrol the streets of the major towns. "Apparently confident that the danger of a Turkish intervention had passed, Makarios announced on January 1, 1964 that he had abrogated the Treaties of Alliance and Guarantee."[37] The visiting British Commonwealth Secretary, Duncan Sandys, warned Makarios that his unilateral act would precipitate Turkey's intervention. This prompted the Archbishop to change his announced position by stating that he intended to terminate the Treaties by appropriate means.[38] Nonetheless, this apparent reversal did not undermine Makarios' determination: in April 1964, he once again declared the Treaty of Alliance (which allowed Turkey, as well as Greece, to station a contingent of troops on Cyprus) invalid. As expected, the Turkish government denounced the move and insisted on the Treaty's validity.[39]

Two thousand British peace-keepers were unable to keep the peace in the face of organized fighting by the warring parties. As the situation deteriorated, fears of escalation and the spectre of a Greco-Turkish war over Cyprus prompted Britain and the United States to engage in vigorous diplomatic efforts to bring the fighting to an end. Unwilling to assume lone responsibility for peace-keeping, the British Government proposed a larger NATO force. The idea was acceptable to Turkey, the Turkish-Cypriots and, with some reservations, to Greece. However, in spite of determined efforts by the United States to win his endorsement, Makarios rejected the idea. The Greek-Cypriot leader feared that Turkey had a larger influence within the Western alliance than Greece and that a NATO solution would be more favourable to Turkey than to Greek-Cypriots and Greece. Instead, he sought the involvement of the United Nations where he could capitalize on the support of non-aligned and Communist bloc countries opposed to NATO's involvement. Subsequently, upon the initiative of the British and American governments, the United Nations Security Council authorized a peace-keeping force to be sent to Cyprus. The United Nations Force in Cyprus (UNFICYP) became operational on March 27, 1964, with nearly 7,000 troops contributed by various countries. Three days earlier, Secretary-General U Thant had appointed Sakari Tuomioja as mediator, a Finnish diplomat who had previously served as his country's premier.

United Nations troops could not use their arms except in self-defence. Also, they could not search or disarm Greek or Turkish-Cypriots or remove fortifications; neither could they stop the flow of weapons or military personnel that both sides secured from abroad. Furthermore, they were denied full freedom of movement.

In spite of these restrictions, however, the Peace Force managed to defuse many potential conflicts and prevented a large number of local disputes from escalating. However, it was unable to prevent the flare-up of large-scale fighting and further loss of life. Although Turkey repeatedly threatened intervention to restrain the Greek-Cypriots, as one observer wrote, "...each time that Turkey threatened, or appeared to threaten invasion without carrying it out, the credibility of the threat was bound to diminish."[40]

That was only part of the Turkish government's problem. It also had to cope with mounting domestic pressures to relieve the Turkish community. Ever since the beginning of the December 1963 hostilities, Turkish leaders were under pressure from Turkish-Cypriots, opposition parties, and public opinion to aid their compatriots on the island. Turkish papers frequently carried reports of the slaughter of innocent Turkish-Cypriot civilians, including women and children, and charged that Greek-Cypriots were carrying out a "genocide."

Inönü, who in the face of the Cyprus crisis was able to patch together another coalition government, was a former hero of the Turkish War of Independence. He was greatly respected by the military, who were among the groups pressing for intervention. Some writers have argued that the veteran Turkish leader was not keen on intervention.[41] The likelihood of a wider war with Greece and the possibility of Soviet intervention on the side of Greek-Cypriots troubled him. Furthermore, at the time Turkey did not possess landing craft for an amphibious operation in Cyprus. George Harris described Inönü's attitude concerning military intervention in these terms:

> Inönü had shown himself throughout his career to be wary of foreign adventures. His wariness had not decreased over the years. Inönü understood the game of world politics from long experience at the top of government. He could appreciate the complex problems that would

inevitably accompany any Turkish landing on Cyprus; there is evidence that in the councils of war that took place at this time his was the voice to question whether Turkey was prepared to deal with the ultimate implications of intervention or even to carry out the operation itself.[42]

Nonetheless, in spite of the huge risks involved in sending the military, Inönü relented; he informed the United States of his government's decision to intervene on June 4, 1964. The American response, contained in a sternly worded letter to Inönü from President Johnson, was not entirely surprising in its opposition to Turkey's intervention. However, what was unexpected and particularly offensive to the Turkish leaders was Johnson's characterization of the obligations of Turkey and the United States in their bilateral and Alliance relationship. The U.S. President stated that Turkey had an obligation to consult the United States before taking any action in Cyprus. Further, he questioned Turkey's freedom to act by reminding Inönü of the conditions governing the sale of American arms to Turkey:

> I must tell you in all candour that the United States cannot agree to the use of any United States supplied military equipment for a Turkish intervention in Cyprus under present circumstances.[43]

But, from Ankara's perspective, the most aggravating statement in Johnson's letter dealt with American obligations to Turkey in the case of Soviet intervention provoked by the contemplated Turkish action in Cyprus:

> I hope you will understand that your NATO allies have not had a chance to consider whether they have an obligation to protect Turkey against the Soviet Union if Turkey takes a step which results in Soviet intervention without the full consent and understanding of its NATO allies.[44]

Johnson's letter caused serious offence in Ankara but, nevertheless, had the desired American objective of dissuading the Turks from intervening in June 1964. Still, continued assaults on Turkish-Cypriot positions by Greek-Cypriot forces kept the pressure on Turkey to achieve concrete results. A few months later, Turkey seized an opportunity to lend more credibility to its threats of intervention.

During the first week of August 1964, Greek-Cypriot forces launched a major offensive against the only outlet to the sea (at the Erenköy and Mansoura beachhead) controlled by Turkish-Cypriot fighters. In spite of the United Nations troops in the area, Greek-Cypriot forces overran several Turkish-Cypriot villages. Before they took control of the coastal positions, however, the Turkish Air Force intervened and, in a series of raids on August 8 and 9, stopped the Greek-Cypriot advance, inflicting heavy losses on the

Greek-Cypriot forces and causing some damage to several Greek-Cypriot villages in the area.

When the Turkish Air Force began its bombing operation to stop the Greek-Cypriot advance, Makarios appealed to Greece, the Soviet Union, and Egypt for military help. No such help came. Soviet leader Khrushchev expressed a willingness to negotiate military assistance, but he also urged Makarios to "use all efforts to prevent bloodshed."[45] More significantly, Greece did not send her Air Force to confront Turkish jets. In his book dealing with the events of this time, Andreas Papandreou described the position of his father's government in the following terms:

> Makarios demanded that we dispatch our Air Force to provide his cover. We did not, not because we did not wish to, but because it was technically impossible. Cyprus was far from Greek air bases, and our fighters would have had no more than two minutes' flying time over Cyprus. We would therefore only have provoked Turkey into further action, without offering substantive aid to the Cypriot ground forces.[46]

While George Papandreou was criticized by Greek-Cypriots and Greeks alike for his government's passivity during the Turkish air raids, he accused Makarios of breaking an agreement that no military operation would be started against Turkish-Cypriots without the prior consent of the Greek government.

Actually, Papandreou supported Greek-Cypriot goals, including Enosis, more enthusiastically than his predecessors. Even before the Erenköy events, he had reached an agreement with Makarios to send a large clandestine military force to Cyprus in order to help deter a Turkish military intervention. As Andreas Papandreou wrote later:

> At the April meeting between Makarios and Papandreou an important, indeed a critical decision had been made. Cyprus was quite far from Greece. Greece's commitment to Cyprus, therefore, that it would come to its assistance in case Turkey landed troops did not amount to much. If Greece were really able to contribute militarily to the defence of Cyprus, it would have to do so before the Turks attacked. In fact, if Greece, by shipping troops and arms to Cyprus in a clandestine way, could raise the cost of a Turkish landing, it might well be in a position to prevent it. This was my father's proposal, and Makarios accepted it.[47]

An estimated 12,000 mainland Greek troops were subsequently stationed on the island.[48] These troops would no doubt make a Turkish landing much more difficult and costly and to that extent served as a considerable deterrent to Turkey.

The Turkish government was profoundly disturbed by the support Greece's Papandreou government gave to the Greek-Cypriot leadership. In Turkish eyes, by endorsing Makarios' unilateral renunciation of the Zurich-London settlement, Papandreou shared in the blame for the strife on the island. Rather than fulfill Greece's obligation to maintain the Zurich-London arrangements, as Turkey pressed it to do, Papandreou's government decided to back the course chosen by the Greek-Cypriot leadership.

In Opposition, it will be recalled, Papandreou had condemned the Zurich-London Accords and the abandonment of Enosis. When in office, he had to be more circumspect. Indeed as *The Times* quoted, "the majority government of Mr. Papandreou [soon] manoeuvred itself to an unwieldy position for fear of exposing itself to the same criticism that Mr. Papandreou, while in Opposition, had hurled against the previous Government over Cyprus."[49] Of course, politicians are often obliged by the imperatives of office to repudiate commitments made in Opposition. Nonetheless, Papandreou still chose to cater to Greek national sentiments on the Cyprus issue and renew the quest for Enosis. For the Turks, particularly, Papandreou's relative lack of restraint in office was a major departure in Greek policy toward Cyprus.

At international forums, namely at meetings of NATO and the United Nations, Greek officials stressed the sovereign rights of the Greek Cypriot-controlled Cyprus government to change its own Constitution and remove treaties that undermined its sovereignty. In addressing Greek audiences, however, Papandreou went further, by publicly declaring his support for Enosis. In a speech he made at the Thessaloniki University, Papandreou declared that "Enosis will come. It is coming. It is common knowledge that the Cyprus problem can only be solved through Enosis. The only obstacle is the absurdity of Turkish demands."[50]

In yet another speech, he declared with rhetorical flourish at the Officers' Club in Salonika: "Enosis is coming, and with Cyprus as a stepping stone Hellenism will continue its advance into the Middle East in the steps of Alexander the Great."[51] At a more practical level, Papandreou dispatched a team of economic experts to the island to study the economic repercussions and adjustments of Enosis. As *The Economist* remarked, "whether a marriage will be arranged between the kingdom of Greece and the republic of Cyprus is very much in the balance, but at the moment the Greek government is certainly going through all the motions of a bridegroom presumptive."[52]

Papandreou forfeited the understanding and cooperative relations the Karamanlis Government had maintained with Turkey over Cyprus. But as the strife on Cyprus continued and the condition of the Turkish community deteriorated, Ankara insisted on bilateral talks with Greece to help restore Turkish-Cypriot rights. Papandreou, though, had agreed with Makarios that the United Nations, and not Greece and Turkey, could legitimately involve itself in the settlement of the dispute.

In the aftermath of his controversial letter to Inönü, President Johnson invited both Inönü and Papandreou to the United States for talks on Cyprus. During the latter's visit to Washington, Johnson reportedly told Papandreou that, having stopped the Turks from taking direct military action over Cyprus a number of times, the American government could not do so again.[53] Within NATO's Permanent Council, the Greek government was reprimanded for sending large numbers of troops and equipment to Cyprus and warned that military aid would be suspended if it did not engage in direct talks with the Turkish government to end the crisis.[54] In spite of considerable American and NATO pressure, however, Papandreou stuck to his position and refused to discuss the issue directly with the Turkish leader. Papandreou opposed direct talks with Turkey for he felt that to do so would constitute an admission that the Cyprus question was a Greek-Turkish problem. He was unwilling to accept that Ankara had any legitimate interest in Cyprus, except on the question of the Turkish community's rights as a minority group.[55]

On the other hand, Papandreou did not always approve of Makarios' brinkmanship and supported a less provocative course on the island to deny Turkey the justification for military intervention; hence, his admonition of the Archbishop during the Erenköy offensive in 1964 for taking initiatives which threatened to bring Greece into a war with Turkey. Earlier, in December 1963, when the Greek-Cypriot leaders decided to launch a major attack on the Turkish community, Papandreou rejected the Greek-Cypriot call for the Greek contingent to be ordered to neutralize the Turkish contingent. As Paul Rahe explained:

> In the crunch, Greek Prime Minister George Papandreou was unwilling to take that risk: he had only recently been able to oust Constantine Karamanlis from power, and he was in the midst of an electoral campaign in Greece. In those circumstances, he could hardly afford to quarrel with Makarios which is what allowed Makarios a relatively free hand that fateful December. But, by the same token, Papandreou could hardly risk a confrontation with Turkey, and there was no telling whether a move by the Greek army against the Turkish army in Cyprus might not become a *casus belli.*[56]

In addition, during the tense first half of 1964, when the danger of Turkish intervention appeared high, Papandreou asked the Greek-Cypriot leader to restrain the extremists in the Greek community. As *The Economist* of April 15, 1964 reported:

During the recent discussions between the Greek Prime Minister, Mr. Papandreou, and Archbishop Makarios it was made abundantly clear that if the Greek government is to support the archbishop in his campaign for self-determination, then as a *quid pro quo* he must cooperate as far as possible with the United Nations.

Although he refused to meet with Turkish leaders to discuss a settlement for Cyprus, Papandreou appeared more understanding than Makarios of the need for some accommodation of Turkish interests in a future settlement. *The Economist* recognized the differences between the Papandreou and Makarios governments when it stated that "in over-simplified terms, the Greek government may be prepared to settle for a 90 percent victory, while Archbishop Makarios and the Greek Cypriots want 100 percent."[57]

The differences between the Greek and Greek-Cypriot leadership can be illustrated by comparing their reaction to the Acheson Plan. Dean Acheson, the veteran American diplomat, had been assigned by President Johnson to find a formula for resolving the Cyprus issue and ensuring that Greece and Turkey would not fight over it. By this time, American officials had decided that a formula that provided for Enosis, with concessions to Turkey, stood the best chance of gaining acceptance by the principal parties; such a settlement would have the added advantage of keeping the island within NATO and neutralizing Makarios, whose appeals for Soviet and non-aligned support had alienated Washington.

Acheson's plan provided for Enosis in return for a military base for Turkey in the northeast corner of the island and the creation of one or two Turkish-Cypriot cantons with local autonomy. The plan also called for the cession to Turkey of the tiny island of Castellorizon off the Turkish coast in the Mediterranean; further, it provided for compensation for those Turkish-Cypriots who wanted to leave the island. The Turkish government thought the plan worthy of discussion and so did the Greek government; in particular, Papandreou favoured the revised version of the plan calling for Turkey to be granted a long-term lease rather than sovereign rights for a base. He was quoted as saying to his colleagues that "we are being offered an apartment building and subletting only one penthouse to our neighbours, the Turks."[58] The idea of leasing a base was unacceptable to the Turks, but it was the Greek-Cypriot leadership who scuttled the plan. Makarios categorically condemned Acheson's solution as a plan of partition and pressured Papandreou to reject the plan. Eventually, the Greek Premier bowed to Makarios' insistence and rejected the Acheson offer. However, Makarios' rebuff and conduct did not sit well with many Greek officials; he was publicly blamed by Greek Deputy Prime Minister Stephanopoulos for rejecting an offer for Enosis.[59]

Makarios was able to carry the Greek-Cypriot masses with him, but Papandreou was wary of merely reacting to the Archbishop's initiatives. Following the Greek-Cypriot operation in August 1964, which had provoked Turkey to launch air-raids, Papandreou "laid down to Makarios the doctrine of the National Centre."[60] As he elaborated later to the Greek-Cypriot leader,

> No decision shall be taken in Cyprus that may lead directly or indirectly to hostilities without our approval. The opinion of Athens must be final for it is Athens that bears responsibility of the whole of Hellenism.[61]

Furthermore, Papandreou did not trust Makarios' commitment to Enosis.[62] The Greek leader believed that although Makarios paid lip service to union with Greece, he actually preferred to be the leader of an independent state. As his son Andreas Papandreou put it, "He (Makarios) always talked about Enosis — but he always acted in the direction of independence."[63] Given these suspicions, Papandreou sent Grivas to Cyprus in 1964 to keep Makarios on the Enosis track.

As commander of the National Guard, Grivas insisted on taking his orders from Athens and not from the elected Greek-Cypriot government headed by Makarios. This meant that the Greek-Cypriot National Guard was under the control of Greece, as were the 12,000 illicit Greek troops that had been smuggled onto the island in 1964. Greek-Cypriot recruits wore Greek army badges and took the same oath as the army in Greece, pledging allegiance to the Greek King rather than Makarios or Cyprus.[64] It was worrisome enough for Makarios that he could not command the National Guard, but he was also concerned that it could be used against him. Although this did not happen until July 1974 when the Greek junta ordered Makarios' overthrow, the possibility of Grivas' doing so was a matter of speculation for several years.[65] Makarios tried, but failed, to have Grivas replaced as commander of the National Guard in 1966, at a time when short-lived governments without a strong mandate alternated in Athens.[66] Grivas reveled in Makarios' failure declaring, "There is only one army in Cyprus — the Greek army."[67]

Papandreou had another role assigned for Grivas. He counted on Grivas' strong anti-Communist position to keep Makarios' relations with the Soviet Union in check.[68] In spite of the Greek government's commitment to defend the Greek-Cypriots in the event of Turkey's military intervention, Makarios did not hesitate to appeal for Soviet assistance to restrain Turkey. The Soviet leadership declined to help the Greek-Cypriot government at the time of the Turkish air raids in August 1964, but they did send arms to the Greek-Cypriot government.[69] Although there is no evidence that Papandreou disapproved of Makarios' use of the Soviet card whenever Turkey threatened intervention, he was nevertheless suspicious of the Greek-Cypriot leader's ties with the Soviet bloc and warned him against political commitments to the Soviet Union.[70]

In turn, Makarios did not trust governments in Greece for fear they would succumb to pressure from the Western allies and Turkey to settle for less than the island's total incorporation into Greece. He was particularly disturbed when Papandreou's foreign minister conducted talks with his Turkish counterpart during a meeting of NATO foreign ministers,[71] even though the talks were purely exploratory and achieved nothing. Makarios was even more agitated when the Stephanopoulos and Paraskevopoulos governments conducted a dialogue with Turkey during their brief terms in office, lest these governments agree to some variant of the Acheson plan; i.e., the granting of a military base to Turkey in Cyprus in return for Enosis. When the prominent Greek-Cypriot politician Glafcos Clerides called "the Kanellopoulos government incompetent in its handling of the Cyprus question,"[72] he spoke for the rest of the Greek-Cypriot leaders. There was no love lost between the Greek-Cypriot leadership and the leaders of these caretaker governments.

In writing about the relations between the Greek-Cypriot government and those of George Papandreou and his pre-junta successors, a Greek-Cypriot author offered this assessment:

> ...the Greek Cypriots exerted a strong influence under the parliamentary governments of George Papandreou and Stephanopoulos on Greek politics because they had the sympathy of Greek public opinion. It would not seem unfounded to say that during that period the Cyprus government had the last word, tending to make its policy impinge on the Greek Government rather than the reverse.[73]

By comparison with Greece and her relationship with the Greek-Cypriots, the Turkish government experienced none of the difficulties in dealing with the besieged Turkish-Cypriots. The Greek-Cypriot leaders used non-aligned and Soviet support in their struggle, while Turkish-Cypriots relied exclusively on Turkey. Although Ankara's assistance fell short of expectations, it was Turkey's reluctance to send troops to the island that most disappointed Turkish-Cypriots. Admittedly, the limited Turkish air raids had boosted morale and hopes of future intervention, but Turkey was unable to prevent the erosion of Turkish-Cypriot rights on the island.

The more Turkish-Cypriots were mistreated or threatened by the Greek-Cypriot authorities, the more dependent they became on Turkey. During the Turkish air raids of August 1964, Makarios issued an ultimatum to Ankara and threatened to order indiscriminate attacks on all Turkish-Cypriot communities on the island unless the air raids were halted.[74] As a reminder of how far Makarios would go to realize his ambitions, the threat did not surprise Turkish-Cypriots. In fact, after the outbreak of strife in late 1963, thousands of Turkish-Cypriots abandoned their homes from about 103 villages and settlements and went to live in areas of Turkish concentration. By March 1964, when as many as 25,000 such refugees had moved to these enclaves,[75] the number of Turkish-Cypriots under the authority and protection of the Turkish-Cypriot leadership represented more than one-half of their population.

After the Erenköy events, the Greek-Cypriot government changed its tactics in dealing with Turkish-Cypriots. Rather than initiate major military operations against Turkish-Cypriot enclaves, which risked Turkey's intervention, Makarios initiated an economic blockade during the latter half of 1964, restricting the movement of food and other commercial materials between areas controlled by Turkish-Cypriots and preventing them from obtaining a host of commodities categorized as prohibited materials. Some of these commodities had a direct military application, but withholding others such as fuel, woollen clothing, building materials, and tents, caused serious deprivations for Turkish-Cypriots. In addition, the Greek-Cypriot authorities imposed restrictions on the movement of Turkish-Cypriots and, moreover, frustrated the delivery of Red-Crescent food shipments and other relief materials from Turkey.[76] In 1964, in the aftermath of the Erenköy bombings, Turkey warned that she would "be compelled to take appropriate action" to deliver food supplies to enclaves where such supplies were prevented from entering, but the threat was not carried out.[77]

In his report to the Security Council on September 10, 1964, the Secretary-General of the United Nations reported that "the economic restrictions being imposed against the Turkish communities in Cyprus, which in some instances have been so severe as to amount to veritable siege, indicate that the Government of Cyprus seeks to force a potential solution by economic pressure as a substitute for military action."[78] Although the United Nations Force did much to alleviate the hardships resulting from these restrictions, it was not until March 1968 that most of them were removed.

From the outset, the civil strife ended the participation of the Turkish-Cypriots in the partnership government which the 1960 Constitution had established. This enabled Greek-Cypriots to gain total control of the government. Acting as the government of Cyprus, the Greek-Cypriot leadership proceeded to declare basic provisions of the Constitution null and void, and to legislate without the participation and consent of Turkish-Cypriots.

On April 1, 1964, the Greek Cypriot-controlled House of Representatives passed a Conscription Law creating a National Guard of over 10,000 Greek-

Cypriot conscripts; the training for the force was provided by Greek officers brought from Greece. In November 1964, a new law was enacted providing for unified municipalities. Yet another law, passed in July 1965, abolished the separate communal electoral lists and districts.[79] For all intents and purposes, then, the Makarios government unilaterally established a unitary government in Cyprus exercising full authority everywhere but in the Turkish enclaves.

At the same time that the Greek-Cypriot leaders pursued their policy of exclusion and punitive measures toward the Turkish community, they regularly declared their commitment to uniting the island with Greece. This can be illustrated by the following resolution passed by the Greek-Cypriot House of Representatives on June 26, 1967 (three months after the Greek junta came to power in Athens):

> Interpreting the age-long aspirations of the Greeks of Cyprus, the House declares that despite any adverse circumstances it will not suspend the struggle conducted with the support of all Greeks, until this struggle succeeds in uniting the whole and undivided Cyprus with the Motherland, without any intermediary stages.[80]

Greek-Cypriot leaders have often alleged that Turkey's intervention in Cyprus and encouragement of hard-line policies within the Turkish community made it impossible, or created great obstacles, to reach a settlement to the Cyprus conflict. In the aftermath of the 1963 strife, however, Greek-Cypriots held the upper hand on the island. With the Turkish-Cypriots surrounded in their impoverished enclaves, the Makarios government proceeded to isolate and pressure them to accept Greek-Cypriot rule without the special community rights provided by the Zurich-London arrangements. By offering the Turkish-Cypriots nothing better than terms of surrender, Makarios unwittingly drove them closer to Ankara.

Ultimately, by provoking greater involvement by Turkey, the adversarial and threatening Greek-Cypriot treatment of the Turkish community had far-reaching consequences for the future destiny of the island. Thus, in a fundamental sense, the basic alienation of the two Cypriot communities after 1963 was generated within the island and not outside as has been argued by some authors.[81]

Greek-Turkish Relations Under the Papadopoulos and Ioannidis Juntas and a Major Opportunity for a Cyprus Settlement, 1967-1974

On April 21, 1967, a group of Greek colonels seized power in Athens in a bloodless coup. All of the top coup leaders had served with Greece's forces in Cyprus and thus had first-hand familiarity with the issue. Ankara was one of the first governments to recognize the junta regime, and Turkish leaders hoped that prospects of a Greek-Turkish settlement on Cyprus would be easier with a regime that controlled the press and kept a tight rein on the Opposition which could accuse it of a sell-out. For their part, the new Greek rulers themselves thought that they could make a deal with Turkey to facilitate Enosis with minimal concessions. The fact that the Greek-Cypriot government was opposed to virtually any concession did not deter the new rulers. Accordingly, a few months after seizing power, the leader of the junta, Colonel Papadopoulos, accepted Turkish Prime Minister Demirel's proposal for a summit meeting in September 1967, during which he offered a Turkish military base on Cyprus in return for Turkey's acceptance of Enosis. "Demirel countered with the predictable demand for an area big enough to accomodate most of the Turkish Cypriot community — the old idea of 'double Enosis' or, as the Greek Cypriots saw it, partition."[82] For Turkey, a military base alone was unacceptable; conceding what the Turks wanted was an excessive price for Greece's new rulers to pay: the talks ended in failure.

To the extent that the 1967 Greek offer resembled the earlier Acheson plan (Enosis in return for a base for Turkey) to which the Turkish government was agreeable, it is tempting to speculate as to why the summit meeting failed. One reason that has been cited is that the meeting between the Greek and Turkish leaders was convened with little preparation. In addition, whereas the United States worked hard to make the Acheson Plan acceptable in 1964, there was no such brokerage during 1967, and that may have been the deciding factor in the failure of the Greek bid.

The military junta accepted the Turkish offer for a summit without informing Makarios.[83] Although the outcome of the summit meeting caused relief among the Greek-Cypriots, relations between Nicosia and Athens went sour and deteriorated with time.

In the meantime, after the collapse of the summit talks, an unexpected crisis in Cyprus almost resulted in Turkey's military intervention. In the aftermath of the Turkish air raids of August 1964, the Greek-Cypriot leaders had refrained from large-scale attacks on Turkish-Cypriots. Unlike the more aggressive Grivas, Makarios preferred to chip away at Turkish-Cypriot strength gradually, thus denying Turkey justification for military intervention. In November 1967, however, with the consent of the military regime in Athens, Grivas ordered the Greek-Cypriot National Guard to launch an attack on two Turkish-Cypriot villages, Bogazici and Geçitkale, following a minor incident. Before a cease-fire came into effect the next day, about twenty-eight Turkish-Cypriots had been killed, and severe damage was inflicted on houses and property in both villages.

The Turkish government reacted by sending its jets on warning flights over Cyprus. As public demonstrations took place in Istanbul and Ankara urging military intervention on the island, the Turks mobilized their forces for possible action. As the *New York Times* reported on November 29, 1967:

> The Turks see the moment ripe to get back at the Greeks for all the injury and insult they feel they have suffered in Cyprus since the United States in effect prevented them from invading after communal fighting in December, 1963. Now is the time, the Turks say, for the security of their minority on the island to be assured for once and all, by agreement if possible, by war if necessary.

In an effort to soften Turkish anger, the Papadopoulos junta appointed an experienced diplomat and politician, Panayotis Pipinelis, as Foreign Minister. Nonetheless, Turkish preparations for a landing in Cyprus continued. Indeed, some accounts of the crisis have contended that Turkish troops would have landed on the island in November 1967 but for freak storms in the Eastern Mediterranean.[84]

Turkey's threat to take military action led to intense diplomatic activity among the powers, particularly the United States. The United Nations, through the Secretary General's special envoy Rolz-Bennett, NATO Secretary-General Brosio, as well as United States Presidential envoy, Cyrus Vance, approached all parties in a bid to avert war. " On a single day, 26 November, for example, one was in Ankara, one in Athens, and one in Nicosia."[85] It was Vance who was responsible for the understanding that was reached.

The agreement, reached on November 30, 1967, was largely a matter of Greek compliance to Ankara's demands. The Greek government agreed to withdraw the nearly 12,000 clandestine troops that had been smuggled to Cyprus and to recall General Grivas. For its part, Turkey agreed to disband its forces in southern Turkey that had been readied for landing in Cyprus.

It has generally been assumed that the Greek junta gave in to Turkish demands to avoid a war with an adversary whose army is three times its size. This is only a partial explanation. On Cyprus itself, the Greeks had a substantial advantage: the presence of a substantial Greek force would have made a Turkish landing difficult and costly. Indeed by accepting to withdraw this force as part of the settlement negotiated by Vance, Greece lost a very important deterrent against Turkey's future military intervention on the island; the withdrawal made it considerably easier for Turkish troops to gain control of northern Cyprus seven years later, in the aftermath of the Ioannidis coup of 1974. In addition, the withdrawal could be interpreted as a major step away from Enosis. The several thousand Greek troops on the Island, and the various steps — real and symbolic — to integrate Greek and Greek Cypriot soldiers were the strongest tangible ties between Greece and Cyprus. If the excess Greek forces were withdrawn, the continued independence of the island would appear more likely. On the other hand, withdrawal would also imply that the Treaty of Alliance was still valid and, therefore, that the 1960 Accords would be the starting point for negotiating a new settlement.[86]

When the crisis broke out on Cyprus in November 1967, the Greek junta had only been in power for about half a year. It was weak and internationally unpopular. Also, given its firm orientation towards NATO and the United States, the Greek regime was susceptible to American pressures to make concessions and avoid a war with Turkey. It was essentially for these reasons that it backed down and accepted most of Turkey's terms.

By winning major concessions from Greece, Turkish leaders could justify calling off their military intervention. But the Demirel government was widely criticized by many Turks for losing a favourable opportunity to use force and solve the Cyprus problem once and for all. By this time, the Turkish army had been provided with the landing craft that were needed for an amphibious operation in Cyprus, and the Turkish military apparently favoured intervention. However, Prime Minister Demirel and the Foreign Ministry were reportedly reticent to involve the country in a war provided that major political concessions could be extracted from the Greek military regime.

Throughout the negotiations conducted by Vance and the other diplomats, Makarios "was again displaying all his old qualities of 'brinkmanship'."[88] The Archbishop raised no objection to the withdrawal of Greek troops and Grivas' recall because his hand was thereby strengthened in Cyprus. However, he made the task of the negotiators difficult by rejecting a number of other agreements reached between Ankara and Athens. For example, the Greek government had accepted Turkey's demands that the Greek-Cypriot National Guard be disbanded, but Makarios successfully resisted this,[89] much to his later regret. He also turned down a proposal by the United Nations Secretary-General U Thant to give wider powers to the Peace Force. Furthermore, he rejected a reported understanding between Greece and Turkey for the Turkish-Cypriots "to be allowed to maintain a police force and have a degree of self-government in their own areas."[90]

According to Nancy Crawshaw, "the Kophinou [Geçitkale] crisis was a turning-point in the island's post-colonial history."[91] The Greek-Turkish dialogue that had started before the November crisis had failed to bring about a Cyprus settlement. One of the most important consequences of the 1967 crisis was a period of disengagement from the affairs of the island by

Greece and Turkey and the assumption by the two Cypriot communities of the major responsibility in the search for a settlement. The sobering effect created by the crisis brought about a period of calm and reassessment in Cyprus. Turkey's threat of invasion and ability to exact concessions from Greece demonstrated to Greek-Cypriots, yet again, that Enosis could not be effected in the face of determined Turkish opposition. Moreover, the Greek junta's unpopularity among Greek-Cypriots, and the removal of Grivas, strengthened the position of those in the Greek community who preferred to give negotiations a chance rather than continue with the strife indefinitely. In the presidential election held in February 1968, Makarios received an exceptionally strong mandate by winning 95 percent of the votes against the rival candidate, Dr. Evdokas, who had campaigned on a platform based on Enosis. The United Nations and other governments urged Makarios to make conciliatory gestures toward the Turkish community and to take the first step as the stronger party. His government's pacification measures, which removed irritating restrictions on Turkish-Cypriots, were intended to create a conciliatory atmosphere and to serve as an inducement to the Turkish-Cypriots. Restrictions were removed on the movement of Turkish-Cypriots and also on the movement of goods to and from the Turkish areas.

The Turkish-Cypriots had their own incentives to reach a negotiated settlement. However contented they were with Turkey's ability to force Greece to withdraw her troops and General Grivas from the island, they were disillusioned over her inability or unwillingness to intervene by force to bring about a fair settlement. In addition, the weariness resulting from the economic deprivations brought on by the strife gave added reason to the Turkish-Cypriots to modify some of their declared aims (in particular, their demand for a federal solution based on geographical separation) and to engage in direct talks with a view to reaching a settlement.

The Turkish leadership officially designated Rauf Denktash as their representative in the proposed talks. Although he did not attain the top position in the Turkish community until the early 1970s, Denktash was widely viewed by most Turkish-Cypriots as a vigorous defender of their rights. The Makarios government viewed him as a hard-liner and preferred someone more conciliatory to deal with. When Denktash went to Turkey soon after the 1963 December outbreak of strife, the Greek-Cypriot government banned his return to the island. Contrary to Greek-Cypriot hopes, however, Denktash retained his preeminent standing in the Turkish community. In October 1967, he made an attempt to enter the island secretly but was apprehended and detained by the Greek-Cypriot authorities; he was subsequently allowed to return to Turkey following demands for his release by the Turkish government. As part of Makarios' conciliatory pacification programme, Denktash was allowed to return to Cyprus to assume his role as chief negotiator for his community.

The Greek-Cypriot side chose Glafcos Clerides as their negotiator. Clerides had solid credentials as a Greek-Cypriot nationalist: he had been a member of EOKA and defended many of its fighters brought to court by the British authorities during the EOKA insurgency before independence. He also had been one of the principal architects of the Akritas Plan. Nonetheless, he had a reputation for flexibility and had good personal relations with Denktash.

The preparation of the groundwork for the talks was helped by Osorio-Tafall, the Special Representative of the Secretary-General in Cyprus. An agreement was to be sought within the framework of an independent unitary state. Accordingly, it was agreed by the two sides that Enosis, or any solution based on the geographical separation of the two communities (i.e., partition or federation), could not form the basis of negotiations. At the same time, there was an agreement in principle to provide some form of local autonomy to assuage Turkish-Cypriots' concerns over security. Clerides and Denktash held a preliminary meeting in Nicosia on June 2 and initiated the talks formally on June 24, 1968.

Inasmuch as both sides looked to direct talks as the most realistic means of achieving a settlement, the intercommunal talks aroused some modicum of hope. Furthermore, external support for the negotiations was substantial, not the least by the mainland governments. Nonetheless, there was an enormous gap in the bargaining strength of the two sides that influenced both the substance and the conduct of the negotiations. Ultimately, this asymmetry was instrumental in the failure of the talks, in spite of six years of protracted bargaining.

In the intercommunal talks, the bargaining position of the Greek-Cypriots was much stronger than that of the Turkish-Cypriots. In the aftermath of the December 1963 strife, considerations of safety had obliged Turkish-Cypriots to withdraw from the bi-communal administration. Consequently, as previously stated, Greek-Cypriots assumed exclusive control of the Republic's institutions. This Greek Cypriot-controlled authority was recognized as the Government of Cyprus internationally by all states except Turkey. Makarios sought to use this advantage in every conceivable sphere to weaken the Turkish-Cypriot position and to deter Turkey's intervention.

The Greek-Cypriot government consistently followed a non-aligned policy and supported the position of non-aligned states at the United Nations. Since his attendance at the Bandung Conference as an observer in 1955, Makarios had worked hard to develop ties with many non-aligned leaders. Most non-aligned states supported the position of the Makarios government at the United Nations General Assembly and at the non-aligned conferences.[92] In part, this diplomatic aid was the reward for Makarios' diligent work in non-aligned councils. In addition, and more importantly, most of these Afro-Asian states identified easily with the Greek-Cypriot majority because they too faced demands for political community rights by self-differentiating ethnic communities within their borders.

Turkish-Cypriots, on the other hand, had no say in Cypriot foreign policy or in any other aspect of the Republic's government. Thus, they had to rely on Turkey alone to express their case internationally. As a member of NATO, however, Turkey was unable to match the diplomatic support which the Greek-Cypriot government obtained from the bulk of the non-aligned states. Moreover, in spite of the threat to the Turkish-Cypriot community by the Greek-Cypriot authorities, and Greece's support of Greek-Cypriot policies that contravened the 1960 Constitution and treaties, Turkey's NATO allies balked at taking sides, much to the chagrin of Turkey.

The Makarios government also used the advantage of its control of the airport and all the ports to import large quantities of arms, including some heavy armaments. As Crawshaw stated, "The United Nations accepted the massive importation of arms by the Cyprus Government as a legitimate right in the defence of the state; Turkish efforts to bring in arms were stigmatised as 'smuggling'."[93] This, and the four-to-one numerical advantage Greek-Cypriots enjoyed, enabled them to exercise considerable military pressure locally on Turkish-Cypriots, even though Turkey was able to exact some restraint due to its military strength in the wider context.

Not only were the Turkish-Cypriots militarily weaker, and unable to present their case effectively in the international arena, they were also poorer and falling further behind the Greek-Cypriots. Ironically, in spite of the strife, the Greek-Cypriot economy experienced remarkable growth after 1963. Kyriacos Markides, using figures provided by the Greek-Cypriot authorities, reported that between 1960 and 1970 the per capita income in Cyprus grew by an average of 7 percent a year;[94] unemployment reached a low of 0.9 percent. Indeed, Greek-Cypriot enterprises experienced labour shortages; in these circumstances, taking advantage of improved safety conditions after 1968, an estimated 10,000 Turkish-Cypriots travelled from their enclaves to work as common labourers for Greek-Cypriot employers.[95]

However, island-wide figures showing remarkable economic growth and prosperity applied only to Greek-Cypriots, who traditionally had enjoyed higher income levels and standards of living. By contrast, high unemployment and economic stagnation prevailed in the Turkish-Cypriot enclaves; this further widened the economic gap between the two communities and caused much bitterness among the Turks.

Markides reported that "whereas in 1961 the economic condition of the Turks was 20 percent below that of the Greeks, by 1973 it was 50 percent below."[96] The economic blockade imposed by the Makarios government (which was applied with varying intensity for a period of nearly four years), and the losses of income derived from government sources (namely the salaries of civil servants and grants for Turkish-Cypriot education), created serious economic difficulties for the Turkish community. Furthermore, the accommodation of nearly 25,000 refugees, the majority of whom were unable to derive any income from the land and property left in Greek-held areas, aggravated Turkish-Cypriot economic woes. These were only partly eased by the financial subsidies provided by Turkey.

In spite of their substantial weaknesses, however, the Turkish-Cypriots did have a major trump card. They were in control of their enclaves (where they maintained their own government, courts, police force, and a small army of recruits led by officers from Turkey) and provided a host of services for their people. Greek-Cypriots resented this state of *de facto* partition, and the Turkish-Cypriot reliance on Turkey which made it possible. Admittedly, the total area of the enclaves constituted a mere 2 percent of the island's territory,[52] but the prospect of the consolidation of a separate Turkish-Cypriot administration heavily subsidized by Turkey was unpalatable to the Greek-Cypriot leadership.

Nevertheless, the terms the Greek-Cypriot side sought in the intercommunal talks reflected their paramount strength. Makarios pressed for the acceptance of a drastically amended Constitution in conformity with the thirteen points he had proposed in 1963. This meant reducing Turkish-Cypriot representation in government in a ratio proportionate to their numbers. More significantly, the Greek-Cypriot leadership sought to replace the special community rights of the Turkish-Cypriots enshrined in the Constitution by substituting a human rights code applicable to all citizens of the Republic, without regard to ethnic origin.

Turkish-Cypriot leaders contended that the breakdown of intercommunal government and the ensuing events demonstrated that the "paper guarantees" of the Constitution were not sufficient to protect the rights and security of the Turkish community. Ideally, they wanted to separate the Turkish community from the Greek-Cypriots to ensure maximal protection. This separatist position was adopted soon after the civil strife began in 1963. Later, during 1964-1967, Turkish-Cypriot spokesmen revised their position to a more diluted form of separation, calling for a federal system in which one or more Turkish cantons would exercise considerable autonomy while Greek-Cypriots exercised preponderant power at the federal level; nevertheless, this solution still envisaged the "exchange" of an unspecified number of Greek and Turkish-Cypriots; in any case, they were unacceptable to Greek-Cypriots.

As a reflection of their weaker bargaining position, Turkish-Cypriot leaders made further concessions in the course of the post-1968 intercommunal talks. In a bid to make their demands more palatable to the Greek-Cypriots, they advocated local autonomy without a population exchange to be applied in areas of Turkish-Cypriot concentration. Furthermore, in the course of the negotiations, Turkish-Cypriots made other concessions. They agreed to Greek-Cypriot demands to reduce Turkish-Cypriot representation in the government from 30 percent (as provided in the 1960 Constitution) to 20 percent, which reflected their ratio of the total population. In addition, they consented to reduce the veto power of the Turkish Vice-President to matters more directly related to Turkish-Cypriot interests.

The most succinct description of the Turkish-Cypriot plan for local autonomy has been provided by Patrick as follows:

(1) local government districts which would be autonomous, with such autonomy so written into a constitution that it could not be altered by the central government where Greek-Cypriots would be in a majority;
(2) the boundaries of the autonomous districts would be drawn primarily according to communal considerations;
(3) these districts, depending on their ethnic character, would be directly responsible either to a Greek-Cypriot or to a Turk-Cypriot co-ordinating authority;
(4) these co-ordinating authorities would, in partnership, form the basis of the central government.[98]

Given the fundamental importance of security to the Turkish-Cypriots, local autonomy was the crux of the negotiations dealing with the internal structure of the government. However, the Greek-Cypriot side had equally fundamental objections to it. In their eyes, the Turkish-Cypriot proposals envisaged a structure that would be "expensive, inefficient and guaranteed to irritate rather than soothe inter-communal feelings."[99] Moreover, and more seriously, the Greek-Cypriot leadership believed that the application of the Turkish-Cypriot proposals on local autonomy would create "a state within a state" and a prelude to future partition. In spite of intensive negotiations on the subject, the central issues remained unresolved, and an impasse was reached by the end of 1971.

While talks on local autonomy continued, another issue of fundamental importance — the question of external guarantees — was left in the background. Turkish-Cypriots viewed Turkey's guarantee as essential for their security. From the Greek-Cypriot point of view, however, the rights of the guarantor powers (as conferred by the Treaties of Guarantee and Alliance) infringed on the prerogative of Greek-Cypriots to rule Cyprus on the basis of majority rule and decide its future destiny. Accordingly, they argued for the removal of external guarantees, their real target being Turkey's guarantees.

Ultimately, the failure to reach an understanding on the local government issue precluded exhaustive negotiations on the issue of external guarantees. However, another familiar issue, Enosis, again re-emerged to undermine the talks. During the presidential election campaign in 1968, and on several other occasions, Makarios made a distinction between the "desirable solution" (Enosis) and the "feasible solution" (independence). Nevertheless, in spite of their undertaking to exclude Enosis from the settlement being sought in the intercommunal negotiations, Makarios and other Greek-Cypriot spokesmen continued to express their commitment to it as an ideal. In April 1971, for example, in a speech which he made during a ceremony to unveil the statue of an EOKA hero, Makarios declared: "Cyprus is a Greek island. We shall maintain it as a unified island until we have handed it back to Greece."[100] By rekindling Turkish-Cypriot fears of ultimate Greek-Cypriot intentions, these statements seriously hampered intercommunal negotiations. Denktash repeatedly protested and asked for assurances that the Greek-Cypriot side would agree to exclude Enosis as a future form of settlement. However, Makarios and other Greek-Cypriot leaders could not bring themselves to close the doors to Enosis. During the first three years of the intercommunal talks, the Greek and Turkish governments avoided taking any steps that might be construed as interference in the intercommunal process of finding a settlement. After averting a possible war during the November 1967 crisis, discussions which took place between Athens and Ankara generated some optimism concerning the resolution of their bilateral disputes: Cyprus was the most important issue by far, but other irritants such as the treatment of their ethnic minorities were also taken up. Veteran Greek Foreign Minister Pipinelis and Prime Minister Papadopoulos went so far as to talk effusively about the desirability of realizing a Greek-Turkish federation, an idea which Venizelos and Atatürk had broached during the Greco-Turkish rapprochement nearly three decades earlier. In an interview which he gave to the Turkish paper *Milliyet* on July 1, 1968, Papadopoulos declared: "If I had magic power I would do everything possible to bring about a federation and would immediately lead our people in that direction."[101]

Papadopoulos' conciliatory statements encouraged Turkish officials, but the improved climate in the mainland governments' dealings failed to advance the intercommunal negotiating process in Cyprus. As usual, the Greek-Cypriot leadership was very sensitive to the possibility of a Greek-Turkish deal over the heads of the Cypriots and an imposed solution, but Makarios resisted any pressures to alter the Greek-Cypriot agenda.

After three years of intercommunal talks, the negotiating parties acknowledged that they were deadlocked. The Turkish government was getting more and more disillusioned, as were the Turkish-Cypriots, about reaching an agreement. At the NATO meeting in Lisbon in May 1971, Greek

Foreign Minister Palamas met with his Turkish counterpart, Osman Olcay. "They said later, in separate interviews, that the intercommunal talks could not go on indefinitely, and Palamas added that, if no agreement was reached soon, Greece and Turkey would consult on how to handle the problem."[102] Some Greek-Cypriot authors[103] have alleged that the Greek and Turkish Foreign Ministers had reached a firm Cyprus agreement in Lisbon to be put into effect without Makarios' consent. There is, however, no evidence of any such agreement.

What evidence exists only indicates that the Papadopoulos junta preferred to improve its relations with Turkey by defusing the Cyprus issue and believed that the Makarios government could be more forthcoming in the negotiations with the Turkish-Cypriots. In a letter which he wrote to Makarios dated June 18, 1971, Papadopoulos repeated a proposal which he had apparently made before that the Archbishop

> offer the Turkish Cypriots a 'ministry of local government', since this was virtually all that Denktash wanted. Papadopoulos added that, far from weakening the fabric of the Republic, the presence of such a minister in the Cabinet would emphasize the unity of the state.[104]

The junta leader added by saying " I do not claim that our proposals would be definitely accepted by the Turkish side, but they would render our case unassailable."[105] He concluded by warning that "if Makarios insisted on breaking the common front, the Greek Government would have to act in the national interest and the interests of Cypriot Hellenism, however 'painful' that might be."[106]

Makarios responded by rejecting the Greek leader's warnings and his counsel on the appropriate concessions to the Turkish-Cypriots and his warnings.[107] By this time (1971), relations between the Makarios government and the Greek regime had soured considerably; during the next two years, however, the rift between the two governments became more serious and open. The issue of how to settle the Cyprus dispute was by no means the only subject on which the Makarios and Papadopoulos governments differed. To begin with, the Athens regime revived the concept of the "National Centre." Much as they were belittled by many Greeks for their claim, the leaders of the Greek junta saw themselves as guardians of the Hellenic Christian civilization. In a similar way, as *Ethnarch*, Makarios was the standard-bearer of Christian Hellenism in Cyprus. But the junta leaders merely saw him as an opportunist "red priest," who compromised Hellenic interests by allying himself with the enemies of the Greek nation.

Papadopoulos and his associates held Makarios responsible for the spread of Communist influences among Greek-Cypriots; in particular, they were suspicious of the electoral support which AKEL, the Communist Party of Cyprus, gave to the Archbishop. In addition, they deplored his policy of cultivating cooperative relations with the Soviet Union and his role in the non-aligned movement. In keeping with the thinking of their political leaders in Athens, Greek officers of the National Guard accused the leftist forces in Cyprus of undermining Hellenic nationalism and thereby Enosis.

The Greek military rulers were further aggravated by the anti-junta criticism that was commonplace in the uncensored Greek-Cypriot press. As Markides stated:

From the day the colonels took over in Greece, the leftist and liberal press in Cyprus continuously denounced the 'fascist dictatorship' and called for the restoration of democracy in the mother country.[108]

Some of Makarios' Cabinet Ministers were viewed as hostile by the Athens regime. In February 1972, during a strained period in Athens-Nicosia relations, Greek leader Papadopoulos successfully pressured Makarios to replace three members of his cabinet who were unpalatable to Athens.[109] It was at this time that Papadopolus revived the concept of "National Centre" with which Papandreou had first confronted Makarios. In a letter which he wrote to the Archbishop, Papadopoulos demanded that the Greek-Cypriot leadership accept the principle that "Athens is the centre of Hellenism, of which Cyprus is only a part, and that therefore Athens should have the upper hand in dealing with the Cyprus problem."[110]

From Athens' perspective, the Greek-Cypriot leader's links and collaboration with the Greek regime's enemies represented more than minor irritants. As a royalist, Makarios did not hide his preference for constitutional monarchy in Greece, which meant the restoration to power of King Constantine deposed by the junta. Also, it is worth noting that before the July 1974 coup, Makarios invited Athanasiadis Novas, a former premier and one-time close associate of King Constantine, for a state visit to Cyprus. Apparently, Novas' visit "seemed to confirm the rumours that the formation of a Greek government in exile was imminent."[111]

Thus, from the Greek military rulers' point of view, not only did Makarios fail to show requisite political respect and play an auxiliary role vis-a-vis the "Hellenic Centre," he was willing to align himself with politicians who were bent on undermining and overthrowing the military regime. It is not surprising then that the Greek military rulers felt justified in making life hard for Makarios and weakening his government in Cyprus; available evidence shows (mostly covert) support for the Archbishop's adversaries after 1971. As Couloumbis observed, "the pressure from the Greek military regime against a progressively independent, verging on the defiant, Makarios gathered momentum in the early 1970s."[112]

The same author has also aptly stated that "the Athens junta concluded that the Archbishop's Achilles heel could be found in his 'betrayal of Enosis'."[113] Officially, the Greek regime supported the search for a solution on the basis of an independent Republic. By covert means, however, it lent support to Makarios' Enotist adversaries in Cyprus by projecting the Archbishop as one who had betrayed Hellenism. It is widely believed that the Greek regime lent support to Grivas (who secretly returned to the island in 1971 and established a new underground organization called EOKA B) to wage a campaign for Enosis as had the previous EOKA in the 1950s. Although numerically small, Makarios' opponents had the advantage of support from armed elements of the National Guard and the police force; moreover, Grivas's pro-Enosis campaign gathered increasing momentum and support from discontented elements, particularly on the right.

The Turkish government, as well as the Turkish-Cypriots, were mere spectators to the quarrel between Makarios and the Athens regime. Papadopoulos and some other senior members of his regime regularly professed friendship with Turkey and their belief in the need to heal the Greek-Turkish rift over Cyprus. But Turkish hopes for a settlement were repeatedly disappointed on the island, and for this the Turks pinned the major responsibility on the Greek-Cypriot leadership.

The United Nations helped revive the talks after they had broken down. When they started again in June 1972, Turkey (as well as Greece) became more directly involved by providing a constitutional advisor. But the renewed talks merely sputtered on without creating any serious expectation of a breakthrough. By this time, the Turks were resigned to a slow erosion of their rights and influence on the island.

In the meantime, Bülent Ecevit's left-of-centre Republican People's Party emerged as the winner in Turkey's elections in October 1973, although he failed to get an overall majority of parliamentary seats. Ecevit managed to put together a coalition with the National Salvation Party (a small party of right-wing fundamentalists) by mid-January. When Ecevit presented his government's programme to Parliament on February 1, he spoke of the need for a "federal" solution. The Greek-Cypriots protested the call since it implied the geographical separation of the communities. Turkish government spokesmen responded by denying that the settlement which they advocated would create a geographically based federation.[114] "One of Ecevit's principal foreign policy advisors wrote that in Cyprus the Ecevit government sought not a sharing of land, but a sharing of government duties and authority."[115] However, when Ecevit repeated his call for a federal solution on March 27, the Greek-Cypriot leadership suspended the talks for a few months. It is possible that Ecevit's call for a federal form of settlement represented a hardening of Turkey's position on Cyprus. On the other hand, Turkey was not in any position at the time to exert the type of leverage on the Greek-Cypriot leadership or on the Greek government to get the kind of terms it deemed desirable.

A few months before Ecevit struck an uneasy coalition government in Ankara, a group of discontented military leaders led by Brigadier Ioannidis overthrew the government of Colonel Papadopoulos in November 1973. According to Crawshaw, "the new dictators were more fanatical in their nationalistic ambitions, more reckless in their methods and incredibly blind to the possible reactions of Turkey."[116]

In an interview he gave to Oriana Fallaci after the Cyprus war in 1974, Makarios described a meeting which he had with Ioannidis in the following terms:

> In 1963 or 1964 he (Ioannidis) had been in Cyprus as an officer of the National Guard, and one day he came to see me, accompanied by Sampson, in order to 'explain to me secretly a plan that would settle everything'. He had bowed to me, he had kissed my hand most respectfully, then: 'Beatitude, here's the plan. To attack the Turkish Cypriots suddenly, everywhere on the island. To eliminate them one and all. Stop.' I was flabbergasted. I told him I couldn't agree with him, that I couldn't even conceive of killing so many innocent people. He kissed my hand again and went away in a huff.[117]

As the strongman of Greece, this same Ioannidis displayed the type of ruthlessness and recklessness which Makarios described in his interview. Less circumspect than Papadopoluos, his predecessor, Ioannidis kept up the pressure on Makarios by aiding EOKA B on Cyprus. Ultimately, the Archbishop decided to deal with the escalating terrorist acts of EOKA B by publicly confronting the Athens regime for the first time. This was clearly an act of desperation.

In a letter which he addressed to the Greek head of state Gizikis, Makarios accused the Greek government of plotting to kill him: "More than once I have sensed and on occasion almost felt, the invisible hand stretched out from Athens seeking to destroy my human existence."[118]

Beyond this grievous accusation, Makarios charged the Athens regime of blatant intervention on the island through its support of EOKA B and the encouragement of opposition groups and the control of the National Guard. Before the dispatch of his letter, the Greek-Cypriot leader had planned to reduce the number of Greek officers of the Guard and demanded of Greece that Greek-Cypriot officer trainees be approved by his government. This was an attempt to wrest control of the National Guard from Greece and, in his letter to Gizikis, Makarios reiterated his demand for the withdrawal of the bulk of the officers from Greece.

Instead of replying to Makarios, the Ioannidis junta ordered the National Guard to overthrow him. In a bloody coup that began on July 15, 1974, the

National Guard seized the presidential palace. Although Makarios narrowly escaped his attackers, large numbers of his armed and civilian supporters were killed in the take-over. The junta appointed as president Nicos Sampson, a well-known former EOKA fighter with a reputation as a Turk-killer. In less than a week, the Turkish government landed troops in northern Cyprus. The Ioannidis regime collapsed within a few days of Turkey's intervention in Cyprus, and former Premier Karamanlis flew in from Paris to assume charge and restore democratic government.

Since the Ioannidis coup provoked Turkey's military intervention and war of 1974 that effectively partitioned the island, Greek-Cypriots and Greeks have understandably held the Greek military regime responsible for provoking Turkey's military intervention and for the subsequent misfortunes of Greek-Cypriots. Furthermore, in a related thesis, the conduct of the Athens regime has been shown as proof that external powers and interests, and not Cypriots, determined the destiny of Cyprus. Although favoured by several authors,[119] these interpretations are inadequate.

To begin with, it is misleading as well as unfair to treat the Papadopoulos and Ioannidis regimes as indistinguishable, as has been done by most authors. Although they had much in common, they differed in terms of their policies and approach towards Cyprus as well as Turkey.

Both Papadopoulos and Ioannidis believed that Makarios was dedicated to remaining the leader of an independent Cyprus rather than working toward the island's union with Greece. However, Papadopoulos had a realistic assessment of what it would take to bring about Enosis; i.e., he understood that the price of Enosis involved making concessions to Turkey. In spite of his unsuccesful bid to have the Turks accept Enosis (with concessions) in the course of the September meeting at the Greek-Turkish border, he did not rule out reaching an understanding on union at some time in the future as the Turkish-Cypriots' (and Turkey's) status on the island weakened with the passage of time. Moreover, Papadopoulos understood the nature of the stand-off which existed between Greeks and Turks in Cyprus. In particular, he had learned a sobering lesson in November 1967 when, in response to Grivas' attack on two Turkish-Cypriot villages, Turkey was only dissuaded from landing troops by substantial Greek concessions; he thus avoided a situation whereby Turkey would be provoked to intervene on the island. This meant that the Turkish enclaves were to be left alone and that no unilateral attempt should be made by Greece to change the ultimate destiny of the island.

Ioannidis, on the other hand, failed to grasp the significance of Turkey's commitments in Cyprus. Either he did not believe that Turkey would send military force to the island to prevent Enosis, or he expected the United States to keep Turkey in check should the latter consider intervention. He

failed to appreciate that Washington had substantially weakened its leverage by checking the Turks earlier in 1964 and 1967. He also attempted to
bring about union at a time of deteriorating relations with Ankara over the
issue of continental shelf and oil rights in the Aegean Sea.

The need to differentiate between the Papadopoulos and Ioannidis juntas
has also been suggested by Zenon Stavrinides, a Greek-Cypriot scholar, in
the context of evaluating Greek-Cypriot and the Greek military regime's
responsibility for the events of 1974. In his words

> ...the following conjecture may be suggested. Whereas Colonel Papa-
> dopoulos, who ruled Greece from April 1967 to November 1973, was
> very keen to see some sort of compromise settlement in Cyprus, his
> successor Brigadier Ioannidis was bent on bringing about Enosis.[120]

Ultimately, it was Ioannidis, and not Papadopoulos, who went so far as
to order the National Guard to assassinate Makarios and overthrow his
government. Nonetheless, as has been widely reported, Papadopoulos
himself provided clandestine support to Makarios' adversaries in Cyprus,
although there is no evidence that he did so during the first three years of his
regime in Athens. Also, no evidence has appeared that the two unsuccessful
attempts at Makarios' life (in 1970 and 1973) were made at the Greek
leader's behest. Grivas, Makarios' most formidable opponent, did not return
to Cyprus until 1971 to mount a serious challenge to the Archbishop's
authority. Grivas and the Colonels had a common interest in accusing the
Archbishop of having betrayed Enosis and of collaborating with Communists at home and abroad. However, although Papadopoulos and Ioannidis
collaborated with Grivas, the EOKA leader was no mere instrument of either
of the two dictators. While in Cyprus, the legendary hero of EOKA had a
long-standing reputation of defying government authority, including direc-
tives from Greece; he was also known to be in favour of the restoration of
monarchy in Greece. For all the animosity towards Makarios, he did not seek
to remove him from power by assassination, nor could he be directed to do
so by Athens. In fact, Grivas' differences with the Papadopoulos junta deteriorated to such an extent that he accused the Greek dictator of plotting to
kill him.[121] It is more than coincidental that the Ioannidis junta resorted to
removing Makarios from power by assassination after Grivas died on the
island in January 1974.

Even if Makarios' enemies in Cyprus had been successful in their
attempts to assassinate him during the Papadopoulos era, one should not
necessarily assume that the outcome would have been the same as when
Ioannidis attempted to depose and kill Makarios and install Sampson as
successor. Although this involves arguing hypothetically, Turkey would not

necessarily have sent its troops to the island if one of the previous attempts on Makarios' life had been successful, provided that it secured adequate assurances over the protection of Turkish-Cypriot rights and Turkey's guarantor powers. After all, Makarios was strongly resented by the Turks as a bitter enemy who had repeatedly frustrated Turkey's attempts to salvage Turkish-Cypriot rights and Turkey's standing on the island since 1963. As long as his replacement did not bring about Enosis, there was no imperative for Turkey to respond with military force. If, for example, Makarios had been replaced with Clerides, the veteran Greek-Cypriot negotiator, it would not have been difficult to assuage Turkey's anxieties over the Turkish community. By contrast, given his record of killing many Turkish-Cypriot civilians, Sampson was certain to provoke intense suspicions and active reaction by Turkey. This too was overlooked by Ioannides, notwithstanding the fact that Sampson had not been his first choice.

Just as it is sweeping and misleading to treat the Papadopoulos and Ioannidis regimes as one and the same, it is equally simplistic and erroneous to assign the responsibility for the conditions that brought about the 1974 governments in Greece and Turkey. It is true that Ioannidis committed a huge error of judgement by not anticipating Turkey's intervention in July 1974 when he ordered the coup against Makarios in Cyprus. Nonetheless, neither he nor other Greek leaders should bear the sole or even the major responsibility for the pursuit of Enosis that ultimately led to the war of 1974 and the territorial division which followed. At the very least, the failure to come to terms with renouncing Enosis must be borne jointly by Greek-Cypriots and Greece. Indeed, as the previous account has shown, Greek-Cypriot leaders doggedly pursued the Enosis dream after independence in 1960 even when the Greek government of Karamanlis had forsaken the policy of union as unrealizable because of Turkey.

Turkey had repeatedly declared that it would resort to force to avert the island's union with Greece. By sending its Air Force to inflict punitive strikes against Greek-Cypriot forces in August 1964, it had demonstrated its capacity to engage in military action on the island only forty miles from its southern coast. Later, during the November 1967 crisis, it once again demonstrated its leverage by forcing the military regime in Athens to withdraw the Greek troops that had been illicitly stationed on the island. For Makarios and his associates (although not for militants like Grivas), these lessons were sobering enough to force them to avoid major attacks on the Turkish-Cypriots. But neither Makarios nor other Greek-Cypriot "realists" could go so far as to give up the ideal of Enosis even when it was patently apparent that there could be no deal with Turkish-Cypriots without renouncing Enosis. This is why, in spite of years of hard bargaining between Greek and Turkish-Cypriot negotiators between 1968 to 1974, no agreement could be reached on such fundamental issues as local autonomy and the exclusion of Enosis as an option.

Some Greek and Greek-Cypriot authors have contended that the inter-communal negotiations had virtually resolved substantive Greek-Turkish differences on Cyprus. In his book on the relations between Greece, Turkey, and the United States, Couloumbis wrote that "by early summer of 1974, the negotiators had reached an agreement on most important issues; some relatively minor questions remained to be ironed out."[122] Similarly, in his detailed analysis of the Cyprus dispute and negotiations spanning two decades since 1960, Polyvios Polyviou contended that:

> it is nothing short of remarkable that there was what can only be described as an amazing narrowing of differences on virtually every issue which in its turn makes it almost certain that had it not been for the Greek coup and the Turkish invasion of July 1974 a complete agreement would have been concluded before long.[123]

These claims cannot be sustained by evidence. If these authors were right, then the Cypriot parties would have resolved their dispute before long; hence, the Ioannidis junta's intervention in July 1974 and Turkey's inter-vention it provoked would have been unnecessary. This interpretation has also been favoured by many Greek-Cypriots who want to absolve them-selves of any responsibility for the events of 1974 and the island's subse-quent division. The reality, however, was quite different. As Stavrinides has put it,

> If the negotiations were going so well, and the Turkish-Cypriots were within sight of a settlement which would be acceptable to them, why did Turkey find it necessary to order an invasion whose consequences were bound to be momentous and indeed unpredictable?[124]

Greek-Cypriot leaders were not prepared to offer concessions on local autonomy to Turkish-Cypriots before 1974, which would have secured an agreed settlement, because as the stronger party they did not have to do so. After all, they controlled all state institutions, were internationally recog-nized as the government of Cyprus, and enjoyed wide support among the non-aligned states; at the same time, Greek-Cypriots were the beneficiaries of remarkable economic growth and prosperity. The Turkish-Cypriot en-claves were an embarrassment and a nuisance but no threat to the Greek-Cypriot government; indeed, it was reasonable to expect that the status of the Turkish-Cypriots would further weaken with the passage of time as more of them sought to leave the island for better prospects abroad. Sir Peter Ramsbotham, the former British High Commissioner in Cyprus who had established close working relations with Makarios, offered the following assessment:

> The Archbishop himself seemed to have calculated that time was on his side and that, provided there was no crisis nor excessive pressure on him from Athens, the existing situation was acceptable. In due time, he thought, the Turkish-Cypriots would be absorbed without violence as a privileged minority within Greek Cyprus.[125]

In the aftermath of the traumatic events of 1974, Makarios cited the obstacles of a settlement with the Turkish community in a revealing interview which was quoted in Greek-Cypriot papers:

> I know that some people maintain that with a little more flexibility on our part a solution would have been possible before the Turkish invasion. This is true. But it should be borne in mind that Greece was governed then by a junta, which supported the illegal organization EOKA B in Cyprus. Therefore, it was impossible for me to reach an accommodation with the Turkish-Cypriots, without running the risk of being accused of national betrayal and without violent reactions as a result of the renouncement of Enosis. It must also be noted that the Greek junta and its agents in Cyprus constantly accused me that I was a barricade against the realization of Enosis.[126]

Makarios' admission that more flexibility on his part would have made a deal possible with the Turkish-Cypriots is both remarkable and valid. It is equally valid to identify the Greek-Cypriot Enotists as an impediment to a settlement. But, like most other Greek-Cypriots, he assigns excessive blame on the junta for blocking a settlement on the island. Since 1974, the overthrown and discredited junta has simply become an easy scapegoat for the reverses suffered by Greek-Cypriots and Greece in Cyprus.

All this is not to underestimate the risks involved for Makarios in giving up Enosis and reaching a *modus vivendi* with the Turkish-Cypriots. He would have been accused of betrayal, as indeed he was even without conceding on those central issues that stood in the way of Greek and Turkish-Cypriot reconciliation. Also, as the guardian of his community, he probably wished to avoid causing a polarization among Greek-Cypriots. These concerns obviously weighed heavily in his mind regardless of the Greek military regime's policy.

In any case, the junta's involvement and pressures on Cyprus were not constant. For example, after the withdrawal of Greek troops in 1967 and the start of the intercommunal talks the following year, the Papadopoulos junta supported Cypriot efforts for a settlement; the Athens regime maintained a policy of disengagement for at least three years after 1967 during which the

Greek-Cypriots could have reached a *modus vivendi* with the Turkish-Cypriots. Turkey adopted an equally supportive attitude by supporting substantial Turkish-Cypriot concessions that reduced their ratio of representation in the unitary Cypriot government and diluted the Turkish Vice-president's veto powers. Indeed, all the other external powers with a stake in Cyprus (namely, the United Nations, the United States, Britain, and the Soviet Union) encouraged the intercommunal negotiating process and a settlement based on Cypriot independence.

Thus, in spite of the favourable attitude or active encouragement of all the external actors in the Cyprus issue for a considerable period of time, Makarios saw no substantial incentive to settle with the Turkish-Cypriots on the basis of independence and allow them to exercise local autonomy. The Greek-Cypriot leader's predisposition was that of a Greek nationalist who had dedicated himself to the triumph of Hellenism in Cyprus and the realization of one of its most cherished dreams, Enosis. As such, he viewed both mainland Turks and Turkish-Cypriots as spoilers of the sacred Hellenic mission. Further, like most of his compatriots,[127] he believed in Greek-Cypriot superiority over Turkish-Cypriots.

The intention is not to dwell on the anti-Turkish prejudices of Makarios or his fellow Greek-Cypriots. Most Turkish-Cypriots themselves had negative stereotypes of the other community, viewing Greek-Cypriots for the most part as "facile, manipulative, and untrustworthy."[128] Rather, what is suggested here is that the Greek-Cypriot attitudes toward the Turkish-Cypriots led them to adopt short-sighted policies of discrimination and neglect that alienated members of the smaller community and obliged them to rely even more heavily on Turkey.

In the aftermath of the trauma of the 1974 war, many Greek-Cypriots have re-evaluated their actions and policy toward the Turkish-Cypriots, and some among them have expressed regret for past behaviour. However, as long as the Greek-Cypriots were in a position of strength, as they were during 1964-1974, there was no disposition to help assuage the insecurity of Turkish-Cypriots or address their economic and social needs.

Furthermore, had the course of events in 1974 not prompted Turkey to send its troops to Cyprus and thereby undermine the prospects of the island's union with Greece, it is questionable whether Makarios could have brought himself to renounce the cause of Enosis which he had so passionately pursued for decades.

Notes

1. Woodhouse, *Karamanlis*, p. 87.
2. Averoff, *Lost Opportunities*, p. 368.
3. Woodhouse, *Karamanlis*, p. 87.
4. Feroz Ahmad, *The Turkish Experiment in Democracy, 1950-1975*, London: Royal Institute of International Affairs, 1977, p. 404.
5. Alexandris, *The Greek Minority*, p. 276.
6. *Ibid.*
7. *Ibid.*
8. Andreas G. Papandreou, *Democracy at Gunpoint: The Greek Front*, New York: Garden City, 1970, p. 139.
9. Markides, *Rise and Fall*, p. 59.
10. Crawshaw, *Cyprus Revolt*, p. 365.
11. Averoff, *Lost Opportunities*, p. 322.
12. *The Times*, April 2, 1963.
13. Zenon Stavrinides, *The Cyprus Conflict: National Identity and Statehood*, Nicosia: Stavrinides Press, pp. 63, 145.
14. *The Guardian*, February 14, 1962.
15. Reddaway, *Burdened*, p. 130.
16. *Ibid.*
17. Patrick, *Political Geography*, pp. 37-8.
18. The Akritas Plan was first published in the Greek-Cyprist Newspaper, *Patris*, on April 21, 1966. For the text of the Akritas Plan, see the memoirs of Greek-Cypriot leader Glafcos Clerides, *Cyprus: My Deposition*, Vol. 1, Nicosia: Alithia Publishing, 1989, pp. 212-19. Most Greek and Greek-Cypriot authors have avoided any reference to the Akritas Plan.
19. *The Times*, January 5, 1962.
20. Patrick, *Political Geography*, p. 37.
21. Mayes, *Makarios*, p. 152.
22. See Rauf R. Denktash, *12'Ye Bes Kala Kıbrıs (Moment of Decision in Cyprus)*, Ankara, 1966.
23. *Ibid.*
24. Nihat Erim, *Bildigim ve Gördügüm Olçüler Içinde Kıbrıs* (The Cyprus Issue As I Have Known It), Ankara: Ajans Turk Matbaacılık Sanayii, 1976, p. 274.
25. Averoff, *Lost Opportunities*, p. 395.
26. *Ibid.*
27. *Ibid.*, pp. 396-7.
28. See *The Times*, January 5, 1963.
29. Erim, *Kıbrıs*, p. 274.
30. Averoff, *Lost Opportunities*, p. 426.
31. Woodhouse, *Karamanlis*, p. 87.
32. Averoff, *Lost Opportunities*, p. 429.
33. Reddaway, *Burdened*, p. 131.
34. Glafcos Clerides, the Greek-Cypriot leader, expressed such views to the author during an interview in Cyprus on October 25, 1985. Also see Clerides, *My Deposition*, pp. 130, 137, 208, 328.
35. Crawshaw, *Cyprus Revolt*, p. 366.
36. *New York Times*, January 2, 1964.

37. Sharon Wiener, *Turkish Foreign Policy Decision-Making on the Cyprus Issue*, Ph.D. dissertation, Duke University, 1980, p. 89.

38. Stephens, *Place of Arms*, pp. 185-6.

39. Wiener, *Turkish Foreign Policy*, p. 89.

40. Philip Windsor, *Nato and the Cyprus Crisis*, London: International Institute of Strategic Studies, Adelphi Paper No. 14, 1964, p. 10.

41. Wiener, *Turkish Foreign Policy*, pp. 96-110. See also George Harris, *Troubled Alliance: Turkish-American Relations in Historical Perspective, 1945-1971*, AEI Hoover Policy Studies, 1972, p. 114.

42. Harris, *Troubled Alliance*, p. 113.

43. "Document: Correspondence Between President Johnson and Prime Minister Inönü, June 1964 as released by the White House, January 15, 1966," *The Middle East Journal*, Vol. XX, No. 3, Summer 1966, p. 387.

44. *Ibid.*

45. As reported in *The Guardian*, August 11, 1964.

46. Papandreou, *Democracy at Gunpoint*, p. 148.

47. *Ibid.*, p. 132.

48. Patrick, *Political Geography*, p. 426.

49. July 23, 1964.

50. As reported in *The Times*, October 28, 1964.

51. Woodhouse, *Karamanlis*, p. 173.

52. December 5, 1964.

53. Papandreou, *Democracy at Gunpoint*, p. 134.

54. See *The Sunday Times*, July 19, 1964, and *The Guardian*, July 14, 1964.

55. Papandreou, *Democracy at Gunpoint*, p. 133.

56. Paul Rahe, "Revelations," *Institute of Current World Affairs*, October 31, 1986.

57. August 1, 1964.

58. Couloumbis, *Troubled Triangle*, p. 47.

59. Markides, *Rise and Fall*, p. 128.

60. Kyle, *Cyprus*, p. 11.

61. Markides, *Rise and Fall*, p. 129.

62. See the *Observer Foreign News Service*, November 22, 1967.

63. Papandreou, *Democracy at Gunpoint*, p. 131.

64. Ehrlich, *Cyprus, 1958-1967*, p. 103.

65. Campbell & Sherrard, *Greece*, p. 280.

66. See the *New York Times*, April 12, 1966. See also Papandreou, *Democracy at Gunpoint*, p. 239.

67. Purcell, *Cyprus*, p. 370.

68. Campbell & Sherrard, *Greece*, p. 270.

69. *The Guardian*, August 11, 1964, and *The Times*, August 17, 1964.

70. Papandreou, *Democracy at Gunpoint*, p. 140. See also George Ball, *The Past Has Another Pattern*, New York: W.W. Norton & Co., 1982, p. 353. See also Reddaway, *Burdened*, p. 233.

71. Papandreou, *Democracy at Gunpoint*, p. 141.

72. Purcell, *Cyprus*, p. 373.

73. Leontios Ierodiakonou, *The Cyprus Question*, Stockholm: Almquist & Wiksell, 1971, p. 296.

74. See *The Guardian* , August 10, 1964. See also the *New York Times*, August 10, 1964.

75. Patrick, *Political Geography*, p. 456.

76. Purcell, *Cyprus*, pp. 370-1.

77. U.N. Document S/5954 (1964), para. 8.

78. U.N. Document S/5950 (1964), paras. 63-4.

79. Kyriakides, *Cyprus: Constitutionalism*, pp. 114-15.

80. Reddaway, *Burdened*, p. 196.

81. See, for example, Kitromilides, "Co-Existence to Confrontation": "...the decisive factors in the escalation of conflict [in Cyprus] and the consequent distortion of ethnic relations, have been external, not domestic," p. 60. See also Adamantia Pollis, "Colonialism and Neo-Colonialism: Determinants of Ethnic Conflict in Cyprus," in P. Worsley and P. Kitromilides (eds.), *Small States in the Modern World: The Conditions of Survival*, Nicosia: Zavallis Press, 1979. Pollis wrote: "The history of Cyprus makes evident that the principal determining factors for ethnic conflict have not been cultural or religious differences, but the policies pursued by interested powers external to Cyprus." p. 73.

82. Mayes, *Makarios*, p. 187.

83. *Ibid.*

84. See, for example Crawshaw, *Cyprus Revolt*, p. 377.

85. Ehrlich, *Cyprus, 1958-1967*, p. 112.

86. *Ibid.*, pp. 106-7.

87. Mayes, *Makarios*, p. 189.

88. *Ibid.*, p. 190.

89. Kyle, *Cyprus*, p. 13.

90. Mayes, *Makarios*, p. 190.

91. Crawshaw, *Cyprus Revolt*, p. 378.

92. See, for example, the General Assembly resolution passed on December 18, 1965, by 57 votes and 5 against. The resolution read, in part, as follows: (The General Assembly "... takes cognizance of the fact that the Republic of Cyprus, as an equal member of the United Nations, is, in accordance with the Charter, entitled to and should enjoy full sovereignty and complete independence without any foreign intervention or interference." See Public Information Service, *Cyprus: The Problem in Perspective*, Nicosia, 1969, Appendix V, p. 44.

93. Crawshaw, *Cyprus Revolt*, p. 370.

94. Markides, *Rise and Fall*, p. 78.

95. See Stavrinides, *Identity and Statehood*, p. 81.

96. Markides, *Rise and Fall*, p. 31.

97. Kyriakides, *Cyprus: Constitutionalism*, p. 112.

98. Patrick, *Political Geography*, p. 174.

99. *Ibid.*

100. *Ibid.*, p. 175.

101. As quoted in Young, *Greek Passion*, p. 427.

102. Mayes, *Makarios*, pp. 212-13.

103. See Attalides, *Cyprus: Nationalism*, p. 132. See also Polyviou, *Conflict and Negotiation*, p. 150.

104. Mayes, *Makarios*, p. 213.

105. Salih, *Diverse Nationalism*, p. 66-7.

106. Mayes, *Makarios*, p. 213.

107. *Ibid.*

108. Markides, *Rise and Fall*, p. 137.

109. *The Times*, June 26, 1972.

110. *New York Times*, February 13, 1972.

111. Markides, *Rise and Fall*, p. 140.

112. Couloumbis, *Troubled Triangle*, p. 77.

113. *Ibid.*

114. Wiener, *Turkish Foreign Policy*, p. 327.

115. *Ibid.*

116. Crawshaw, *Cyprus Revolt*, p. 388.

117. Oriana Fallaci, *Interview With History*, London: Michael Joseph, 1974, p. 318.

118. Crawshaw, *Cyprus Revolt*, p. 388.

119. Among these writers are Polyviou, Attalides, and Markides, whose works have been cited in this chapter.

120. Stavrinides, *Identity and Statehood*, p. 113.

121. C.M. Woodhouse, *The Rise and Fall of the Greek Colonels*, New York: Franklin Watts, 1985, p. 123.

122. Couloumbis, *Troubled Triangle*, p. 76.

123. Polyviou, *Conflict and Negotiation*, p. 152. Turkish-Cypriot leader Denktash has denied that there was a "near agreement." See Rauf R. Denktash, *The Cyprus Triangle*, London: K. Rustem, p. 58.

124. Stavrinides, *Identity and Statehood*, p. 112.

125. Peter Ramsbotham, "Impressions of Archbishop Makarios, 1969-1971," in J.T.A. Koumoulides (ed.), *Cyprus in Transition: 1960-1985*, London: Trigraph, 1986, p. 103.

126. Quoted in Markides, *Rise and Fall*, p. 126.

127. See Vamik Volkan, *War and Adaptation: A Psychoanalytic History of Two Ethnic Groups in Conflict*, Charlottsville: University Press of Virginia, 1979, p. 34. Volkan has quoted from a paper by J.H. Tenzel and M.S. Gerst entitled "The Psychology of Cross-Cultural Conflict: A Case Study," presented at the 125th Annual Meeting of the American Psychiatric Association, Dallas, Texas, May 1, 1971. Tenzel and Gerst wrote in their paper: "The Greek Cypriot openly believes in his cultural superiority over the Turkish community. A public comment to one of these investigators that this cross-cultural study was invalid because 'it compared the biggest cultures to no culture at all' while extreme, is nevertheless indicative of feelings held by a large segment of the population even though only occasionally expressed."

128. Volkan quoted from a study by J.H. Tenzel and M.S. Gerst in which the investigators commented on the problems involved in the political negotiations between Greek and Turkish-Cypriots: "The Greeks would see the Turks as being cautious and overly suspicious and less inclined to be trustworthy, while the Turks would see the Greeks' actions as being facile and manipulative and thus also untrustworthy." *Ibid.*

4

1974 and After: New Realities for Cyprus, Greece, and Turkey

The Ioannidis Coup and Turkey's Intervention

The Greek junta leader Ioannidis initiated the coup against Makarios during a period when there was considerable disarray within the ranks of the senior members of the military regime. However, the timing of the coup was dictated by the Greek-Cypriot leader's open challenge to the junta. By overthrowing Makarios, and effecting *de facto* Enosis, Ioannidis hoped not only to remove a troublesome adversary, but also to win a diplomatic victory for his beleaguered regime. In spite of Turkey's record of opposition to Enosis and threats of going to war to avert its realization, Greece's junta leader discounted the likelihood of Turkey intervening on the island. He believed that the United States government would not let Turkey use force.

Ioannidis's belief had some basis in fact: Turkey was prevented from sending the military to the island during the 1964 and 1967 crises as a result of United States pressure. Furthermore, Turkey appeared resigned to the slow erosion of the Turkish community's status on the island in the aftermath of the post-1963 developments.

However, after United States President Johnson's blunt and offensive letter forced the Turks to call off their military intervention in 1964, a consensus had developed in Turkey that the country's leaders had erred by yielding to American pressures; they had failed to protect a vital national interest. In July 1974, after the Greek coup brought Sampson to power, Washington dispatched Undersecretary of State Joseph Sisco to Ankara in a bid to dissuade the Turks from intervening. Turkish Prime Minister Ecevit told him bluntly:

> Ten years ago… you committed an error and so did we. Your mistake was to tie our hands and stop us. Our mistake was that we listened to you. We will not commit the same error as ten years ago.[1]

In retrospect, Ioannidis' miscalculation appears all the more remarkable since Turkey's then Prime Minister Ecevit had already shown a capacity to defy the United States government. He had lifted the ban on the cultivation of poppies in Turkey, weeks before the anti-Makarios coup. According to Feroz Ahmad, "from his earlier pronouncements it was clear that his government would attempt to be more independent in its relations with the outside world, especially the United States."[2] Furthermore, soon after he came to office in January 1974, Ecevit began to challenge the *status quo* in the Aegean by challenging Greece's claims on the continental shelf issue.

Yet Ecevit's own personality may have encouraged perceptions that he would be unlikely to resort to war as an instrument of policy. A former journalist and an accomplished poet, Ecevit had a reputation for being a humanitarian "man of feelings."[3] Before he became prime minister he studied Hindu mysticism and translated T.S. Eliot's poems into Turkish. In one of his poems he described the common bonds and affinity between the Greek and Turkish peoples: "... The wild spirit flowing in our veins is the same/ we have cursed each other.../ But there is still love between us."[4] After being informed that the decision to send Turkish troops to Cyprus had been made, American Ambassador Macomber appealed to Ecevit to reconsider by asking how a humanitarian person like him could sanction the use of force and the loss of lives.[5]

Although it could safely be assumed that any Turkish government would have felt bound to prevent Cyprus' union with Cyprus, external pressures, particularly from the United States, might have prompted a different leader than Ecevit to forsake the use of force in favour of diplomatic instruments. Ecevit, however, saw in the situation created by the Greek coup an opportunity to put an end to years of frustrating wrangling over the rights of the Turkish community and to attain a position of strength in Cyprus. In addition, he expected that a successful intervention would be enormously popular with the Turkish public and thus generate considerable approval for his Republican People's Party. If all went well, he could free himself from the restraints of the difficult coalition with the National Salvation Party and be in a strong position to attain his goal of building a Scandinavian-type welfare state in Turkey. According to Sharon Wiener:

> A careful analysis of the evidence suggests that Ecevit did have an impact on the outcome of the 1974 crisis. His political outlook, willingness to break with tradition, and nationalism all supported an intervention on the island and a determination to seek a permanent solution to the Cyprus problem.[6]

Although the Athens regime denied responsibility for the overthrow of Makarios, the evidence that the junta directed the coup was overwhelming. At first, Turkish Prime Minister Ecevit appealed to Britain (as one of the guarantors of Cypriot independence) to cooperate with Turkey and take joint military action on the island. Ecevit flew to London personally on July 17 to put the case to Prime Minister Wilson. The British government, however, was unwilling to commit troops, nor would it allow the use of British bases for Turkish troop landings.

Ecevit was concerned that unless Turkey acted without delay, it ran the risk of forfeiting a rare opportunity for intervention. He worried that the junta-backed Sampson regime might consolidate itself in Cyprus. The Turkish leader was upset that Washington failed to denounce Sampson. The Turks also took note of press reports in the United States suggesting that the United States was about to recognize the Sampson regime. Regardless of whether Washington had any such intentions, Ankara was anxious to act without delay.[7]

For a few days, Undersecretary Sisco shuttled between Greece and Turkey to find a diplomatic formula to avert war. He conveyed to Athens the Turkish government's demands which included the removal of Sampson from the presidency, the recall of Greek officers to Greece, and guarantees of safety for the Turkish community with a land corridor under their control to link up the Nicosia enclave with the coast.

The Greek junta leader rejected these terms. All that Ioannides was prepared to do was to replace the Greek officers in Cyprus with new ones from Greece. This was an inadequate response for Turkey, and Sisco understood the ultimate futility of his mission. In the early hours of July 20, 1974, the Ecevit government dispatched troops to the island and began what it called a "peace operation." In justification of its action, the Turkish government cited its rights under the Treaty of Guarantee:

> In the event of any breach of the provisions of the present Treaty, Greece, the United Kingdom, and Turkey undertake to consult together, with a view to making representations, or taking the necessary steps to ensure observance of those provisions.
>
> In so far as common or concerted action may prove impossible, each of the three guaranteeing Powers reserves the right to take action with the sole aim of re-establishing the state of affairs established by the present Treaty.[8]

While troops embarked from landing craft on a beach near Kyrenia, paratroops were dropped into the largest Turkish enclave, stretching north from Nicosia toward Kyrenia. The primary objective was to link up the forces embarking from Kyrenia with those who moved north from the principal Turkish enclave extending from Nicosia. This was not accomplished until July 23, the day when Turkey agreed to a cease-fire, because of the effective resistance put up by the Greek-Cypriot National Guard. The

Turkish and Greek contingents (stationed under the Treaty of Alliance) clashed directly when the former made an abortive attempt to "break through to the Nicosia-Kyrenia road"[9] to prevent the landed troops from reaching the Nicosia enclave of the Turks.

There was concern in Ankara that the direct engagement between mainland Greek and Turkish forces would prompt Greece to extend the war beyond Cyprus. In fact, such a war was only narrowly averted. On the day that Turkish troops landed on Cyprus, Greek junta leader Ioannides ordered the armed forces to mobilize and wage war against Turkey, but the Greek military high command refused to comply. Instead, senior Greek generals — many of whom held higher rank than Ioannidis — asked that the junta give way to a government of national unity. Following a meeting with leading civilian politicians, it was decided to call upon former Prime Minister Karamanlis to lead the nation. He arrived from Paris, where he had lived in self-imposed exile for eleven years, to a tumultuous welcome from the Greek people.

The impact on the Greek regime of Turkey's military intervention was its collapse and the restoration of democratic government in that country. For the same reason, the Sampson regime in Cyprus also fell but not before bloody fighting between supporters of Makarios and those of the junta. Hundreds of Greek-Cypriots perished during this fighting.[10] Glafcos Clerides, the Speaker of the Greek-Cypriot House of Representatives, became the acting president.

During its exercise of power in Greece, the junta was never popular internationally and had provoked widespread antipathy to its action in Cyprus. From the perspective of the Turkish government, this was helpful in winning understanding, and even sympathy, for the military response in July. By aborting Enosis, the Turks appeared to preserve the island's independence. However, with the junta's demise, and the emergence of Karamanlis as leader, Greece was no longer an international pariah. Indeed, Greece's Western allies were so concerned that Karamanlis and the forces of democracy prevail in Greece that they began to lean on Turkey not to add to the new government's difficulties by making further military advances on the island. This, at any rate, was the Turkish government's view. The Greek government felt, on the other hand, that the United States had tilted towards Turkey before, during, and after the events surrounding the coup and the military intervention.

In fact, most Greeks and Greek-Cypriots have subscribed to the notion that the United States conspired to create the conditions that made Turkey's intervention possible in order to bring about the island's partition between Greece and Turkey. Even those who do not blame Washington directly for plotting the events of July 1974 argue that the United States failed to lodge sufficiently strong warnings to Ioannidis not to undertake the coup against Makarios. Further, critics of the United States policy have argued that the United States did not exercise as much pressure as was needed to prevent Turkey's military intervention or, at the very least, the second operation in August.

These beliefs are at best arguable or, as in the case of the allegation that Washington encouraged the Ioannidis coup, totally without foundation. It should be recalled that the Cyprus crisis occurred during the final days of the Watergate investigations when President Nixon was preoccupied with defending his actions. Nevertheless, the Turkish intervention unleashed a wave of anti-American and anti-NATO sentiment in Greece and among Greek-Cypriots. On August 19, 1974, Greek-Cypriot gunmen assassinated United States Ambassador Rodger Davies.

From the Turkish side, the situation after the cease-fire on July 23 was far from satisfactory. By securing Kyrenia, Turkish forces had gained a foothold and secured access to the sea for the Nicosia enclave. On the other hand, most Turkish enclaves and a majority of the Turkish-Cypriot population remained outside the Turkish-controlled area. In anticipation of further action, more materiel and troops were brought in from Turkey.

In the meantime, an intense diplomatic campaign by the United States to prevent renewed fighting on the island as well as a possible Greco-Turkish war resulted in an agreement for the three guarantor powers to hold an urgent conference in Geneva. The foreign ministers of Greece, Turkey, and Britain deliberated in the first Geneva conference held from July 25 to 30, 1974. The declaration issued at the end of the conference called for the observance of the cease-fire, the evacuation of the Turkish enclaves occupied by Greek and Greek-Cypriot forces, and the exchange of military personnel and civilians detained during the hostilities. In addition, the guarantor powers called for another conference, this time with the Greek and Turkish-Cypriot representatives, to re-establish constitutional government. As an astute observer noted, the declaration made two observations, "one upholding the 1960 constitution, the other appearing to abandon it."[11] The call for the Turkish Vice-President to resume his functions was based on the continuing validity of the 1960 Constitution and was consistent with the Greek position that there should be a return to the constitutional order created by the Zurich-London accords. On the other hand, the statement noting "the existence in practice of two autonomous administrations, that of the Greek Cypriot community and that of the Turkish Cypriot community"[12] was included in the declaration upon Turkish insistence. It conformed with their intention to seek a constitutional framework based on two separate and autonomous entities united at the federal level.

During a press conference he gave on July 28, 1974, Turkish Prime

Minister Ecevit stated that "...no one should think or speak as if nothing new has happened in Cyprus, as if nothing has changed there. A lot has changed irrevocably in Cyprus since the morning of 20th July."[13]

For Greece and the Greek-Cypriots, the new reality was unpalatable and difficult to accept. With the junta and the Sampson regime gone, they hoped to galvanize enough pressure on Turkey to limit her gains on the island and to restore the constitutional order that existed before July 1974. Greek-Cypriot leader Clerides argued that Turkey had sent her army to Cyprus by citing her authority under the Treaty of Guarantee and that such intervention could only be justified by restoring the 1960 constitution. Also, at the second Geneva conference, the Greek and Greek-Cypriot representatives protested that Turkish troops had extended their control considerably beyond the cease-fire lines established on July 23, 1974.

However, neither Turkey nor the Turkish-Cypriots had any intention of allowing a return to the subverted 1960 Constitution and the state of affairs that prevailed before 1974. Turkish-Cypriot leader Denktash argued that the 1960 Constitution had enabled Greek-Cypriots to discriminate against and threaten the security of Turkish-Cypriots. Accordingly, a new constitutional structure had to be created that made it possible for both sides to feel secure.

Both Denktash and Turkish Foreign Minister Günes bitterly complained at the time of their meeting that tens of thousands of Turkish-Cypriots were kept as hostages and badly treated by Greek-Cypriot forces. The Turkish side then put forth two alternative federal plans. The first, offered by Denktash, called for a bi-zonal federation with the envisaged Turkish state in the north covering 34 percent of the island's territory. This was clearly unacceptable to the Greek and Greek-Cypriot representatives in spite of a hint from Denktash that he would agree to reduce the size of the envisaged Turkish zone below 34 percent.[14]

Both the Turkish-Cypriot leadership and the Turkish government felt strongly that a clear separation of the two communities was essential to ending the security problem of the Turkish community. They also believed that the creation of two autonomous units in a federal system would avoid the kind of conflicts that had characterized the short-lived bi-communal government.

However, they were persuaded, primarily by the United States government, that a less drastic federal plan involving the resettlement of fewer people was more likely to be accepted by the Greek side. The United States feared that a breakdown of the Conference would prompt the Turks to renew their advance in Cyprus and once again bring Greece and Turkey to the brink of war. Intensive diplomatic activity and "heavy inputs"[15] by Kissinger yielded the "Günes Plan," named after Turkey's Foreign Minister. The plan called for the creation of six Turkish-Cypriot cantons in different parts of the island covering about one-third of the island's territory. In order to bolster the prospects for a federal settlement and avert a breakdown of talks, the United States issued a formal statement on the same day as it was put forth:

> The United States position is as follows: we recognise the position of the Turkish community in Cyprus requires considerable improvement and protection. We have supported a greater degree of autonomy for them. The parties are negotiating on one or more Turkish autonomous areas. The avenues of diplomacy have not been exhausted and therefore the United States would consider a resort to military action unjustified. We have made this clear to all parties.[16]

From the Turkish point of view, the bi-zonal plan was far preferable to the Günes Plan (with its scattered cantons) in terms of meeting Turkish-Cypriot security needs; also, one single unit in the north would be easier for Turkey to defend in any future contingency. From the Greek-Cypriot point of view, both plans were fundamentally flawed since they involved population movements and separate communal administrations. However, the Turks were determined to press their plan and demanded that the Greeks decide on the acceptability of the cantonal plan without delay.

For Mavros, the Greek Foreign Minister, it was politically more astute to leave the decision on the issue to the Greek-Cypriots, thus avoiding accusations of conceding to the division of the island under the threat of Turkish guns. However, this did not make things easier for Greek-Cypriot leader Clerides. He protested to Denktash that while he was in favour of a federal structure providing wide autonomy for Turkish-Cypriots, he would be branded as a traitor by fellow Greek-Cypriots if he went back to the island on that day and said, "My friends, we have divided the island and left 34 percent of its territory to Turks."[17] On the other hand, Clerides argued that he could make the federal principle acceptable to the Greek-Cypriot people gradually.[18]

But this was not acceptable to the Turkish-Cypriot or the Turkish representatives who insisted that the Günes Plan was offered on a take-it-or-leave-it basis. Günes did not even accept Clerides' request for thirty-six to forty-eight hours for consultations with the Greek government, Makarios, and other Greek-Cypriot community leaders; he feared that Makarios and others would merely stall as in the past, and nothing would be achieved by extended negotiations. The Conference ended in failure on August 14, 1974, amid British and Greek accusations that the Turks had not allowed more time for a possible agreement in Geneva.

George Kousoulas, a Greek-American author of a text in international relations, has cited the Geneva conference as a textbook illustration of erroneous problem definition. During the conference, the Greek side defined the problem in terms of the island's illegal invasion by the Turkish army and asked for the removal of these forces. In the face of the Greek capabilities at the time, this objective was clearly unattainable. Yet the Greek side did not revise its objectives — the definition of the problem — to adjust its course of action to the actual capabilities. Turkey, on her part, defined the problem in terms of providing protection to the Turk-Cypriot community on Cyprus. Such protection, they argued, could be accomplished through some form of a federal structure, with the Turk-Cypriots having their own separate region. Had the problem been stated by both sides in terms of an equitable division of territory, reflecting the actual composition of the island population (80 percent Greek-Cypriot and 18 percent Turk-Cypriot) a solution could have been easier to find, especially given that at the time of the conference the Turkish army occupied only a very small area on the north coast of Cyprus. The Greek-Cypriots, however, insisted on their definition of the problem and rejected the concept of a federal state.[19]

Kousoulas' argument is sound as far as it goes. On the other hand, one should not underestimate the political risks which leaders face when they are called upon to renounce a national goal and make sacrifices. This was the basic dilemma of Clerides who knew that to agree to the Turkish plan would mean committing political suicide.

On August 14, 1974, shortly after the breakdown of talks at Geneva, the Turkish army launched its second operation on Cyprus. Before another cease-fire came into effect three days later, Turkish troops had brought just over one-third of the island under their control. In Athens, immediately after the Turkish advance, the Karamanlis government called for a meeting of the war council to decide on an appropriate response. The Greek Prime Minister proposed to engage the Turkish forces in Cyprus and, possibly, on other fronts. He specifically suggested dispatching three Greek submarines to Cyprus to attack Turkish ships and fighter aircraft from Greece to take action against targets on the Turkish mainland.[20] But the Greek army chiefs did not concur, arguing that the state of readiness of the armed forces was inadequate and engaging the Turks in distant Cyprus was impractical. Karamanlis still explored other methods of military response. He ordered that a division with armoured vehicles be dispatched to Crete, to be sent on to Cyprus. Stating that he and Defence Minister Averoff intended to accompany the convoy, he then unsuccessfully appealed to Britain to protect the passage of the convoy from Crete to Cyprus.[21]

In spite of these gestures, Karamanlis understood the futility of fighting the Turks in Cyprus. His hope was not so much to turn the tide against Turkey but to provoke the direct involvement of the United States to end the hostilities, thereby limiting Turkey's gains. Like the rest of his countrymen, and Greek-Cypriots, he was bitter that the United States and the Western Alliance had not stopped the Turks. Within four hours of the Turkish advance on August 14, 1974, he ordered Greek forces to withdraw from NATO command, although Greece continued to be a member of the Alliance.

For Greece, as for the Greek-Cypriots, Turkey's successful military intervention and radical alteration of the *status quo* in Cyprus was humiliating. By its action on the island, Turkey did not merely turn a monumental blunder of the Ioannidis junta to its advantage; it also demonstrated the helplessness of Greece in stopping Turkey's troops on the island. This laid to rest the cherished Greek dream of Enosis. In the aftermath of the 1974 war, Archbishop Makarios lamented that what he called the Turkish invasion of Cyprus was the greatest blow to Hellenism since the Asia Minor disaster of 1922, when the Turkish nationalist forces defeated the invading Greek armies in Anatolia.

Turkey's leaders emerged from the 1974 war on Cyprus with a huge sense of accomplishment that they had redressed years of humiliating reverses in the island. By taking a bold inititiative, and finally defying powerful Allied pressures against military intervention, they successfully averted Cyprus' union with Greece and thereby protected a vital national interest; further, by maintaining a substantial military force on the island, they ensured that Turkey would be in a strong position to determine the terms of any future settlement.

Greeks in Greece and Cyprus saw Turkey's action differently. Privately, and even sometimes publicly, Greek leaders were willing to acknowledge that they "understood" Turkey's initial military intervention in July 1974. However, Turkey's later advance, after the collapse of the junta and the Sampson regimes, appeared to Greeks to be an unwarranted, aggressive act intended to secure territorial control over part of the island as a prelude to seizing the rest of the island at some future date. Prime Minister Karamanlis also believed that by ordering the second offensive soon after he had taken over the leadership in Greece from the discredited Colonels, Ecevit had dealt a blow to his efforts to maintain control and restore democracy while junta supporters still held influential positions.[22]

Turkey's action in Cyprus coincided with a greater assertiveness over its interests and rights in the Aegean. Because of Turkey's use of military force in Cyprus, and the declared willingness to do so in the Aegean, Greeks have accused Turkey of being an expansionist power with designs not only on Cyprus but also on Greece's eastern Aegean islands.

The Impact of the United States Arms Embargo

Turkey's initial intervention in July 1974 was favourably received by most states. Its action created the salutary outcome of causing the downfall of the Greek junta and its hand-picked regime in Cyprus. However, Turkey was severely criticized for its second operation; nearly 180,000 Greek-Cypriots became refugees[23] when they fled advancing Turkish forces and moved to the Greek-held south. As a result, much of the island experienced great economic and social disruption.

By bringing about 36 percent of the island's territory under their control in the north, some of which could be bargained away in future negotiations, the Turks acquired substantial leverage in dealing with Greek-Cypriots and Greece. However, given Turkey's support for a separate autonomous Turkish-Cypriot entity in the north and Greek-Cypriot resistance to such an arrangement, neither side put much store in early negotiations. Consequently, the Greek and Greek-Cypriot governments sought to pressure Turkey by diplomatic means.

The Greeks capitalized on the international censure against Turkey's second offensive in order to obtain diplomatic support at international forums such as the United Nations and the conference of the non-aligned states, where Greek-Cypriots had always been well-received. In the United States, the newly-mobilized Greek lobby, representing nearly 3,000,000 Greek-Americans,[24] succeeded in persuading Congress to impose an arms embargo on Turkey in February 1975.

The successful imposition and maintenance of an embargo of United States' military aid and sales to Turkey until 1978, against the wishes of the Executive, was made possible due to a convergence of forces: the desire of a well-organized ethnic lobby to influence United States policy-making in favour of Greece and the Greek-Cypriots, and the wish of a substantial group of Congressmen led by liberal Democrats to assert Congressional rights in foreign policy-making in the immediate aftermath of the Watergate crisis. Congressional action on the embargo was largely the result of accumulated frustrations and resentment felt by many legislators at having been by-passed by the Executive (specifically President Nixon and Secretary of State Kissinger) in deciding major foreign policy issues.

The leading advocates of the embargo included not only Greek-American congressmen; namely, John Brademas, Paul Sarbanes, Peter Kyros, Gus Yatron, and Skip Bafalis, but also such senators as Benjamin Rosenthal, Thomas Eagleton, Adlai Stevenson III, Charles Percy, and Edward Kennedy. In his study of the Greek lobby's role in the imposition of the Turkish arms embargo, Paul Watanabe noted the special links that had developed between the Greek lobby and Senators Percy and Kennedy;[25] the latter proved especially helpful in publicizing the plight of Greek-Cypriot refugees by virtue of his position as chairman of the Judiciary Committee's Subcommittee to Investigate Problems Connected with Refugees and Escapees.

The advocates of the embargo used a combination of legal, political, and moral arguments to make their case. In making their legal arguments, embargo advocates cited the Foreign Assistance Act of 1961 (PL 87-195) and the Military Sales Act of 1968 (PL 90-629), both of which stipulated that military hardware and services were only provided to recipient countries for self-defense. These laws also provided the termination of sales and aid to any country that "substantially violated" the conditions, and it is on this basis that a cut-off of military sales and aid to Turkey was demanded.

In political terms, the pro-embargo legislators argued that the United States had tilted towards Turkey during the Cyprus crisis and had alienated Greece, which was forced to withdraw from the military wing of NATO. In the following excerpt from one of Senator Eagleton's speeches, the Senator marshalled legal and political arguments to denounce Secretary of State Kissinger. It was typical of the position taken by the embargo advocates:

> We are told to ignore the law, we are told that Henry does not like the law; that Henry will have his hands tied, just as Henry said we would tie his hands if we terminated the Cambodian bombing... our distinguished Secretary of State is famous for his tilts. He tilts toward the junta in Chile. He tilts towards Thieu in Vietnam. His most famous tilt was the pro-Pakistan tilt. His current tilt, his Turkey tilt, is no wiser than the other tilts.[26]

Thus, embargo advocates argued that the United States should apply pressure (and sanctions, if necessary)[27] to force Turkey to withdraw from Cyprus and to allow for a fair settlement (i.e., one that would protect Greek-Cypriot interests). Finally, a combination of legal and moral arguments was developed by referring to the invasion of a sovereign island by Turkey's army and to the enormous humanitarian problems arising from the large number of refugees.

For Turkey's leaders, the imposition of the embargo was as unexpected as it was infuriating. Turkish spokesmen argued that no one in the United States (or in other allied countries) had raised a murmur when illegal Greek forces, including a tank unit[28] equipped with American arms, were stationed on the island. They also complained that Turkey's allies had neglected the plight of Turkish-Cypriots in spite of years of oppression and threats to their security by the Greek-Cypriots supported by Greece.

Since most of Turkey's military equipment had been procured from the United States, Turkey was unable to buy the spare parts and replacement equipment its army required and could not easily switch to alternative suppliers; this adversely affected the effectiveness of the Turkish military. Some European armaments were purchased, however, necessitating greater expenditures than would have been the case without the embargo, but these fell short of meeting Turkey's needs.

Congressional supporters of the embargo hoped that the embargo's punitive effects would make the Turks more yielding on Cyprus. But the angry reaction in Turkey over the measure threatened to cause irreparable damage to Turkey's relationship with the United States and NATO. As many Turks saw it, Turkey was being punished by its chief ally for having gone into Cyprus to protect its vital national interests. In 1975, in spite of his preference for maintaining close ties with the United States, Turkish Prime Minister Demirel felt obliged to retaliate by closing down several of the American installations in Turkey. Nevertheless, the skill with which the United States Executive handled the issue helped cushion the damage to Turkish-American relations. From the beginning, the Executive portrayed the embargo as a Congressional act taken against the wishes of the Executive. In the final analysis, however, Ankara held the United States Administration responsible for its removal although, clearly, most Turkish leaders (and the Turkish military) wished to avoid the severing of Turkey's ties with the United States. Indeed, the Turkish government played a helpful role in the Carter administration's bid to remove the Congressional embargo "by occasional conciliatory gestures ..., including the July 1978 Turkish-Cypriot offer to permit resettlement by Greek Cypriots of the coastal town of Varosha."[29]

In the final analysis, contrary to the hopes of its sponsors, the Congressional arms embargo and the pressures it created for Turkey did not yield major Turkish concessions for a Cyprus settlement. Governments in Ankara refused to make concessions that could be tied to the embargo pressures. For example, although Turkey stated that it would withdraw its troops as part of an overall Cyprus settlement agreed upon by Turkish and Greek-Cypriots, it refused to do so before then. In any case, embargo or not, there was resistance to giving up the gains of 1974 without an agreement securing vital Turkish interests.

Greece wanted the pressure of the embargo to be maintained as long as possible for two reasons. First, it sought to take advantage of the embargo to procure various types of military hardware to improve Greek military capabilities vis-a-vis Turkey. Second, it hoped that a continuation of the embargo would yield Turkish concessions on Cyprus. Accordingly, it protested to the United States government when the Carter administration eventually persuaded Congress to lift the arms ban in 1978. Nevertheless, it is is doubtful whether the Karamanlis government, then in office, would have preferred for the embargo to cause so deep a rift as to prompt Turkey to leave the Western alliance.

In terms of its effect on the relations between Greece and Turkey, the embargo created an additional focus for their diplomatic jockeying. It also delayed the beginning of substantive talks on the Cyprus issue for two primary reasons: it encouraged Greek-Cypriot (and Greek) hopes that pressures and sanctions on Turkey would help to facilitate a pro-Greek settlement. On the other hand, the humiliation caused by the embargo and the belief that it hardened the Greek and Greek-Cypriot position in negotiations stiffened Turkey's and Turkish-Cypriot resistance.

In Search of a Cyprus Settlement

In spite of both Greece and Turkey's preoccupation with Cyprus as a major foreign policy problem, since 1974 both have avoided the appearance of negotiating a Cyprus settlement. This was a sensitive issue with the Greeks on account of the junta's coup in Cyprus in 1974, and the sour memories of the Zurich-London accords, which were settled without meaningful Greek-Cypriot participation. The Greek authorities have repeatedly stated that although Greece has an interest in the island because of its large Greek population, Cyprus is not a bilateral problem between Greece and Turkey, given that the island is an independent state whose future should be decided by the Cypriots themselves. Hence, the post-1974 adoption in Greece of the slogan "Cyprus decides, Greece supports." Since 1974, the Greek and Greek-Cypriot governments focused primarily on increasing international pressures on Turkey by supporting the lobbying effort of Greek-Americans in Washington and, owing to the Greek-Cypriot government's high standing among the non-aligned states, by obtaining favourable resolutions at the United Nations, non-aligned, and Commonwealth conferences.

These efforts obtained considerable success but did not make the Turks any more yielding on the fundamental questions. During his post-1974 leadership, Karamanlis' overriding ambition was to make Greece a full member of the European Community so as to assume a rightful place among the Western European states. He also expected that full membership would strengthen Greece's democratic institutions. Furthermore, there was the barely articulated expectation that, within the Community, Greece would be in a more advantageous diplomatic situation in dealing with Turkey.

Although an associate member since 1963, and a candidate for full membership since 1987, Turkey has been concerned that Greece will use the unanimity rules to block its full membership. Greece has made it plain that it expects a favourable settlement in Cyprus before it will endorse Turkey's bid for full membership. In the meantime, Greek leaders have used the Community institutions to berate and isolate Turkey. A case in point was Greek Premier Papandreou's attempt during the EEC summit in June 1986 to postpone the normalization of relations between the Community and Turkey following the restoration of a civilian elected government there. He cited Turkey's military presence in Cyprus and other issues such as the human rights record of the military government in Ankara during 1980-1983 as causes for concern.[36]

Despite Greek insistence that their compatriots in Cyprus decide a future settlement for the island, both Karamanlis, and especially Papandreou, have sometimes differed with, and sought to influence, Greek-Cypriot leaders both on the approach to and terms of proposed settlements. During a visit to Athens by Greek-Cypriot leader Kyprianou in April 1983, Greek President Karamanlis "bluntly accused Cyprus of discouraging Western states' past efforts to help by 'negative and provocative behaviour'."[31] He went on: "In order to define our policy in practice, we must define in a clear and concrete manner our basic objectives. A struggle with ill defined, contradictory and unattainable targets is inconceivable."[32]

When Papandreou became Prime Minister in 1981, he upgraded Greek interest in Cyprus. As he had done during his years in Opposition, he used the issue domestically to blame the right-wing as well as the United States for the Cyprus events of 1974. In this context, he repeatedly threatened to open the so-called "Cyprus File" by launching an investigation to discover those responsible for the Cyprus coup, so that they could be penalized. In Cyprus, too, Greek-Cypriot politicians, particularly of the left, have demanded the opening of the "Cyprus File." However, in both Greece and Cyprus, such investigations were not pursued lest they "jeopardize national interests."[33]

As with his predecessor, Papandreou argued that the key issue in Cyprus was the continued "occupation" of the island's north by Turkish troops and that the appropriate policy was to internationalize the dispute. As an affirmation of his government's strong interest in Cyprus, Papandreou became the first Greek leader ever to visit Cyprus in February 1982. He encouraged Greek-Cypriots not to yield from their positions.

The irritation caused by Papandreou's hard line toward Turkey and among the Turkish-Cypriots probably delayed a Cyprus settlement. For several years, the Greek leader argued against any Cyprus talks until Turkey withdrew her troops from the island, even though this position was modified later. But while his bid to internationalize the Cyprus issue in order to generate increased diplomatic pressure on Turkey appealed to Greek-Cypriots, many Greek-Cypriot politicians did not endorse his desire to terminate the protracted dialogue between Greek and Turkish-Cypriot representatives: the Communist Party (AKEL) and Clerides' Democratic Rally (DISY), which together represented a majority of the Greek-Cypriot electorate, continued to support intercommunal talks as representing the most realistic avenue toward a settlement.[34]

In the circumstances, Papandreou did not press the issue too hard. In spite of his reputation for weak leadership and his practice of frequent consultations with Athens, Greek-Cypriot leader Kyprianou continued on with the protracted intercommunal talks on the island. Indeed, what many observers consider to have been the most promising intercommunal negotiations since 1974 (which culminated in the January 1985 summit meeting of the Cypriot leaders) took place during Papandreou's first term in office. Yet, Papandreou was held at least partly responsible (by Turkey, Turkish-Cypriots, and some Greek-Cypriots) for encouraging a hard line and supporting Kyprianou's refusal to sign the draft agreement during his summit meeting with Turkish-Cypriot leader Denktash in 1985.

The overriding objective for Greece, as well as the Greek-Cypriots, has been to bring about the withdrawal of Turkish troops on Cyprus or at least to obtain an agreement which ties their departure to a specific timetable. As Groom has stated, Turkey's military presence

> reminds Greeks and Greek Cypriots of the humiliation brought upon them by the Colonels in Athens and Nicos Sampson in Nicosia. It is a humiliation they feel can be purged best by securing the withdrawal of Turkish troops from Cyprus.[35]

It is widely acknowledged in Greece and by the Greek-Cypriots that the ideal of Enosis can no longer realistically be pursued. The war of 1974 has thus belatedly forced Greek-Cypriots and Greece to come to terms with their cherished ideal, the pursuit of which has cost them dearly. On the other hand, the fact that Turkey attained a powerful position on the island in 1974 and gained substantial bargaining power for herself and Turkish-Cypriots has not changed the Greek view of Cyprus as a Hellenic island with a small Turkish minority.

Greek-Cypriot leaders have always been willing to grant Turkish-Cypriots substantial minority rights but have strongly resisted the idea that Turkish-Cypriots are entitled to community rights on the same level as Greek-Cypriots. In particular, the notion that Turkish-Cypriots would exercise near-sovereign rights over a portion of the island (as implied in the Turkish-Cypriot concept of a bi-zonal federation) has been fundamentally objectionable to Greeks.

Even the concept of intercommunal talks which implies the equality of the two negotiating parties has been difficult for Greeks to accept. Partly for this reason, and partly because they preferred to define the Cyprus problem as having been caused by Turkey's invasion, Greek-Cypriot leaders repeatedly — and unsuccessfully — sought to negotiate directly with Turkey by arguing that Ankara and not Turkish-Cypriot leaders determined policy regarding Cyprus. As seen by Turkish-Cypriots and Ankara, this is based on a policy of denying that Turkish-Cypriot political needs and aspirations are as legitimate as those of Greek-Cypriots.

Turkish leaders have rejected the Greek-Cypriot approach, arguing instead for intercommunal negotiations on the basis of both communities' equality, as demanded by Turkish-Cypriots. The mainland governments were to play a supportive role. The Turks have also refused to recognize the Greek-Cypriot government (which continues to enjoy international recognition as the Republic of Cyprus). To them, it is merely an administration representing the Greek community. Further, Ankara has used its diplomatic influence, albeit with scant success, to win acceptance for the position that there are two legitimate administrations on Cyprus and that the Turkish-Cypriots be allowed to have an equal say at the United Nations, the Council of Europe, and other international forums.

The Turks have been determined to protect their position of strategic superiority in Cyprus and not to forfeit the gains of 1974 without concrete arrangements for the Turkish community. Essentially, this has meant supporting the Turkish-Cypriot demand for a loose bi-zonal federation, ensuring that their kinsmen would be masters within their own province or federated state.

Since 1974, Turkey has channelled substantial financial aid to help develop the infrastructure and economy in the north, in the hope of eliminating Turkish-Cypriot reliance on the Greek-Cypriots who have traditionally dominated the island's economic life. Although it is not as robust as the economy of the south, Turkish-Cypriot economic growth and standard of living have shown substantial improvement over the past decade. There is a new-found confidence about future economic prospects and much greater activity in the construction and tourism sectors.

However, the Greek-Cypriots' economic embargo since 1974 has added to Turkish-Cypriot difficulties substantially, particularly by making it difficult for British and European tourists to visit the north. Due to its continued recognition as the legitimate government of Cyprus by most of the world states, the Greek-Cypriot administration has dissuaded British and European governments from allowing direct flights to the Turkish-Cypriot airport in the north. As a result, tourists to northern Cyprus have to travel to Turkey before they can reach the island. Moreover, tourists who visit the Greek-Cypriot south are strongly discouraged from visiting the north. Greek-Cypriots have also employed punitive measures to impede Turkish-Cypriot trade with other countries. Under Greek-Cypriot law, it is illegal for foreign ships to call upon the Turkish-Cypriot port of Famagusta, and ships' masters have been threatened with imprisonment for loading or unloading cargo there.[36]

The Turkish-Cypriot government has been denied a share of the considerable development aid which the internationally recognized Greek-Cypriot regime has received from foreign governments and various international agencies such as the World Bank. Consequently, it has turned to Turkey, which has provided most of the investment in the north and, on average, has chanelled $40,000,000 annually — up to 40 percent of the current Turkish-Cypriot budget.[37]

The heavy reliance of Turkish-Cypriots on Turkey has led Greece and Greek-Cypriots to argue that Turkish-Cypriot leaders merely obey the dictates of Ankara, and that it is Turkey that has set the agenda for the Cyprus negotiations. This view is not borne out by the evidence. As Groom has stated: "It is evident that the Turkish Cypriots are heavily dependent on Turkey but they can act independently."[38] The Turkish-Cypriot leadership has not always seen eye to eye with the Turkish government,[39] and has been the initiator of major policies. For example, the idea of establishing an independent state in the north came from the Turkish-Cypriot leadership. Indeed, such a state would have been created earlier than in 1983 had it not been for Turkey's reticence over taking such a step.

Turkish-Cypriot President Denktash has been the leader of the Turkish community for more than two decades. His charismatic leadership and political skills, including his ability to define national goals for his community, has enabled him to exercise considerable influence with Ankara as well as other actors with a stake in Cyprus. Denktash has cultivated and secured a privileged relationship with the Turkish media, the military, and (to a lesser extent) with the Foreign Ministry in Ankara;[40] these connections have been a considerable asset for him in dealing with successive Turkish administrations.

In addition to making a concerted effort to create a viable economy in northern Cyprus independent of the Greek-Cypriot south, Turkish-Cypriots and Turkey have acted jointly to bolster the population of the north by welcoming settlers from the Turkish mainland. In part, these Turkish settlers were economic migrants from Turkey to meet labour shortages, particularly in the citrus groves, soon after the 1974 war.[41] These Anatolian immigrants have been settled in northern Cyprus in villages previously inhabited by Greek-Cypriots. This has prompted Greece and the Greek-Cypriots to accuse Turkey and the Turkish-Cypriots of colonizing the north with settlers in order to change the demographic character of Cyprus. Greek-Cypriot spokesmen have repeatedly argued that Turkish settlers would have to return to Turkey as part of an overall settlement.

The settlers issue has been controversial even among the Turkish community in Cyprus. Relations between Turkish-Cypriots and immigrants (most of whom came from peasant communities in Anatolia) have not been smooth. Allegations of discrimination by the immigrants ultimately led to the creation of a political party to represent their interests. Called the New Birth Party, its appeal is mainly to the Turkish immigrants. (In the parliamentary elections of 1985, the party captured four of the fifty seats in the Turkish-Cypriot parliament.)

According to a British parliamentary report of 1987, the number of Turkish settlers is estimated by the British government and foreign observers at 35,000 out of a total population of 150,000 in northern Cyprus.[42] The issue of the settlers has certainly added to the many problems which face the negotiators for a Cyprus settlement. However, it is unlikely that the Turkish settlers will constitute a major impediment to reaching a *modus vivendi* in the future.

For Turkey and the Turkish-Cypriots, security is of much greater concern. Thus, Turkish leaders have repeatedly stated that Turkey would not give up her powers as a guarantor (as provided in the Zurich-London Accords). Turkish-Cypriots feel particularly strongly that Turkey's continued guarantee is essential for their security.

As for the presence of Turkish troops, Turkey has pledged itself to the principle of withdrawal once a final Cyprus settlement is reached and the security needs of the Turkish community no longer require their presence. The Greek-Cypriots have secured many resolutions at the United Nations and at conferences of the non-aligned nations calling for the departure of non-Cypriot forces from Cyprus. These resolutions have not made Turkey any more amenable to withdrawing its forces from the island before Turkish-Cypriots' security needs are satisfied. Turkish officials believe that any premature withdrawal would leave the Turkish-Cypriot area in the north at the mercy of the much larger Greek-Cypriot National Guard. Whereas Turkish-Cypriot security forces number 4,500, there are an estimated 11,000 to 12,000 men in the Greek-Cypriot National Guard.[43] In addition, Turkish-Cypriots' meagre financial resources would necessitate substantial assistance (from Turkey) to obtain military hardware comparable to those secured by the Greek-Cypriot government. Moreover, the effectiveness with which Greek-Cypriot fighters resisted Turkish troops when they intervened in 1974 has not been forgotten on the Turkish side. For all these reasons, Turkish-Cypriots have been unwilling to concede even the possibility that all Turkish troops could be withdrawn in the future.

Indeed, the Turkish-Cypriot leadership quarrelled on the issue with Ankara in 1984 when Turkey accepted the principle of withdrawal in response to the United Nations' efforts to draw up a draft agreement for the endorsement of the Cypriot communities.[44] Currently, there are an estimated 27,000 Turkish troops on Cyprus.[45] Both Turkish-Cypriots and Turkey believe that maintaining a residual Turkish military force will be necessary for the foreseeable future. In the circumstances, Turkish-Cypriots and the Turkish government recognize the principle of their being a Greek contingent as was provided by the Zurich-London agreements.

From the beginning, Turkish-Cypriots, with Turkey's backing, sought to define the terms of a settlement by insisting on a bi-zonal federal system for the island to be negotiated by the two communities on the basis of equality. As early as 1975, during their meeting in Vienna, Turkish-Cypriot leader Denktash and Greek-Cypriot negotiator Clerides had agreed that all remaining Turkish-Cypriots living in the south would be allowed to join their kinsmen in the north.[46] As a result of this move, almost all Turkish-Cypriots are now concentrated in the north thus further strengthening their case for a bi-zonal arrangement. Also in 1975, the Turkish-Cypriots proclaimed the establishment of the Turkish Federated State of Cyprus, thus formalizing the Turkish part of the yet unformed Cyprus federation which would consist, according to the Turkish-Cypriot definition, of two equal parts.

For the Greek-Cypriots, all this smacked of partition and was thus thoroughly unpalatable. Nevertheless, an acceptance of the federal principle gradually appeared as a necessary price to pay for the sake of securing the removal of Turkish troops and recovering some Turkish-controlled territory in the north thus relieving the refugee problem. In February 1977, the Greek-Cypriot leadership formally accepted the federal concept when Makarios and Denktash met and agreed on the following set of guidelines:

(1) We are seeking an independent, non-aligned, bi-communal federal Republic;

(2) The territory under the administration of each community should be discussed in the light of economic viability or productivity and land-ownership;

(3) Questions of principles such as freedom of movement, freedom of settlement, the right of property and other specific matters are open for discussion taking into consideration the fundamental basis of a bi-communal federal system and certain practical difficulties which may arise for the Turkish Cypriot community;

(4) The powers and functions of the central federal government will be such as to safeguard the unity of the country, having regard to the bi-communal character of the State.[47]

As a statement of principles, the Makarios-Denktash guidelines were a step forward in the process of Cyprus negotiations, but each community's understanding of federalism differed fundamentally, and no significant bridging of the gap has occurred for several years. In any case, Makarios died a few months after the agreement on guidelines and was succeeded by Spiros Kyprianou, who was opposed to the acceptance of the principle of federation. Another high-level meeting in May 1979, this time between Denktash and Kyprianou, yielded a ten-point agreement on procedures for pursuing intercommunal talks on the basis of the 1977 guidelines,[48] but substantive exchanges did not follow until the early 1980s.

Greece and Turkey have not played a direct role in the intercommunal negotiations and, for the most part, have reacted to a string of initiatives made by other external actors: namely, by the United Nations, the United States, and (less frequently) Britain and the Soviet Union. Clearly, it is difficult to envisage a Cyprus settlement which does not enjoy the support or consent of Greece and Turkey. On the other hand, since 1974, as during the previous decade, it has been the Greek and Turkish-Cypriots who have taken the lead both in defining the terms of a possible settlement and in conducting negotiations. As long as Greece and Turkey's minimal objectives are satisfied, it will be the Cypriot communities that will ultimately decide the fate of negotiations for a settlement.

Of the external powers with a stake in the Cyprus dispute, the United States has enjoyed considerable influence over Greece and Turkey (both of which are major recipients of American aid) and the Cypriot communities, in spite of occasional bilateral strains that have limited her leverage. As the senior member of the Western Alliance with a strong interest in limiting the damage of the Cyprus issue in NATO, the United States has made energetic attempts to help the negotiating process, usually in step with United Nations diplomacy. This has not been an easy task for the United States given the strong suspicions of partiality expressed by one party or the other at various times. During the 1960s, it was usually the Turks (as the weaker party) who expressed disappointment over what they believed to be Washington's reluctance to press Greek-Cypriots and Greece to facilitate a settlement protecting Turkish-Cypriot rights. After 1974, the tables were turned, with Greeks and Greek-Cypriots complaining of American reticence to pressure Turkey to obtain favourable terms for them.

For American policy-makers Cyprus was a "bleeding ulcer" in need of treatment, and the stakes were substantial enough to justify the risks of offending one or both parties: without a Cyprus settlement, further deterioration in Greek-Turkish relations could not be ruled out, and thus NATO's southern flank, already in disarray, could be irreparably damaged. In the aftermath of the island's separation into two political units with all Turkish-Cypriots concentrated in the north, American officials believed that a compromise settlement could be negotiated by the parties in Cyprus (with mainland support and American encouragement) based on Greek-Cypriot acceptance of the federal arrangement and Turkish-Cypriot territorial concessions. United States diplomats believed, or hoped, that if agreement on the basic principles was reached by the leadership of the island communities, then the parties could reconcile their positions by bargaining at the negotiating table on such issues as the size of the envisaged Turkish-Cypriot province and the powers of the central government.

In order to expedite this process, United States President Jimmy Carter dispatched elder statesman Clark Clifford in 1977 to encourage the parties to make more concrete proposals than had been on the table thus far.[49] Although the Clifford mission did not yield a breakthrough, Washington still believed that additional diplomatic efforts could help break the Cyprus deadlock. However, in view of Greek-Cypriot and Greek suspicions of American partiality towards Turkey, the United States government often took care to act discreetly; the proposals officially presented as the Anglo-Canadian initiative of November 1978 were principally drafted by State Department counsellor Matthew Nimetz (hence, the preference of some writers to refer to them as the Nimetz Plan).

The plan called for a bi-zonal federation, a principal Turkish-Cypriot demand, but also addressed major Greek-Cypriot concerns by proposing "a considerable amount of geographic adjustment in favour of the Greek-Cypriots,"[50] and the withdrawal of non-Cypriot (read Turkish) troops as part of a final settlement.[51] The plan also provided for the inclusion in the envisaged federal constitution of the so-called "three freedoms" (freedom of movement, freedom of settlement, and freedom of ownership) on which Greek-Cypriots have been insistent. Although Turkish-Cypriots were unenthusiastic about the plan, it was the Greek-Cypriots who formally rejected it, prompting American officials to make veiled statements critical of Greek-Cypriot attitudes.[52] In subsequent years, Greek-Cypriot leaders apparently regretted their rejection of Nimetz' proposals; in any case, principal elements of the plan were incorporated in later United Nations-sponsored proposals that Greek-Cypriots have accepted, albeit reluctantly.

In spite of the disappointment in Washington over the failure of the Nimetz Plan, United States diplomacy has continued to play an important, though discreet, role in support of the United Nations Secretary-General's initiatives for a Cyprus settlement. The Reagan administration was credited with persuading Turkey's Head of State Evren to secure major Turkish-Cypriot concessions in December 1984;[53] namely, to abandon demands for a rotating presidency and to agree to limit the size of the Turkish-Cypriot province to less than 30 percent.[54] These concessions paved the way for the United Nations' January 1985 summit between the Greek and Turkish-Cypriot leaders.

Compared with the United States, the Soviet Union has been much less active in the Cyprus dispute. For the most part, the Soviets have reacted to others' initiatives for a settlement. One exception was the Soviet proposal for the convening of an international conference in August 1974 when Turkey embarked on a second military operation on the island. The idea was revived again in 1986, calling for the participation of Greece, Turkey, and the permanent members of the Security Council, to discuss international guarantees and the de-militarization of the island.[55] However, in both instances, Turkey declined to participate in a forum in which it would be pressured (particularly by the Soviet Union) to withdraw its troops from northern Cyprus before the intercommunal process yielded a settlement that satisfied Turkish-Cypriots' security needs.

Like the United States, the Soviet Union has not been particularly interested in the internal arrangements of a Cyprus settlement. The overriding Soviet interest in Cyprus has been the island's continued independence and non-alignment. This is why Soviet governments have consistently opposed Enosis, as well as partition of the island between Greece and Turkey, because such solutions would bring Cyprus into NATO. Thus, the Soviet government condemned the Greek-inspired coup of July 1974 and supported Turkey's initial intervention which caused the collapse of the Sampson regime. But once the Sampson regime fell and Enosis was aborted, it opposed any further military advance by Turkey that threatened to bring about the island's partition.

It is generally assumed that the Soviet Union has benefitted from the Cyprus dispute's negative impact on Greek-Turkish relations and the resultant damage to NATO's southern flank. On the other hand, the Soviets have acted with restraint and have not engaged in activities that might exacerbate conditions in Cyprus. Although AKEL — the Communist Party of Cyprus that coordinates its policies closely with the Soviet government — has opposed formulas for a Cyprus settlement put forth by the Western countries (such as the 1978 Nimetz Plan), it has supported a more flexible Greek-Cypriot approach to the intercommunal negotiations. From the Soviet point of view, an agreed settlement would strengthen the island's independence and presumably enhance prospects for Communist influence in the island by opening up the prospect of easier collaboration between Communists in both communities. The Communist Party of Greece (KKE) has also pursued a policy supportive of Greek-Turkish accommodation, particularly in recent years. The party had long blamed "imperialist" powers (i.e., the United States) for the confrontation and costly arms race between Greece and Turkey.[56]

Obviously, other than supporting Cypriot independence, Soviet and American interests diverge in Cyprus. Nonetheless, their support for the involvement of the United Nations there has been an important element in containing the Cyprus dispute and in the search for settlement formulas. The United Nations has played an important and unique role, thanks to its long-standing mandate for peace-keeping and peace-making on the island for over three and one-half decades. Its role in facilitating the high-level meetings of Greek and Turkish-Cypriot leaders owes much to the involvement of the Secretary-General who, through his Special Representative on the island, has provided a supportive diplomatic framework that has encouraged the leaders of the two communities to identify points of agreement before seeking to reduce their differences.

United Nations officials have focused their efforts at a trade-off whereby Greek-Cypriots will exchange their acceptance of a bi-zonal federal system for Turkish-Cypriot territorial concessions. Once the constitutional and territorial aspects of the issue are settled, the other overriding issue of security, including the question of external guarantees and Turkish troop withdrawals, would be tackled. But reaching an agreement on the territorial issue will involve much more than determining whether or not a cluster of villages would remain under Turkish-Cypriot control or come under Greek-Cypriot administration. In the same way, in seeking an agreement on the powers of the federal and the two constituent governments, there has been more at stake for each party than determining, for example, whether the provinces or the federal government should be granted residual powers. The two communities are far apart in their expectations of what a settlement would do for them and in their vision of the future of the island. This constitutes a fundamental impediment to realizing a final settlement.

In spite of what they view to be the disaster of 1974, Greek-Cypriots still consider Cyprus to be an indivisible Greek island; after all, Greek-Cypriots have been the majority community for centuries and all corners of the island bear witness to their past and present existence. Greek-Cypriots assert that they are entitled to exercise majority rule. As it is, they have forsaken their ideal of Enosis and accepted the federal principle demanded by the Turkish-Cypriots; from their perspective, this represents an enormous concession.

The Turkish-Cypriot federal plan aims at creating two politically equal states loosely connected with each other. For the Greek-Cypriots, however, this undermines the basic indivisibility of the island. To endorse that form of a settlement is tantamount to accepting the imposition of a minority of 20 percent (or 18 percent, to go by Greek-Cypriot sources) on the majority of 80 percent. By the same logic, the Greek-Cypriots resist the Turkish-Cypriot demand for political equality, given the considerable variance in their proportion of the total population.

The outlook and assumptions described above help to explain the Greek-Cypriots' approach to negotiating a federal settlement for Cyprus after 1974 and their resistance to accepting an exclusive Turkish-Cypriot political entity in northern Cyprus. For their part, Turkish-Cypriots have consistently rejected the majority-minority approach of the Greek-Cypriots. As one of the island's two communities, they feel that they are entitled to the same rights as the Greek-Cypriots.

For years, they have been aggravated by the Greek-Cypriot approach to the intercommunal talks, which proceeded from the assumption that, as the majority community, they were entitled to exercise the decisive political power on the island. They have been equally frustrated by the international community's recognition of the Greek-Cypriot administration as the legitimate government of all of Cyprus. In addition, the economic embargo employed by the Greek-Cypriot government on the Turkish-Cypriot area since 1974 has created major economic problems in the north and has generated considerable bitterness.

It was as a result of these accumulating frustrations that the Turkish-Cypriot leadership decided to establish, unilaterally, the Turkish Republic of Northern Cyprus in November 1983. In doing so, they served notice that if their quest for political equality in a federal Cyprus could not be fulfilled, they would opt for outright independence. They were careful, however, not to close the doors on a federal settlement; as they saw it, this would be negotiated between two equal states.

The Turkish-Cypriots have no wish to return to the 1960 Constitution that had established a partnership government between the two communities. Greek-Cypriots violated this partnership, the island's independence, as well as the Constitution that set up the Cyprus Republic by seeking to unite the island with Greece. In the process, they mistreated Turkish-Cypriots for their opposition to Enosis, and numerous members of the Turkish community became victims of Greek-Cypriot violence between 1963-1974; hence, their insistence on a loose bi-zonal federation providing maximal powers for their province and as much separation from the Greek-Cypriot state in the south as can be reconciled within a federal arrangement.

Given these conflicting perspectives, it is not surprising that intercommunal negotiations have failed to bridge differences sufficiently, despite unwavering external encouragement. To say this, however, is not to minimize the significance of the narrowing of the gap between the two parties that has occurred, thanks in no small part to the persistence of United Nations diplomats.

United Nations diplomacy in Cyprus has benefitted from the fact that, before he became Secretary-General, Javier Perez de Cuellar acquired considerable expertise on the Cyprus issue by virtue of his previous posting as the United Nations Special Representative on the island during 1976-1977. De Cuellar and his colleagues did not believe that the declaration of independent statehood by Turkish-Cypriots made a settlement much harder than before. Indeed, some observers (as well as Turkish-Cypriots) believe that the threat of a permanent Turkish-Cypriot state becoming consolidated in northern Cyprus spurred the Greek-Cypriots to reconsider their options. In any case, both sides accepted the Secretary-General's call for "proximity talks" in August 1984. This bid to breathe new life in to the negotiating process, "strongly backed by the United States and Britain,"[57] achieved promising results, especially in the third round held during November 1984 when the Turkish-Cypriots made substantial concessions (mentioned earlier) by giving up their demand for a rotating presidency and agreeing to reduce the territory under their control from 36 to 29 percent.

The Turkish-Cypriot demand for a rotating presidency had been consistent with their claim for political equality, and thus their concession on this issue was significant. However, most parties interested in a settlement viewed the territorial concession to be much more encouraging. As Groom stated:

> Of great significance was the Turkish Cypriot agreement to a territorial adjustment to 29 percent (less than the magical 30 percent and only 1 percent more than the 28 percent for which Archbishop Makarios had been willing to settle).[58]

In past negotiations, Turkish-Cypriots had argued that the territory under their administration ought to be large enough to be economically viable[59] and should also reflect Turkish-Cypriot land ownership. In previous discussions concerning territory, Turkish-Cypriots had been resistant to lowering their share below 32 percent.

Greek-Cypriots have officially stated their opposition to Turkish-Cypriots administering a territory larger than their share of the overall population in Cyprus. Nonetheless, some Greek-Cypriot leaders have privately acknowledged this to be an untenable position. Before he died in August 1977, Archbishop Makarios unofficially stated that he would settle for the Turkish-Cypriots having 28 percent of the island's territory (as indicated above) in the envisaged federal system. Accordingly, Western and United Nations diplomats believed that if the Turkish-Cypriots could have been persuaded to reduce the size of their envisaged province's territory to less than 30 percent, this would have helped to create a breakthrough. It was on this premise that President Reagan appealed to President Evren of Turkey in late 1984, and the latter persuaded Turkish-Cypriot leader Denktash to agree, thus setting the stage for a major diplomatic initiative.[60]

What the United Nations Secretary-General managed to secure by the end of the third round of the proximity talks was an agreement by both sides to a document spelling out the basic elements for a federal, bi-zonal Republic (see Appendix 2). The federal government would have a Greek-Cypriot president and a Turkish-Cypriot vice-president. At the same time, the two communities would have equal standing in the federal government. The federal cabinet positions would be divided on a seven-to-three basis, with the proviso that the Foreign Ministry or other major portfolio would be assigned to a Turkish-Cypriot. The agreement provided for a federal legislature with two chambers: the Lower House would have a seven to three ratio in favour of Greek-Cypriots, but there would be equal representation in the Upper House. Legislation on major matters would require separate majorities in both chambers.

It was agreed that a transitional government would be established and funds provided in order to bring about an economic equilibrium between the two provinces or federated states, as well as facilitating the resettlement of displaced persons. The Varosha area and six other territories were to be administered by the United Nations on an interim basis.

The draft agreement did not resolve all outstanding issues between Greek and Turkish-Cypriots. Such important issues as the precise boundaries of the two provinces or states, the withdrawal of non-Cypriot (Turkish and Greek) troops,[61] the question of guarantees, and the three fundamental freedoms (the freedom of movement, of settlement, and property ownership anywhere on the island) were left, together with lesser details, to be settled by working committees after the draft agreement was signed by the two Cypriot parties. Incomplete though the agreement was, as Groom observed, "nothing like this had been seen before and it justified the Secretary-General's jubilant tone to the Security Council."[62]

So confident was the Secretary-General that the document represented the breakthrough for a final agreement, he believed that at the summit meeting in New York on January 17, 1985, the two parties "could set the seal 'in an hour'."[63] Nor was de Cuellar alone in his high expectations. Even Greek Prime Minister Papandreou, with a reputation for a hard line in Cyprus, acknowledged on January 2, 1985 that the Turkish-Cypriots had "undoubtedly made significant steps in the direction of a viable and just settlement of the Cyprus problem."[64] Greek-Cypriot leader Kyprianou "is reported to have commented 'everything is fine; our side has obtained the best possible conditions'."[65]

However, contrary to virtually universal expectations, the January 1985 summit meeting failed, leaving behind a trail of controversy and accusations. Turkish-Cypriot leader Denktash and de Ceullar believed that the purpose of the summit was to sign the Secretary-General's draft agreement and then move on to set up working committees to finish the task. Greek-Cypriot leader Kyprianou, however, wanted to use the draft agreement as a basis for further discussions. Indeed, to the dismay of the Secretary-General and the Turkish-Cypriot leadership, he went so far as to re-open all the major issues on which agreement had already been reached.[66]

Upon returning home from New York, Kyprianou was censured by a vote of two-thirds of the legislators in the Greek-Cypriot House of Representatives for his inept handling of the summit talks and for missing a major opportunity for a settlement. In Greece, however, the Papandreou government stood by the Greek-Cypriot leader, and Greek public opinion gave no indication of disappointment. This was not because a Cyprus settlement would be unwelcome, but because the terms were seen as not favourable enough. In Turkey, there was no disappointment but rather considerable relief among the public, based on the widespread belief that the Turkish government had made excessive concessions. Turkish and Turkish-Cypriot leaders, however, blamed Greek-Cypriots and Greece for the failure of the summit. They believed that Papandreou was more interested in exploiting the Cyprus issue and decrying Turkey's "occupation troops" on the island to score diplomatic points against Turkey than in endorsing an accord. They believed he wanted to aid the Greek lobby's major objective of limiting military aid to Turkey.

The Greek-Cypriot leader's failure to accept the Secretary-General's draft agreement at the 1985 summit has given a considerable boost to the Turkish-Cypriots' international standing, and Turkey has also benefited from this; they were seen as the parties willing to compromise.[67] Even the United Nations Secretariat was not unduly reticent in laying the blame on Kyprianou. In analyzing the outcome of the 1985 summit, Groom has observed:

> ...it is not only the Greek Cypriots who have noted differences of substance between the Secretary General and the Greek Cypriot side. So have major Western Powers and they are pressing Kyprianou hard to pursue his concerns with Perez de Cuellar's framework failing which Kyprianou will forfeit their sympathy. This puts the Turkish-Cypriots, so often condemned in international fora, in an unaccustomed position of a degree of international approval.[68]

The events surrounding the 1985 Cyprus summit have helped ease the international diplomatic pressures that Greek-Cypriots and Greece have quite successfully mobilized against Turkey and the Turkish-Cypriots. In general, especially since the mid-1980s, there has been wider international receptivity to the Turkish position on Cyprus, particularly in the West. Admittedly, the support for the Greek-Cypriot government is still high among the non-aligned and Communist bloc states. Turkish diplomacy has been making greater diplomatic inroads by cultivating closer ties with neighbouring Middle Eastern states and assuming a larger role in meetings of the Islamic Conference. In spite of its secular orientation, it is largely because of the sense of isolation over the Cyprus issue that Turkey has turned to the Islamic world. Greece's attempts to undercut Turkish diplomacy among the Arab states of the Middle East have been unsuccessful, despite the special efforts by Papandreou, who put much emphasis on securing Arab links in an attempt to isolate Turkey.

In the future, Greek and Greek-Cypriot expectations of maintaining international pressures on Turkey and the Turkish-Cypriots will have to come to terms with the fact that, with the passage of years, the world community is tiring of the Cyprus problem. Thus, at the March 1983 summit of the non-aligned states in New Delhi, United Nations Secretary-General Perez de Ceullar did not even mention Cyprus in his survey of world problems that require attention.[69]

Although the island is divided into two, the problems of Cyprus are dwarfed by those of neighbouring Lebanon and other trouble-spots in the world. After all, there has been practically no case of political violence involving Greek and Turkish-Cypriots since 1974, and virtually all refugees have been comfortably resettled and provided with employment. Unprecedented economic growth in the south has brought new levels of prosperity to Greek-Cypriots and has further widened the gap between the two communities; at $6,800, the per capita GNP in the south in 1987 was more than twice the $2,900 for the Turkish-Cypriots.[70] In these circumstances, Greek and Greek-Cypriot appeals to the conscience of the international community will likely generate diminished levels of sympathy. Thus, the Greek-Cypriot government decided to drop its plans to introduce the Cyprus issue on the agenda of the General Assembly in the fall of 1987 when soundings indicated that past levels of support would not be forthcoming.

There is a consensus, especially among the Western countries, that any future attempt by the Greek-Cypriot government to internationalize the Cyprus dispute and avoid the intercommunal negotiating process shepherded by the United Nations will be counter-productive. Thus, Greek-Cypriot proposals for an international conference to deal with the issues which the 1985 summit could not resolve have failed to win much support.

Since the failure of the January 1985 summit, it was expected that the United Nations Secretary-General would strive to revive the intercommunal talks. The initiative of Greek and Turkish leaders that began at Davos in January 1988 improved prospects for renewed initiatives on Cyprus. In August 1988, Turkish-Cypriot leader Denktash met with the newly elected Greek-Cypriot leader Vasiliou at a meeting convened by Secretary-General Perez de Ceullar in Geneva. Since then, the two Cypriot leaders have regularly met on the island in a new bid to reach agreement for a new settlement.

The current talks began without any preconditions. Essentially, they have been based on the Denktash-Makarios guidelines of 1977 and the 10-point procedural agreement reached between Denktash and Kyprianou in 1979 (referred to earlier). During the first eighteen months of these talks, there has been little discussion on the respective boundaries of the envisaged federated states. On the other hand, there has been an intense debate on the exercise of the so-called three freedoms, the freedom to travel, freedom to settle, and freedom of property.

The Greek-Cypriot position is that a final settlement in Cyprus has to provide for the exercise of what appears to them to be basic human rights. In the Cypriot context, this would pertain to the right of Greek-Cypriots to move freely, to own property, and to settle in the envisaged Turkish-Cypriot province in the north. How could you have a country, the Greek-Cypriots ask, where the people of one province are barred from settling or buying property in another?

These prerogatives, which Greek-Cypriots want to exercise in all of Cyprus, are the very rights Turkish-Cypriots want restricted in their own province to ensure a demographic majority so that their exercise by Greek-Cypriots in the north would not undermine Turkish security, character, and autonomous control. As many writers have pointed out, Turkish-Cypriots are afraid of being swamped by Greek-Cypriots.

If one assumes that hardly any Greek-Cypriot would want to settle in a territory ruled by Turkish-Cypriots unless they possessed property rights, then the most important of the three "freedoms" is the one concerning property ownership.[71] Greek-Cypriots do not just have a considerable demographic advantage, they also have a substantial edge in economic resources. Thus, if the freedoms of property ownership and settlement were to be universally recognized without any limits, Turkish-Cypriots could become a minority within their own province and witness the spectacle of the richer Greeks buying up their properties. That would defeat the whole purpose of the Turkish-Cypriot aspiration of being in control of their destiny as a distinct community within an exclusive territory. This, of course, would not rule out engagement in mutually beneficial relations with the Greek-Cypriot province in the south.

On the other hand, the issue pertaining to freedom to travel is of secondary importance. Turkish-Cypriot justification to restrict Greek-Cypriots from travelling to the north is based on security concerns. However, it is envisaged to be temporary until such time as future relations between the two peoples improve to the point where such a restriction would be unnecessary.

In spite of all the failed attempts and lost opportunities for a Cyprus settlement, it would be premature to write off future possibilities. Clearly, it is not difficult to envisage an agreed settlement consistent with Greek and Turkish interests.

For Greece and Greek-Cypriots, the most important aspect of a future settlement is one that ensures the substantial removal of Turkey's military presence on the island. This will help soothe Greece's national pride as well as reduce fears of further Turkish territorial advances on the island. The alternative to an agreed settlement is a permanent Turkish presence in northern Cyprus and the consolidation of the Turkish-Cypriot state. To date, only Turkey has recognized the new state. However, it is probable that the Turkish Republic of Northern Cyprus will gradually win diplomatic recognition among Turkey's traditional allies in the Islamic world; namely, Pakistan, Bangladesh, and Malaysia, with other states following suit in time.

Some writers consider that Turkey is content with the existing *status quo* in Cyprus, but this is arguable. One possible consequence of the continued division of the island would be its future partition between Greece and Turkey. Turkish leaders are not in favour of a formalized partition of Cyprus because that would enable Greece to bring its military to the Greek part of the island and pose a potential threat to Turkey's southern coast. Partly as a result of these considerations, Ankara has not been wholly supportive over the creation of an independent Turkish-Cypriot state in northern Cyprus. Indeed, there is considerable evidence that Turkey has discouraged the Turkish-Cypriot leadership's aspirations of independent statehood since 1974 and delayed its declaration until 1983.[72]

Many Turkish officials acknowledge that the political and economic costs of Turkey's Cyprus commitment have been high, as witnessed by the international disapproval of her policy in Cyprus, the complications with her principal Western allies, and the American aid lost or reduced due to the embargo and continuing efforts of the Greek lobby. It is clear that Turkey considers such costs worth bearing as long as it feels that Greece and Greek-Cypriots are seeking a return to the pre-1974 situation in Cyprus. At the same time, Turkey will accept a settlement that enables Turkish-Cypriots to exercise autonomy under conditions which would prevent the recurrence of Greek-Cypriot political domination or threats to their kinsmen's security.

Furthermore, it is probable that Turkey's application for full membership in the European Community, and the need to avoid Greece's potential veto, will provide an additional incentive for Ankara to resolve the Cyprus problem and proceed with its mission to become integrated with Western Europe. Although this has raised Greek expectations that Turkey could be induced to make concessions on Cyprus it has hitherto resisted, it is obvious that — as is the case with Athens — any agreement must be one Ankara can "live with" and sell to its people. Nonetheless, both Greece and the Greek-Cypriots will seek to use the EEC card to exact concessions from the Turks.

The Greek-Cypriot government's decision to apply for full membership to the EEC (announced in November 1988) is intended to increase pressures on Turkey by raising the prospect of Cyprus' entry before that of Turkey, raising the possibility that Ankara may have to contend with two vetoes. Regardless of whether Greek and Greek-Cypriots' pressures will yield the hoped for results, it is likely that the EEC will play an expanding role in Cyprus.

By and large, it is the Cypriot communities who have set the agenda for negotiations in Cyprus since 1974. Greece and Turkey can encourage and nudge their own kinsmen to reach an accommodation before the island's current division becomes entrenched and irreversible. This does not mean that the Cypriot parties should be rushed into a settlement. However, there are obviously a variety of confidence-building measures that could be supported and tried. For example, the Greek-Cypriot government could terminate the economic embargo placed on economically-strapped northern Cyprus. For its part, Turkey could undertake a withdrawal of its troops on a substantial scale so as to assuage Greek-Cypriot security concerns for the future.

Just as the process of repairing relations between Greece and Turkey promises to be long and difficult, the Cypriot communities too will need time not just to heal old wounds but also to enter into a pattern of cooperative relationships and ensure their success. Since the mid-1950s, Cyprus was instrumental in the unravelling of the Greek-Turkish détente forged in 1930 between Atatürk and Venizelos. Cyprus remains a major testing ground of Greek-Turkish relations. Thus, a *modus vivendi* on the island helped by Turkey and Greece will both mirror their relations in other spheres, and help foster a new course of reconciliation, making it easier to settle their quarrels in the Aegean.

Notes

1. Mehmet Ali Birand, *30 Sıcak Gün (Thirty Hot Days)*, Istanbul: Milliyet Yayınları, 1975, p. 64.
2. Ahmad, *Turkish Experiment*, p. 419.
3. Wiener, *Turkish Foreign Policy*, p. 20.
4. Couloumbis, *Troubled Triangle*, p. 83.
5. Birand, *Hot Days*, p. 64.
6. Wiener, *Turkish Foreign Policy*, p. 323.
7. "One senior American official said that Kissinger told him that the reason the United States had failed to denounce the regime was that he felt to do so would be to give the Turks a 'carte blanche' to intervene." *Ibid.*, p. 311.
8. United Kingdom, *Cyprus*, London: HMSO, Cmnd. 1093, 1960, Appendix B.
9. Crawshaw, *Cyprus Revolt*, p. 390.

10. Andrew Borowiec, *The Mediterranean Feud*, New York: Praeger, 1983, p. 99.

11. Kyle, *Cyprus*, p. 15. See also Polyviou, *Conflict and Negotiation*, p. 158.

12. As quoted in Kyle, *Cyprus*, p. 15.

13. Press conference of Prime Minister Bülent Ecevit, July 28, 1974, *Cyprus Communiques*, Ankara, pp. 23-24.

14. Polyviou, *Conflict and Negotiation*, p. 176.

15. Couloumbis, *Troubled Triangle*, p. 96.

16. As stated in Stern, *Wrong Horse*, p. 101.

17. Birand, *Hot Days*, p. 266.

18. *Ibid.*

19. D. G. Kousoulas, *Power and Influence: An Introduction to International Relations*, Monterey: Brooks/Cole Publishing Co., 1985, p. 103.

20. Woodhouse, *Karamanlis*, p. 218.

21. *Ibid.*

22. Karamanlis asked Ecevit: "Why did you undertake the second offensive against me ?" during their summit meeting in Montreux in March 1978. As reported in Mehmet Ali Birand, *Diyet: Türkiye ve Kıbrıs Uzerine Pazarlıklar, 1974-1979 (Bargaining over Turkey and Cyprus)*, Istanbul: Milliyet Publications, 1975, p. 362.

23. The figure is contained in United Kingdom (House of Commons), *Report from the Select Committee on Cyprus*, Session 1975-1976, London: HMSO, 1976, p. xii. Turkish-Cypriot authorities, however, estimate the number of Greek-Cypriot refugees to be closer to 100,000.

24. The figure has been obtained from *The Economist*, July 3, 1982.

25. Paul Y. Watanabe, *Ethnic Groups, Congress, and American Foreign Policy: The Politics of the Turkish Arms Embargo*, Westport and London: Greenwood Press, 1984.

26. *Ibid.*, p. 127.

27. Couloumbis, *Troubled Triangle*, p. 104.

28. The tank unit is referred to in Michael Harbottle, *The Impartial Soldier*, London: Oxford University Press, 1970, pp. 165-6.

29. Ellen B. Laipson, chapter entitled "Cyprus: A Quarter Century of U.S. Policy" in J.T.A. Koumoulides (ed.), *Cyprus in Transition, 1960-1985*, London: Trigraph Ltd., 1986, p. 74.

30. *Financial Times*, June 24, 1986.

31. The Economist, *Quarterly Economic Review: Cyprus 1983*, 3rd Quarter, p. 19.

32. *Ibid.*

33. Kyriacos Markides, chapter entitled "Problems of Unity and Consensus in a Threatened Society: Cyprus During the Aftermath of the Turkish Invasion," in J.T.A. Koumoulides (ed.), *Greece and Cyprus in History*, Amsterdam: Adolf M. Hakkert Publishers, 1985, p. 55.

34. See *The Economist*, February 27, 1982. See also A.J.R. Groom's chapter entitled "Cyprus, Greece and Turkey: A Treadmill for Diplomacy" in Koumoulides, *Transition*, p. 136.

35. A.J.R. Groom, "Cyprus: Back in the Doldrums," *The Round Table*, Vol. 300, 1986, p. 366.

36. *Foreign Affairs Committee Report on Cyprus*, May 1987, p. xx.

37. *Ibid.*

38. Groom, "Treadmill for Diplomacy," p. 134.

39. David Popper, "Cyprus in Greek-Turkish Relations," paper presented at the Lehrman Institute Conference on Greek-Turkish relations, May 16, 1986, p. 3.

40. These observations have been based on discussions with diplomatic sources in Cyprus on the basis of non attribution.

41. Oguz Korhan, who was the Minister of Agriculture in the Turkish-Cypriot government in 1974, explained to the author that at the time nearly one-half the Turkish-Cypriot population were still under Greek-Cypriot contol in the south.

42. *Foreign Affairs Committee Report on Cyprus,* 1987, p. xvii.

43. *Ibid.,* p. xix. In addition, the International Institute of Strategic Studies has estimated the number of Greek-Cypriot reservists to be 60,000. *Ibid.* The United Nations, however, has estimated the number of Greek-Cypriot reservists to be 50,000.

44. This observation is based on confidential interviews conducted in northern Cyprus during September 1985.

45. See the International Institute of Strategic Studies, *The Military Balance, 1988-89,* London, 1988, p. 87.

46. Necati M. Ertekun, *The Cyprus Dispute and the Birth of the Turkish Republic of Northern Cyprus,* London: K. Rustem, 1981, pp. 39-42.

47. See United Nations, Secretariat, *Report of the Secretary-General Pursuant to Paragraph 6 of Security Council Resolution 401 (1976),* (S/12323), April 30, 1977, para. 5.

48. For the text of the ten-point agreement, see United Nations, Secretariat, *Report by the Secretary-General on the U.N. Operation in Cyprus* (for the period December 1, 1978 to May 31, 1979 (S13369), May 31, 1979, para. 51.

49. Laipson, "Quarter Century," p. 74.

50. See the text of the twelve-point plan published in *The Middle East Economic Digest,* December 1, 1978.

51. *Ibid.*

52. *New York Times,* March 11, 1979.

53. Groom, "Doldrums", pp. 362-3.

54. Laipson, "Quarter Century," p. 78.

55. *The Economist,* February 1, 1986.

56. According to Kitsikis, "the KKE supported for the first time in November 1986 a campaign in favour of the establishment of Greco-Turkish friendship" following the meeting in the Greek part of Cyprus between the Greek and Turkish Communist party leaders, General Secretaries Florakis and Kutlu. See Dimitri Kitsikis "Populism, Eurocommunism, and the KKE: The Communist Party of Greece" in Michael Waller and Meindert Fennema (eds.), *Communist Parties in Western Europe: Decline or Adaptation,* Oxford: Basil Blackwell Ltd., 1988, p. 113.

57. Groom, "Doldrums," p. 362.

58. *Ibid.*

59. See the Denktash-Makarios guideline agreement cited in footnote 47.

60. Groom, "Doldrums," p. 363.

61. There are an estimated 2,800 Greek troops. See the *Military Balance, 1988-89,* p. 87.

62. Groom, "Doldrums," p. 363.

63. *Ibid.*

64. *Ibid.*

65. *Ibid.*

66. *The Times*, January 22, 1985. Also, at one point Kyprianou even denied the existence of an official document — his spokesmen publicly referred to it as a "ghost document." *Ibid.*

67. *Ibid.*

68. Groom, "Doldrums," p. 378.

69. The Economist, *Quarterly Economic Review: Cyprus 1983,* 2nd Quarter, p. 15.

70. *The Ottawa Citizen,* September 2, 1988.

71. Unofficial surveys conducted in the south have indicated that few Greek-Cypriot refugees, or others, would be interested in moving to settle in the federated northern state ruled by Turkish-Cypriots. Information on these surveys was provided to the author by diplomatic sources stationed in Cyprus on the basis of non attribution.

72. This is based on confidential interviews with various observers in Turkey and northern Cyprus.

5

The Aegean Dispute and Additional Strains in Greek-Turkish Relations

The Aegean dispute between Greece and Turkey centers on the delineation of sovereign rights in the Aegean Sea. The determination of maritime boundaries is an undertaking of considerable complexity especially when unusual geographical configurations and islands are involved. It is essentially a political process usually accomplished by direct negotiations between disputing states. In recent years, however, states have made increasing use of arbitral and judicial tribunals in resolving such disputes.

The essence of the Aegean dispute is the overlapping Greek and Turkish national interests in the area. The Greeks view the Aegean as a Greek sea dotted with over 2,000 islands that (with two exceptions in the northern Aegean) are Greek. On the other hand, Turks consider that, as an Aegean nation, Turkey is entitled to an equitable share of the resources in the Aegean. For historical reasons, Greek-Turkish relations have been characterized by mistrust and hostility. Moreover, the resolution of the Aegean dispute has been further complicated by the Cyprus dispute which has strained Greco-Turkish relations since the mid-1950s.

Geographically, the Aegean Sea has some very special characteristics. It is a "semi-enclosed" sea, with two coastal states, Greece and Turkey.[1] However, it also constitutes an important international sea-route for traffic passing via the Dardanelles to Istanbul and further to the Black Sea. Another important characteristic is that the Aegean is dominated by islands throughout its length. It is this factor (particularly Greece's eastern Aegean islands close to Turkey's coast) which poses particular problems in the delimitation of maritime boundaries. There is a large variation in the size, population, and location of the eastern Aegean islands, all of which are potentially relevant factors in determining maritime boundaries. Some of these islands have substantial populations such as Lesbos with a population of 88,601 and Rhodes, whose population stands at 87,831; on the other hand, the tiny island of Kastellorizon, which is only one mile off Turkey's southwestern coast, has a population of 222 and an area of only 3.5 square miles.

At Lausanne in 1923, it was decided that the mostly Greek-inhabited Aegean islands, which had been ruled by the Ottoman Empire for centuries, would come under Greek rule; most of these islands had, in any case, passed to Greek control during the Balkan wars of 1912-1913. Thus, with the exception of Gökçeada, Bozcaada, and the tiny Rabbit Islands (Tavsan Adalari) at the entrance of the Dardanelles, all of the 2,200 Aegean islands and islets have been under Greek sovereignty. It was also decided, however, that Turkey's security concerns warranted the demilitarization of the eastern Aegean islands. The equilibrium established by the Lausanne Treaty in the Aegean did not pose any large problems for the two neighbours for one-half a century.

Since the early 1970s, however, Greek and Turkish differences over the Aegean have developed into a full-fledged conflict and become of serious significance. The issues over which Greece and Turkey have quarrelled in the Aegean consist of the following: sovereign rights over the continental shelf, the limits of the territorial sea, sovereign airspace (as well as the control of the military and civil air traffic control zones), and the re-militarization of the Greek islands in the eastern Aegean.

The Development of the Continental Shelf Issue

According to the 1982 United Nations Convention of the Law of the Sea (Article 76), the "continental shelf" of a coastal state:

> comprises the sea-bed and subsoil of the submarine areas that extend beyond its territorial sea throughout the natural prolongation of its land territory to the outer edge of the continental margin, or to a distance of 200 nautical miles from the baselines from which the breadth of the territorial sea is measured where the outer edge of the continental margin does not extend to that distance.[2]

The continental shelf dispute emerged in the aftermath of the search for oil in the Aegean. On November 1, 1973, Turkey granted twenty-seven permits to the State Turkish Petroleum Company to explore for oil in an area to the west of several Greek islands, particularly in the region of Samothrace, Mytilene, and Chios. It was not entirely coincidental that the Turkish exploration plans came on the heels of the Arab oil embargo and a steep rise in petroleum prices following the October 1973 Arab-Israeli war. However, despite the embargo, the Turks were motivated by other considerations.

According to Turkish official statements, Greece had been conducting research and explorations in the Aegean beyond its territorial waters since 1960; in 1973, Turkey decided to stake its own claim to the sea bed. Several weeks after the Turkish grant of exploration rights, an American company discovered modest deposits of oil off the island of Thassos in an undisputed area. The oil find, and expectations of further discoveries, enhanced the two countries' economic interest in the Aegean. The Greek government waited until after the Thassos discovery before launching a protest.[3] In a diplomatic note delivered on February 7, 1974, Athens complained that Turkey's concessions were part of its continental shelf and that Turkey's concessions overlapped areas where Greece had granted oil exploration concessions in 1972. Turkey responded with its own opposing claims in a note of February 27, 1974. Subsequently, there was considerable tension when the Ecevit government decided to send a survey ship, the *Çandarlı*, on May 29, 1974, to conduct research in disputed waters. In anticipation of possible Greek interference, the Turks sent thirty-two warships to escort the *Çandarlı*.

Before the tensions over the Aegean subsided, another crisis broke out in July 1974. This time it was in Cyprus, where the Ioannidis coup against Makarios prompted the Turkish government to invoke Article IV of the Treaty of Guarantee and send Turkish troops to the island. Some observers argued that Turkey's Cyprus victory strengthened its hand in the Aegean: Turkish concessions on the island could be linked to Greek concessions in the Aegean. But the bitterness generated by the Cyprus events were not then conducive to any major initiatives either on the island or in the Aegean. Furthermore, as intermittent talks between Greek and Turkish officials revealed, the two sides differed substantially on the relevant laws and principles which should apply in delimiting the continental shelf as well as the conflict resolution method.

From the beginning of the dispute, the Greek government took the position that, in accordance with international law, it was entitled to most of the Aegean continental shelf. Greek spokesmen have specifically cited the 1958 Geneva Convention[4] on the Continental Shelf in asserting that islands are entitled to generate their own continental shelf. Greece is a signatory of the Geneva Convention whereas Turkey is not. Subsequently, Greece approved and signed the Final Text of the Law of the Sea Conference in 1982, as confirming and lending further support for its position on the drawing up of maritime boundaries. Under the Greek approach, the Greek continental shelf would extend from the Greek mainland to the median line between the Greek islands and the Turkish mainland, thus denying Turkey any continental shelf west of the Greek islands.

Turkey has taken the view that equity is the overriding principle in delimiting Aegean maritime boundaries. The starting point of the Turkish position is that the Aegean Sea, which is semi-enclosed, has special characteristics. The entire sea, and in particular the islands in the eastern Aegean, create special circumstances. In the Turkish view, the Greek islands in the eastern Aegean lie within Turkey's continental shelf which extends naturally from the Anatolian peninsula. These islands are very close to the Turkish coast. The island of Kos, for example, is 124 miles from Athens but only five miles from Turkey's coast. As a look at Map 3 on page 160 will indicate, these islands are several hundreds of miles from the Greek mainland. Thus, Turkish officials maintain that they cannot be considered to be a continuation of the Greek peninsula since there are intervening high seas between them and the Greek mainland. It is Turkey's position that the islands which are close to Turkey's coast do not possess their own shelves. Consequently, Turkish leaders have rejected the Greek claim as fundamentally inequitable. According to one estimate, the application of Greece's formula would confer to it about 97 percent of the Aegean sea bed, leaving Turkey about 2.5 percent, specifically a narrow strip along the Anatolian coast.[5] It is on these grounds that Turkish leaders have accused Greece of wanting to turn the Aegean into a "Greek lake."

The Turkish formula for the resolution of the conflict is to draw a median line through the Aegean archipelago. The Greek government has dismissed such a division as arbitrary and without basis in international law. Greece sees the Aegean dispute primarily as a legal problem, dismissing its equity or political aspects. Furthermore, Greece has objected that the proposed median line would enclave its eastern Aegean islands.

Since Greece considers its case in the Aegean to be stronger on the bases of international law and practice, its basic approach to the resolution of the dispute has been legalistic. It has repeatedly urged that both countries take their case to the International Court at the Hague (hereinafter the World Court) for a binding judgement. Turkey, on the other hand, has not conceded that its case carries any less legal weight. Accordingly, it has cited various continental shelf decisions of the World Court or arbitration tribunals explicitly recognizing equitable principles (such as the 1969 North Sea continental shelf case) or involving the discounting of islands, as was the case in the 1977 Anglo-French arbitration which enclaved the British Channel Islands.

Therefore, Turkey has argued that the Aegean dispute is not just a legal problem, but one that involves important economic, political, and strategic interests for both Greece and Turkey, requiring a political settlement. Turkish leaders have not ruled out a joint appeal to the World Court but only as a last resort and after settling as many of the substantive issues as possible through bilateral negotiations.

These conflicting approaches regarding the proper procedures for tackling their Aegean problems have frustrated attempts to find a settlement since the issue first emerged in late 1973. In February 1975, Greek efforts to find a legal settlement to the continental shelf issue briefly received a boost when the caretaker Turkish Premier Professor Sadi Irmak accepted the

Greek government's proposal for a joint recourse to the World Court. However, Irmak was heavily criticized by Ecevit, then leader of the Opposition. In any case, soon thereafter, Justice Party leader Demirel replaced Irmak and affirmed Turkey's preference for a negotiated settlement. On April 16, 1975, Turkish Foreign Minister Çaglayangil "spelled out the principle that has dominated Turkey's approach ever since: 'Let us talk first — we may reach an agreement — and not go to the Hague'."[6] Even though Turkey preferred a political settlement, Çaglayangil met his Greek counterpart in Rome in May 1975 for preliminary discussions on a *compromis* for joint submission to the World Court. Hopes for a legal settlement were further encouraged a fortnight later when Demirel met Greek Prime Minister Karamanlis in Brussels at a NATO summit. The final communique issued after the Brussels summit included the statement that the two countries'

> problems should be resolved peacefully by means of negotiations and as regards the continental shelf of the Aegean Sea by the International Court at the Hague. They defined the general lines on the basis of which the forthcoming meetings of the representatives of the two governments would take place.[6]

The Brussels communique was subsequently cited by Greece in its application to the World Court as evidence that Turkey had agreed to submit the dispute for settlement by the Court. But serious disagreements emerged in a further exchange of notes between Athens and Ankara which reiterated the standard principles that have become a hallmark of their respective positions on how to resolve their Aegean disputes.

In its note of September 30, 1975, Turkey declared that the submission of the dispute to the World Court required the "explicit consent" of both parties. In a further note of November 18, 1975, Turkey reiterated its position that the Aegean Sea involves vital strategic, economic, and political interests for both parties and,

> ...historically its resources have been shared by peoples of the Anatolian and Greek peninsulas. Ankara also proposed that the parties seek an 'equitable solution', acceptable to both sides, through negotiations. In reply, Greece's note of December 19, 1975, stated that the dispute was limited to 'legal' issues and did not concern vital political or strategic interests; that the positions of the two states on the international legal principles which govern the dispute were 'irreconcilable'; and that the adjudication by the International Court of Justice was now appropriate.[8]

During 1975, the standoff over the settlement avenues discouraged any easing of tensions, and in the following year, domestic pressures were instrumental in the outbreak of a crisis. In Turkey, Prime Minister Demirel had formed his government in the spring of 1975 through an uneasy coalition of his Justice Party and three other minor parties. The Turkish leader was under considerable Opposition pressure to continue staking Turkey's claim to the Aegean sea bed which had begun in late 1973, particularly since Greece continued to assert sovereignty in the disputed continental shelf areas; having failed to challenge the Greeks in the Aegean for more than a decade (until 1973), the Turks wanted to avoid the appearance of acquiescence.

Demirel was attacked by Opposition leader Ecevit, his predecessor who became a national hero in 1974 for sending the Turkish army to Cyprus, for not pressing Turkish claims to the Aegean vigorously. Ecevit also castigated the Turkish premier for accepting Karamanlis' demand to submit the continental shelf issue to the World Court.

Largely in response to Opposition pressure, the Demirel government decided to re-assert Turkish claims to the Aegean sea bed by announcing in February 1976 that a Turkish research ship, the *Hora*, later renamed *Sizmik 1*, would conduct seismic research in disputed waters. In spite of dire warnings from Athens, the Turkish vessel spent three days, August 6-8, 1976, collecting seismic data west of Lesbos in the sea bed claimed by Greece. During its research mission, *Sizmik 1* was escorted by a Turkish warship and shadowed by the Greek navy amid fears that Greek interference might provoke a war. Karamanlis himself came under considerable pressure from his Opposition to take tough action against the Turks, with PASOK's Andreas Papandreou demanding that Greece sink the Turkish vessel. But the Greek leader resisted any recourse to force; instead, in an astute move to defuse the crisis, he launched two separate appeals, one to the Security Council of the United Nations and another to the World Court.

On August 10, 1976, the Greek government requested an urgent meeting of the Security Council on the grounds that Turkey's recent and repeated violations of Greek sovereign rights in the Aegean had endangered international peace and security. On the same day, by unilateral application, Greece also started proceedings at the World Court against Turkey in order to determine the legal rights of Greece and Turkey to the continental shelf. At the same time, Greece filed a request with the Court for interim measures to prevent escalation of the conflict.

In the course of the Security Council debate, Greece repeated its interpretation of the 1958 Geneva Convention as supporting its claims to the Aegean continental shelf and asked the Council to press Turkey "that it must suspend its provocative acts. The United Nations was not in time to stop the tragedy of Cyprus. It can now prevent a new tragedy in the Aegean."[9] In response, the Turkish representative defended his government's position by stating that *Sizmik 1* had conducted its soundings outside the Greek territorial waters in the Aegean. He reiterated Turkey's position that in the absence of an agreed delimitation of the continental shelf, Greece could not claim to have sovereign rights in the Aegean beyond its territorial waters. He also added that a Greek vessel, the *Nautilus,* was conducting research similar to that of *Sizmik 1* in a neighbouring region "at this very moment."[10] Further, the Turkish delegate charged that Greece had violated the Treaties of Lausanne (1923) and Paris (1947) by militarizing the eastern Aegean islands; he also charged that Greece had engaged in illegal acts "aimed at transforming the international air space of the Aegean into national Greek air space, thus depriving Turkey and other countries of their inherent and traditionally established rights to use the international air space over the Aegean."[11] Turkey invited the Security Council to examine Greece's treaty violations and hoped that it would encourage Greece to enter into "meaningful negotiations" with Turkey.

The Security Council did not directly address the substance of the issue but made recommendations concerning the procedure for settlement in such a manner as to give both Greece and Turkey some satisfaction. Thus, Resolution 395 (1976) called for bilateral negotiations (as favoured by Turkey) but also recommended that the contribution of the World Court be taken into account (as favoured by Greece). Paragraphs 3 and 4 of Resolution 395 state that the Security Council:

> 3. Calls on the Governments of Greece and Turkey to resume direct negotiations over their differences and appeals to them to do everything in their power to insure that these result in mutually acceptable solutions; [and]
> 4. Invites the Governments of Greece and Turkey in this respect to continue to take into account the contribution that appropriate judicial means, in particular the International Court of Justice, are qualified to make to the settlement of any remaining legal differences which they may identify in connection with their present dispute.[12]

The ambiguity of the wording of paragraph 4 has been noted by a number of authors.[13] Whether or not it conformed more closely to the Turkish or Greek position is open to debate. On the other hand, it is undeniable that the Resolution and the Security Council's overall handling of the issue "managed to take some steam out of the dispute."[14]

Meanwhile, the World Court considered Greece's request for interim measures of protection; as indicated earlier, this was separate from the Greek appeal to the Court to rule on the rights of Greece and Turkey concerning the Aegean continental shelf. Greece's request for interim measures of protection "sought to prevent both parties from either conducting further research and exploration in the contested areas or taking measures which might endanger their peaceful relations."[15] Greece justified its request for interim measures on two grounds. First, it contended that by granting exploration licences to the Turkish State Petroleum Company and its exploration through *Sizmik 1*, Turkey had caused "'irreparable prejudice' to Greece's right of exclusivity of knowledge about its continental shelf and to the Court's future judgement on the merits."[16] Second, Greece argued that "Turkey was obliged to abstain from any sort of action which might aggravate the dispute, and that Turkey's grant of licences of exploration, if continued, would undermine friendly relations between Greece and Turkey."[17]

Turkey opposed the proposed interim measures on the grounds that its exploration activities did not prejudice any Greek rights in the disputed areas. It further contended that even if its activities harmed Greece's interests, appropriate compensation could be provided. In addition, it objected to the Court's jurisdiction to grant interim relief.

The World Court delivered its judgement on September 12, 1976. It denied Greece's request for interim measures of protection on the grounds that it could not find evidence of "irreparable prejudice" to Greece's rights. At the same time, however, it continued to consider Greece's other submission for judging the rights of the parties in the Aegean continental shelf.

Under Article 36, paragraph 1 of its Statute, the jurisdiction of the Court in contentious cases is dependent on the consent of the parties. Although the Greek application was made unilaterally, Greece alleged that there were two independent expressions of Turkish consent. First, it contended that Article 17 of the General Act on the Pacific Settlement of International Disputes of 1928 (General Act), to which both Greece and Turkey acceded, "when read together with articles 36, paragraph 1 and 37 of the Statute of the International Court, vests the Court with jurisdiction."[18] Article 17 of the General Act requires parties in conflict "to submit to judicial settlement all disputes with regard to which they 'are in conflict as to their respective rights'."[19]

Turkey lodged two objections to the Greek claim: first, that the Act may no longer be in force, and second, that at the time of its accession to the treaty, Greece had made a reservation withholding from the Court disputes "relating to the territorial status of Greece, including disputes relating to its rights of sovereignty over its ports and lines of communication."[20] In its judgement released on December 19, 1978, the Court ruled that the Greek reservation applied to maritime boundary limitations and used it as a basis for rejecting Greece's claim for the Court to exercise jurisdiction over the continental shelf case.

The Court also rejected Greece's argument that the joint Greek-Turkish

Brussels communique was a binding international agreement that required Turkey to submit to the jurisdiction of the World Court. Thus, after nearly two and one-half years of deliberating on procedural questions, the Court was unable to make decisions on the substantive issues of continental shelf delimitation.

For Greece, the decision of the World Court was a significant setback. By then, however, both Greece and Turkey had reached a form of *modus vivendi* by agreeing (in the Berne Declaration of November 11, 1976) to adopt a set of procedures for bilateral negotiations and to refrain from any exploration in areas outside of their respective territorial waters (see Appendix 1).

Although the 1976 crisis over *Sizmik 1's* exploration in disputed waters created a serious danger of military confrontation in the Aegean, it did have a major salutary effect: both the Greek and Turkish governments agreed on the need for adopting a set of procedures to prevent further crises — hence the code of behaviour agreed upon at Berne in November 1976.

What the agreement at Berne did was to freeze the Aegean issues. However, this may not have been the intent or expectation of either of the two countries at the time as they sought to cope with the Aegean crisis. Bilateral negotiations resumed in earnest after Berne, and although no settlement emerged, neither side questioned their usefulness until Andreas Papandreou's PASOK government came to power in Greece in 1981. Indeed, considerable progress was attained on the flight information region (FIR) issue with regard to civilian flights (discussed later in this chapter). Under Papandreou, there was a hardening of the Greek position.

As would be expected, the hardest issue to deal with has been the delineation of sovereign rights of the continental shelf. The Greek and Turkish positions reverted to what they had been at the beginning of the conflict in 1973: Greece arguing that the continental shelf conflict is a legal issue and Turkey insisting that the legal and political aspects of the issue cannot be viewed separately. Greece has welcomed the emergence of the 1982 Law of the Sea Convention,[21] both for its provisions on the territorial sea and the islands' entitlement to continental shelves. Greece contends that its case on the territorial sea issue has been bolstered by the Convention's establishment of the twelve-mile limit as a norm. Turkey, however, together with a few countries like the United States, has not endorsed the Convention's provisions.

In addition, Greece has been amply satisfied with the provisions concerning the continental shelf which were adopted at UNCLOS III (The Third Conference on the Law of the Sea). At the Conference, "Greece sided with the group supporting the equidistance-median line rule of the 1958 Convention on the Continental Shelf,"[22] since the use of the median line method of boundary drawing would give it most of the Aegean sea bed. Turkey, on the other hand, "sided with the group favouring delimitation according to equitable principles as enunciated in the 1969 North Sea Continental Shelf cases and the 1977 Anglo-French Continental Shelf."[23]

The resulting compromise contained in Articles 74 (1) and 83 (1) of the Convention makes no reference to either equidistance or equitable principles, but instead requires achievement of an equitable solution by agreement on the basis of international law, as referred to in Article 38 of the Statute of the International Court of Justice.[24]

Greece has welcomed the reference to international law in Articles 74 and 83, and to Article 38 of the Statute of the International Court of Justice. Turkey, however, has reacted with wariness to the same articles, because the reference to international law may "be used to create a presumption in favour of equidistance or the median line over other methods."[25]

Turkey was similarly disappointed over the provisions which UNCLOS III adopted concerning the legal regime of islands and their entitlement to marine spaces. At the Conference, Greece and the Pacific island nations "introduced draft articles stating that island maritime spaces should be determined by the same rules governing other land territory."[26] Ultimately, Greece's position commanded majority support among the delegates to UNCLOS III as is reflected in Article 121 (2) of the Convention, which provides that islands generate continental shelves and exclusive economic zones in the same manner as "other land territory" except for "rocks which cannot sustain human habitation or economic life of their own."[27] During the Conference, Turkey argued against the adoption of such wording by proposing that:

islands which constitute a source of distortion or inequity in drawing boundaries between opposite or adjacent states shall have marine spaces only to the extent compatible with equitable principles and all geographic and other relevant circumstances.[28]

The Turkish proposal argued against the entitlement of economic zones for islands "situated on the continental shelf of another state if the island's land area was not at least one-tenth of the total land area of the nation to which it belonged."[29] The Turkish proposal also stated that "islands without economic life and situated outside of the territorial sea of a State shall have no marine space of their own."[30]

Having failed to win acceptance for its proposals by a majority of the delegates, the position Turkey has taken with regard to Article 121 (2) on the regime of islands is that it is "an article of general nature which does not predetermine the maritime space to be allocated to islands in delimitation."[31] According to Joel Marsh, Turkey's concern behind this interpretation is that Article 121 contains no provision for determination of the maritime spaces of islands in other than a 'normal' situation; i.e., there is no explicit provision for a situation in which the location of islands may cause them to be disregarded or have diminished effect.[32]

Given its misgivings about various provisions adopted at UNCLOS III, the Turkish government has felt that its vital interests are not safeguarded by the Convention. Accordingly, the Turkish delegate voted against the Convention and has declared that it has no binding effect on Turkey. Greece signed it on the first day.

Notwithstanding UNCLOS III, Turkish officials have been encouraged by the evolving jurisprudence concerning islands and maritime delimitation. Turkish spokesmen approvingly cite the Anglo-French Continental Shelf arbitration (1977) which was the first case where a tribunal addressed the effect of islands on delimitation of a continental shelf boundary. Turkey has been encouraged by the tribunal's decision, which enclaved Britain's Channel Islands which lie close to France's Normandy coastline, and gave partial effect to the Scilly Isles. In an analogous situation in the Tunisia-Libya case (1982), Tunisia's Kerkennah islands were given half effect in delimiting the continental shelf between the two states.

Similarly, Turkey has been encouraged by the World Court's decision in the Gulf of Maine case between the United States and Canada to give only partial effect to Canada's Seal Island and other adjacent islets. More recently,

in the 1985 Libya-Malta Continental Shelf Case, the International Court of Justice ruled that equitable principles required that the tiny uninhabited island of Filfa (belonging to Malta — three miles south of the main island) should not be taken into account at all in determining the boundary between the two countries.[33]

In spite of the discounting or partial effect given to islands in cases decided by the World Court or arbitration commissions in recent years, it is unlikely that Turkey will be any more amenable to the adjudication of the continental shelf issue at the Hague as an isolated legal issue. As Marsh has stated, "Turkey's resistance to adjudication by the Court is based in part on a perception of potential bias against Turkey rather than on legal vulnerability."[34] Understandably, there is considerable reluctance over taking the risk and allowing a third party to decide on an issue of such vital importance. Accordingly, Turkey has preferred to resolve the Aegean issues in bilateral negotiations which would permit trade-offs and presumably secure more favourable terms.

It is precisely because Greek leaders anticipate being pressed to make greater concessions in bilateral negotiations for a settlement that they have insisted on taking the continental shelf case to the World Court. Of course, no party has ever had its boundary case entirely vindicated by the Court. Indeed, given the recent trend in arbitrations, judicial decisions, and negotiations that discount or give partial effect to islands in delimiting maritime boundaries, the Court at the Hague might allocate a greater share of the continental shelf to Turkey than has been contemplated so far by Greek leaders. It is expected that any judicial or arbitral body seeking to decide maritime boundaries in the Aegean would probably consider the weight to be attached to a wide range of relevant circumstances before deciding how maritime boundaries are to be drawn. Barbara Kwiatkowska, a scholar on the law of the sea, has listed such pertinent conditions as:

> geological and geomorphological factors... the general configuration and the length of the coasts, the relationship between the coasts within the general geographical context, as well as the presence of any special or unusual features; the size and position of islands; the unity of mineral deposits; the position of land frontier (in particular its intersection with the coastline) and the existence of other (prior) maritime boundaries; historic rights; security considerations; and the element of a reasonable degree of proportionality between the length of the coasts and the extent of maritime areas to be attributed to these coasts.[35]

Regardless of the disposition of a legal body to create equitable results in delimiting the Aegean continental shelf, Greece has maintained a decided preference for legal adjudication based on its confidence that existing laws and judgements pertaining to maritime boundaries will yield the best results for it. Moreover, as has been aptly argued by Greek spokesmen, a "compromise would encounter less opposition if it were handed down by an external authority."[36]

In addition to reviewing judicial decisions concerning maritime boundaries for possible applications to the Aegean, Greece and Turkey can also draw from the example of dozens of bilateral settlements involving islands and continental shelves. As was the case with several judicial or arbitration cases, islands have also been given half or partial effect in a number of negotiated settlements. For example, Italy and Yugoslavia decided to give partial effect in the case of a number of very small islands in the Adriatic Sea. Similarly, Iran's Kharg Island was given half effect in the delimitation of maritime boundaries between Saudi Arabia and Iran.[37]

In another case of possible application to the Aegean, Australia and New Guinea negotiated what has been described as an imaginative solution to the problem created by the presence of Australian islands, on the "wrong" side of the median line, just south of the main island of Papua, New Guinea. If Australia had claimed a twelve-mile territorial sea for the islands, it would extend its sovereignty over virtually the entire Torres Strait. Both states agreed that the Australian islands would create an "inequitable boundary if given full effect."[38] Accordingly, it was decided that Australia would claim a three-mile territorial sea for the islands and that the islands would not generate their own continental shelf, but instead "sit atop the Papua New Guinea continental shelf."[39]

The enclave approach to the islands adopted in the Australia-Papua New Guinea agreement is certainly favoured by Turkey in the eastern Aegean where Greek islands are close to its coast. But Greece has resisted recognizing any continental shelf belonging to Turkey between its mainland and the eastern Aegean islands. An alternative solution which was discussed by the two parties during talks, before the advent of the Papandreou government in 1981, has been based on the "finger" solution: this would involve Turkey having "four finger-shaped projections into the eastern Aegean between the islands of Samothrace and Lemnos, Lemnos and Lesbos, Lesbos and Chios, and Chios and Samos."[40] (See Map 6 on page 163.) This approach is favourable to Greece since it does not affect the contiguity between the Greek mainland and the eastern islands but does not offer enough continental shelf to Turkey. Yet another solution, put forth by Turkey, calls for joint development (by Greece and Turkey) of the contested sea bed's resources, thereby postponing a decision on the drawing of the maritime boundaries. Although joint development zones have been created between Kuwait and Saudi Arabia, Saudi Arabia and Sudan, Japan and Korea, Malaysia and Thailand, Norway and Iceland, and others, Greece has declined this approach as a solution for the Aegean.

The Territorial Sea

In comparison with the continental shelf question, to which it is interconnected, the territorial sea issue has been far less debated. However, this does not mean that Greece and particularly Turkey's stake in the territorial sea in the Aegean is any less than in the continental shelf.

In the Aegean, Greece has maintained a three-mile territorial sea up until 1936 and a six-mile limit since then. However, it has reserved the right to extend its territorial sea limit to twelve miles in keeping with the practice of most other states. Turkey, like Greece, also maintains a six-mile territorial sea limit in the Aegean, although it maintains a twelve-mile territorial limit in the Mediterranean and the Black Sea. Turkey's position on the issue is that the Aegean is a semi-enclosed sea in which international practice in regard to other seas is not applicable. Even with the six-mile limit, the Turks have felt restricted by Greece through the Aegean Sea's enclosed nature; as

Wilson has pointed out, "already the application of the six-mile limit restricts Turkey to only three places where shipping may enter or leave Turkish territorial waters from international waters."[44] At six miles, Greece exercises sovereignty over 35 percent of the Aegean, compared with 7.6 percent for Turkey (see Map 3 on page 160).

If the territorial sea claimed by both countries were to be increased to twelve miles, the Greek share of the Aegean's sovereign waters would go up to 64 percent, whereas Turkey's share would only increase to 8.8 percent. Also, an extension of the territorial waters to twelve miles would reduce the proportion of High Sea from 56 to 26 percent. (See Map 4 on page 161.) The implications of this for Turkey would be to prevent it from having direct access to international waters: Turkish vessels would have to go through Greek sovereign waters to reach Turkish Aegean ports from the Mediterranean and vice versa. Greek officials have responded to this concern by arguing that "Turkish shipping would be fully protected by the right of innocent passage, but the Turks are not greatly assured by this right, which can be suspended by the coastal state and which does not apply to aircraft."[42]

Furthermore, a twelve-mile extension of the territorial sea would severely restrict the area of continental shelf which Turkey has claimed. It is for these reasons that Turkey has repeatedly warned that it would consider Greece's twelve-mile extension of its territorial waters in the Aegean as *casus belli*.[43]

The legal arguments employed by Greece and Turkey in justifying their case on the territorial sea are nowhere as voluminous or complex as those that pertain to the continental shelf issue. Before the adoption of the 1982 Law of the Sea Conference text, Greece argued that it had the right to increase its territorial sea to twelve miles in accordance with what had (in its view) become a customary rule of international law. Since 1982, it has cited Article 3 of the 1982 Law of the Sea Convention, which provides for the right of states to establish territorial seas of "maximum breadth of twelve miles from the baselines."[44]

Turkey has responded by stating that it has been a persistent objector to the twelve-mile limit and argued "that the twelve-mile limit has not acquired the character of a rule of customary international law."[45] Further, as the Turkish delegate at the Law of the Sea Conference argued,

> the twelve-mile limit is the maximum breadth that may be applied within the general limitation imposed by article 300 which embodies the principle of abuse of right. In the narrow seas, on which Turkey is bordered, the extension of the territorial sea in disregard of the special characteristics of these seas and in a manner which would deprive another littoral State of its existing rights and interests creates inequitable results which certainly call for the application of the principle of abuse of right.[46]

At UNCLOS III, Turkey made a proposal that would have required states bordering enclosed or semi-enclosed seas to determine the breadth of their territorial waters by agreement. Turkey also proposed that

> the territorial sea of one state not cut off the territorial sea of another state from the high seas, and that the right to establish the breadth of the territorial sea be exercised without prejudice to the rights and interests of neighbouring coastal states.[47]

These proposals were not adopted. As Marsh has noted, UNCLOS III left

> ...the twelve-mile limit of Article 3 without explicit modifying provisions. Furthermore, Part IX of the Convention, which defines enclosed and semi-enclosed seas, does not provide special rights for, or limitations on, coastal states with regard to boundary determination in these seas. It merely provides, in Article 123, that coastal states 'should cooperate' in the exercise of their rights and performance of their duties under the Convention. This provision is of some consolation to Turkey in that it at least recognizes enclosed and semi-enclosed seas as special features in the general context of the law of the sea. It does not speak with any precision, however, to Turkey's principal concern that there be potential restrictions on the breadth of territorial waters in these seas.[48]

Although Greece has refrained from extending its Aegean territorial waters to twelve miles, it "would not consider surrendering a right which already accrued to it under international law and practice." In any case, though unexercised, Greece's professed right bolsters its overall negotiating position with Turkey. For Turkey, the issue is of fundamental importance and in any ranking of its Aegean concerns, the maintenance of the six-mile limit would top the list.

Unlike the continental shelf delimitation which does not affect supra-adjacent waters, the possibility of extending the territorial sea in the Aegean to twelve miles does concern third parties who would be restricted by the substantial shrinkage of the High Seas. In particular, the Soviet Union would be adversely affected and has repeatedly communicated its concerns to the Greek government.[50] In addition, although the United States has carefully avoided the appearance of favouring one NATO ally over the other concerning the Aegean issues, given its interests as a global maritime power, it also has discouraged Greece from increasing its territorial sea limit.[51]

Airspace Issues

By presidential decree issued in 1931, Greece has claimed sovereign airspace of ten miles in the Aegean since 1931. Turkey has objected to this claim on the grounds that customary rules and international laws require the airspace to correspond to the territorial sea. Thus, in Turkish eyes, Greece is not entitled to have more than six miles of sovereign airspace in the Aegean.

Greek officials have responded by arguing that, for many years, Turkey had acquiesced in Greece's maintenance of disparity between the breadth of its territorial sea (which was three miles in 1931) and airspace. Turkey has rejected this argument by claiming that Greece did not give proper notification of the ten-mile extension of its airspace until 1975. Since then, Turkey has challenged Greece's exercise of ten-mile wide airspace by periodically sending its aircraft up to six miles from the coast of the Greek Aegean islands. On these occasions, Greece ordinarily sends its own aircraft to intercept those of Turkey. These aerial challenges have long worried Greece and Turkey's NATO allies, but the fact that no serious incidents have occurred may be viewed as an indication that both sides wish to avoid clashes over their Aegean disagreements.

The major Turkish concern with the airspace issue is much the same as with the territorial sea. Turkey already feels confined by the airspace of Greece's eastern Aegean islands. It considers that its acceptance of a ten-mile wide airspace would unduly restrict both its civilian and military aircraft.

Greece, on the other hand, does not wish to give up a right it proclaimed more than one-half a century ago. As for the disparity between the territorial sea and airspace, Greek spokesmen have occasionally suggested (or threatened, as the Turks would view it) that they could remedy it by extending both their territorial waters and their airspace to twelve miles.

In addition to quarrelling about the extent of sovereign airspace, Greece and Turkey have also exchanged accusations concerning air traffic control responsibility in the Aegean. In 1952, the International Civil Aviation Organization (ICAO) assigned to Greece air traffic control responsibility in the Aegean Flight Information Region (FIR). At the time, Turkey's relations with Greece were particularly friendly, both countries having become NATO allies during the same year. Thus, assuming continued friendly relations, Turkey raised no objections to Greece's discharge of FIR responsibility for virtually the entire Aegean with the exception of a narrow strip off the Anatolian coast.

However, in the aftermath of the fighting in Cyprus in July 1974, the FIR arrangements broke down. On August 4, 1974, the Turkish government issued NOTAM 714 (a notice to ICAO for transmission to all air users)

> requiring all aircraft approaching Turkish airspace to report their position and flight plan on reaching the Aegean median line, which lay considerably to the west of the FIR line. The purpose, according to later Turkish explanation, was to enable Turkish military radar to distinguish between innocent flights and potential attackers bound for targets in Asia Minor.[52]

As Wilson noted, Greece refused to accept NOTAM 714 on the grounds that it contravened ICAO regulations. The proposed "report line" could be perceived as serving a political objective since it roughly coincided with the "western limit of Turkish claims to the continental shelf."[53] Accordingly, Greece issued its own NOTAM 1157 which substantially abrogated Greek responsibility for air safety in the Aegean. The result was that world airlines halted all direct flights between the two countries.

The closure of the entire Aegean to international air traffic seriously affected commercial flights to the Middle East and the Far East, thus prompting ICAO to seek a resolution to the crisis. On two occasions, in October 1974 and April 1975, ICAO's Secretary-General Binagi attempted to mediate by proposing the simultaneous withdrawal of both the Greek and Turkish NOTAMs. Although these efforts were unsuccessful, Greece and Turkey nevertheless tried to find a mutually acceptable formula and, according to Wilson, made considerable inroads in narrowing their differences on civilian flights.[54] Further progress on the FIR issues was reported in 1978, although the talks fell short of an agreement. Ultimately, in February 1980, when secret negotiations for Greece's re-entry to NATO's unified command were making progress, Turkey and Greece lifted their NOTAMs, and international civil aviation was resumed in the Aegean.

As with the other aspects of the Aegean dispute, the airspace and FIR issues are related to questions of sovereignty and control in the Aegean. Turkish officials have repeatedly accused Greece of abusing its purely technical FIR responsibilities to gain sovereign rights in the Aegean. One of the major complaints lodged by Turkey relates to alleged Greek actions of unilaterally creating new air corridors without consulting Ankara, as is required by ICAO rules. This has hindered Turkey's access to the Aegean. One of the examples cited by Ankara is the air corridor G18/UG18 (see Map 6 on page 163) which Greece set up in 1985 after consulting Yugoslavia but not Turkey. The Turkish government promptly launched objections by informing ICAO that the new air corridor was close to a prohibited area established at the entrance to the Dardanelles, and that it would adversely affect "its ability to safely conduct naval and air exercises in the Aegean Sea."[55] In the end, ICAO's mediating machinery was able to resolve the dispute to Turkey's satisfaction by winning acceptance for a realignment of the contested air corridor.

The Turkish government has also complained that Greece has failed to consult Turkey when it implemented a 3,000-square mile "control zone" around the island of Lemnos, most of which covered international air space. Greece demanded that all aircraft entering the zone request authorization. On other occasions, the Turks have complained that Greece deliberately sought to interfere with their military exercises either by refusing to issue the appropriate Turkish NOTAMs or by unilaterally amending them. Notwith-standing considerable evidence of Greek obstruction, the Greek govern-ment perceives matters concerning airspace and FIR matters differently. Greece has denied Turkish charges of arbitrary measures and has accused Turkey of seeking to alter the current arrangements in order to gain greater control of Aegean airspace. It has been entirely salutary that where bilateral contacts have failed to resolve their differences on these issues, ICAO has made its neutral authority available to settle problems, as it did over the air corridor issues.

The Remilitarization of the Eastern Aegean Islands

In the course of Greece and Turkey's quarrel over the Aegean maritime and airspace matters during 1974-1975, an issue over which Turkey had complained to Greece during the 1960s re-emerged to burden the agenda of Greek-Turkish disputes.

It will be recalled that at the Lausanne Conference of 1923, Turkey demanded that it be granted sovereignty of Gökçeada, Bozcaada, and Samothrace. In addition, Turkish delegate Inönü pressed for the demilitari-zation of the islands in the eastern Aegean; Turkey was concerned about their possible use as a springboard for Greek attacks on Turkey. Turkey's demands that its security concerns be met were bolstered by the fact that it had only recently experienced an invasion by Greek forces. Ultimately, Turkey was not given Samothrace but granted sovereignty over Gökçeada and Bozcaada because of their strategic location at the entrance to the Dardanelles. The sovereignty over the rest of the Aegean islands had already been decided by the Treaties of London (1913) and Athens (1918) with provisions for their demilitarization. The Treaty of Lausanne confirmed the demilitarized status of the eastern Aegean islands of Mitylene, Chios, Samos, and Ikaria.

Thus Article 13 of the Lausanne Treaty provided that:

With a view to ensuring the maintenance of peace, the Greek Govern-ment undertakes to observe the following restrictions in the islands of Mitylene, Chios, Samos and Ikaria:

1. No naval base and no fortification will be established in the said islands.
2. Greek military aircraft will be forbidden to fly over the territory of the Anatolian coast. Reciprocally, the Turkish government will forbid their military aircraft to fly over the said islands.
3. The Greek military forces in the said islands will be limited to the normal contingent called up for military service, which can be trained

on the spot, as well as to a force of gendarmerie and police in proportion to the force of gendarmerie and police existing in the whole of the Greek territory.[56]

In yet another concession to alleviate Turkish security concerns, Article 4 of the Convention concerning the regime of the Straits, which was annexed to the Lausanne Treaty, provided that the islands situated close to the entrance to the Dardanelles Straits (Gökçeada, Bozcaada, Lemnos, and Samothrace) also be demilitarized. The same stipulation was also made for the Dodecanese Islands when Italy ceded them to Greece in accordance with the Treaty of Paris (1947).

According to Turkish official statements, Greece started militarizing the eastern Aegean islands in 1960, and the first Turkish protest was lodged with the Greek government in 1964, soon after the outbreak of civil strife on Cyprus.[57] Subsequently, Turkey made two further representations to the Greek government on April 2, 1969 and April 4, 1970. In its diplomatic note of April 2, 1969, the Turkish government alleged that in the islands of Mytilene, Chios, Samos, and Ikaria, the "gendarmerie" exceeded the limit foreseen in Article 13 of the Treaty of Lausanne.[58] It was further stated in the aide-memoire that in the islands of Lemnos and Samothrace and the Dodecanese, which were placed under a status of strict demilitarization, military personnel sometimes reached several battalions in one island, not including paramilitary units. Moreover, it was said that the presence of air force units and some special equipment in airports gave these facilities a military character. It was also stated that vessels of the Greek Navy were frequently present in the islands and that these islands contained naval installations.[59]

However, the assurances given by the Papadopoulos junta then in power appear to have mollified Ankara. The Turkish official account of the Greek government's reply is as follows:

> In its reply of 10 May 1969, the Greek Government stated that Greece continued to respect all its treaty obligations emanating from the 1923 Lausanne and 1947 Paris Treaties; that certain measures had been taken on the islands to render police surveillance more effective without infringing upon the provisions of the relevant treaties; that the works mentioned in the Turkish aide-memoire were not of a military nature but aimed at the improvement of port facilities and road network. Furthermore, it claimed that the radar installations in Lemnos were foreseen by NATO plans; that the works undertaken at the airport of the island were aimed at meeting the needs of civil aviation.[60]

In the aftermath of the Ioannidis coup and Turkish military action in Cyprus in 1974, however, the Karamanlis government fortified the islands more heavily.

For Turkey, the issue is not merely one of Greece's violation of its treaty obligations. Although not fearful of a full-fledged Greek invasion, it has had some concern that the islands could be used by Greece for air strikes against targets on the Turkish mainland. As Couloumbis has stated, "the analogy of 'daggers' pointing to the vulnerable body of the Turkish mainland is often made by Turkish officials and experts."[61] Greece, on the other hand, has insisted since the early 1970s that the measures taken on the eastern Aegean islands are purely defensive and intended to deter Turkey's threat. In particular, Greek officials have alleged that the deployment of the Turkish Fourth Army (dubbed the "Army of the Aegean") along Turkey's Aegean coast since 1975, and the presence of landing craft in Turkish ports close to the islands, pose a serious threat to Greece and warrant the counter-measures. Furthermore, statements by several Turkish politicians, including those by Prime Minister Demirel, who pointedly called the islands Aegean and not Greek islands, led Greek leaders to believe that Turkey covets the islands.

In responding and rejecting Turkey's charges concerning its treaty violations, Greece has distinguished between three groups of islands. With respect to Lemnos and Samothrace in the northern Aegean, Greek officials have argued that the Lausanne Treaty provisions are no longer applicable, having been superseded by the Treaty of Montreux (1936) which allowed for the remilitarization of the straits of Dardanelles. This argument has been rejected by Turkish officials who insist that the Montreux Treaty made no mention of Lemnos or Samothrace. On the other hand, in support of their position, Greek officials have quoted the statement made by Turkish Foreign Minister Aras during a debate in the Turkish Parliament in 1936, as follows:

> The provisions concerning the islands of Lemnos and Samothrace which belong to our friend and neighbour, Greece, and which had been demilitarised by the Treaty of Lausanne in 1923, are abolished also by the Treaty of Montreux and we are particularly pleased about this...[62]

Turkish officials have responded to the use of the Aras statement by arguing that the

> ...statement has to be read, as an expression of goodwill in the light of the international political climate prevailing at that time which cannot change, in any way, the provisions of international treaties.[63]

Concerning such other major Aegean islands (namely, Lesbos, Chios, Samos, and Ikaria), Greece argues that the Treaty of Lausanne does not prohibit local self-defence measures. With respect to the Dodecanese, which Italy ceded to Greece in accordance with the Treaty of Paris, Greece contends that Turkey is not entitled to make any claims regarding their armed status on the grounds that it was not a party to the Treaty. Finally, Greek officials have defended the military measures they have taken on the eastern Aegean islands by claiming that the inalienable right of self-defence, as recognized by the United Nations Charter, takes precedence over other treaty obligations.

Greek-Turkish Quarrels and NATO

It is not surprising that the ramifications of the various Greek-Turkish disputes have been felt by the Western Alliance, and especially by the United States, which provides most of the arms for both sides. In 1974, the Karamanlis government pulled Greece out of the military wing of NATO to protest the Alliance's inaction in the face of Turkey's military operation in Cyprus. In the following years, Karamanlis came to believe that to counter Turkey's influence and maintain a proper balance within the Alliance, Greece should return to the NATO fold.

Turkey initially sought to use its power of veto in the NATO military committee to block a return to the pre-1974 arrangements which had placed virtually the entire Aegean under the responsibility of the Greek command. Turkish representatives argued that in the post-1974 circumstances, new arrangements should be made and proposed the use of the Aegean median line to divide responsibilities.[64] Greece rejected this proposal which would have placed its Aegean islands within a proposed security zone controlled by Turkey. Greece also threatened to close the remaining American bases in Greece unless offered satisfactory terms for re-entry.[65] Subsequently, following prolonged negotiations, General Bernard Rogers, NATO Supreme Commander, persuaded Turkey's General Evren (the head of the military government then in power) to drop Turkish objections, and Greece returned to NATO in October 1980.

Although the particulars of the so-called Rogers Plan have remained confidential, it has been widely reported that Greece and Turkey agreed to postpone negotiations on command and control arrangements after Greece's re-entry. According to *The Economist,* "until a new agreement is reached, Nato's south European commander, based in Naples, will assign specific defensive tasks to each country."[66] Apparently, Turkey's General Evren endorsed the Rogers Plan by consulting only the Turkish Foreign Minister and another senior member of the Ministry on the issue.[67] Many Turkish officials have since regretted that Turkey did not use its power of veto to obtain fairer Aegean command and control arrangements. However, General Evren's accommodating position provides an insight into the thinking not just of the senior military brass, but also of Turkey's leadership in general. Regardless of their country's quarrel with its Aegean neighbour,

Turkey's security interests are better served by Greece remaining within NATO than by leaving the Alliance. Although Turkish leaders viewed Greece (since the mid-1970s) as potentially posing the most immediate threat to Turkey's security, they have continued to view the Soviet Union as a larger and more enduring threat. Indeed, the Soviet invasion of Afghanistan in 1979 has exacerbated Turkish concerns vis-a-vis its super-power neighbour to the north.

When Andreas Papandreou came to power in 1981 on a platform calling for radical changes in Greek foreign policy (including withdrawal from NATO and the closing of American bases in Greece), he generated considerable misgivings within the Alliance. Papandreou denounced the Rogers Plan and subjected NATO and the United States to harsh criticism. For example, in 1984 the Socialist Greek leader characterized the United States as a "metropolis of imperialism";[68] by contrast, he stated that "the Soviet Union is not an imperialist power" and commended the Soviets as "a restraining factor in the propagation of capitalism and of its imperialist aims."[69] Although he was not the first Greek leader to blame NATO for being pro-Turkish, Papandreou caused considerable irritation for using NATO meetings to decry the Turkish "threat," particularly during his first term in office.

In spite of his frequent denunciations of NATO, and pre-election threats to leave the Alliance, Greece's Socialist leader sought to involve NATO unsuccessfully as a guarantor of Greece's territorial integrity against the Turkish "threat." To the relief of the Alliance members, Papandreou reversed himself on taking Greece out of NATO on the grounds that to do so would hurt Greek national security. It is obvious that Greece's withdrawal from NATO would result in greater Alliance reliance on the military bases and facilities in Turkey and bring about closer United States-Turkish ties. Also, Socialist or not, Greek leaders paradoxically view the United States both as being pro-Turkish but also as a power that can balance Turkey's hostility towards Greece.

As Bruce Kuniholm has aptly stated " membership in NATO puts Greece in a better position to look out for its own interests and to obstruct Turkish designs in the Aegean."[70] Furthermore, it is believed that many senior military Greek officials would strongly resist forsaking what they consider to be considerable benefits which Greece receives from NATO, such as large-scale American aid and accessibility to advanced military hardware.[71] These considerations helped in negotiating the 1983 Agreement on Defence and Economic Cooperation (DECA) which provided for five more years of American use of bases in Greece as a quid pro quo for United States military assistance. In spite of periodic statements by Papandreou that he would demand the removal of nuclear weapons based in United States installations in Greece, it was widely believed in Washington and Athens that the same imperatives that have made the 1983 Agreement on Defence and Economic Cooperation possible would ensure its renewal.[72]

As much as Turkish leaders prefer Greece remaining within the Western Alliance, they have resented the volume of American aid given to Greece and have complained that Turkey has received scant credit for its greater reliability and contribution to NATO. While it is generally acknowledged by many writers that Turkey's strategic worth to the Western Alliance is greater than that of Greece, the need to avert the alienation of either of the two allies has led the United States and NATO to fashion an even-handed approach to Greek-Turkish disputes. On the other hand, it is probable that the irritation which Papandreou's anti-American and anti-NATO rhetoric has caused in many Western capitals has helped bolster Turkey's standing. In the United States Congress, where Greece and Turkey exert much lobbying effort to influence the levels of aid, the Papandreou government has occasionally provoked criticism as a result of the Greek leader's anti-Western and anti-United States positions. Nonetheless, he was helped considerably by the Greek lobby in the United States.

Greece and Turkey's NATO allies have refrained from becoming involved in the two neighbours' Aegean quarrels. None of them subscribe to Greece's position concerning the Turkish "threat," if by that is meant Turkish territorial designs on Greek territory. With the United States in the lead, NATO countries have regularly appealed to both of their quarrelling fellow-members to resolve their differences amicably. Given that Turkey has favoured a dialogue to deal with bilateral issues with Greece, NATO calls for Greco-Turkish talks have, in practice, appeared to be aimed at Greece more than Turkey.

During 1982-1983, Papandreou withdrew Greece from participation in NATO manoeuvres because the Alliance decided to exclude the island of Lemnos from its planned exercises. NATO's decision on Lemnos was motivated by a desire to avoid becoming involved in the Greek-Turkish disagreements. But Papandreou argued that by excluding the island from its manoeuvres, the Alliance supported the Turkish claim over the militarization of the island. On the other hand, Greece has been an active participant in NATO's Airborne Early Warning System in Europe. According to a newspaper report, by participating in this programme, Greek crews will receive valuable electronics and computer training and perhaps receive additional benefits by monitoring possible violations of Greek-claimed airspace by Turkish aircraft.[73]

There was a significant reduction in Papandreou's anti-United States and NATO rhetoric during his second term, as Greece's economic problems mounted, and its economic reliance on the West has correspondingly increased. Moreover, it is reasonable to expect that the warming trend in the relations between Greece and Turkey since 1988 will discourage further disruptions in NATO's southern flank.

The ready availability of NATO's machinery for conciliation has helped restrain both Greece and Turkey in the pursuit of their bilateral quarrels, although this is rarely acknowledged in Athens and Ankara. As David Barchard has observed, "NATO has ... undoubtedly helped cushion the dispute between the two states since 1974, and in 1980 played a major part in reopening the Aegean to civilian flights."[74] Typically, during Greece and Turkey's last confrontation in the Aegean, in March 1987, an emergency NATO meeting in Brussels produced a mediation offer by the Alliance's Secretary-General. Although the offer was turned down by Greece, parallel behind-the-scenes diplomacy by Washington helped maintain a sense of calm[75] and made it easier to find a face-saving formula to avert a confrontation. Thus, if either Greece or Turkey or both were to leave NATO, there would be a reduction in the diplomatic instruments available for the management of their conflicts.

Preserving the *Status Quo* in the Aegean

Whatever role NATO may play in restraining Greece and Turkey, ultimately the incentives for a settlement of their Aegean issues will have to come from Athens and Ankara. The successful settlement of maritime boundary issues by many states through direct talks suggest that the Aegean disputes are resolvable without recourse to the World Court. Obviously, however, the success of bilateral negotiations presupposes the existence of better relations between the parties than has been the case with Greece and Turkey, especially since the mid-1970s. On the other hand, the negotiating process itself can help ease tensions as well as aid the search for formulas that could settle differences. Indeed, the protracted bilateral talks which were initiated in the aftermath of the 1976 crisis over *Sizmik 1's* research in disputed waters helped to ease the tension.

Not surprisingly, the particular leadership in power in Athens and Ankara have had a bearing on the state of Greek-Turkish relations at any given time, as well as on the prospects for fruitful negotiations in the Aegean. Wilson has argued that during his seven-year leadership of Greece after the Cyprus events of 1974, Karamanlis was "the one person capable of carrying the country with him in acceptance of a settlement involving significant concessions;"[76] during the same period, on the other hand, political leaders in Ankara were hampered by not having a majority government in Parliament and having to rely on coalition partners for support. Two of the minority coalition partners, the National Salvation Party and the National

Movement Party of Alpaslan Türkes took a particularly hard line on Turkish rights in the Aegean; Türkes's inflammatory statements during the late 1970s questioning the sovereignty of the eastern Aegean islands raised Greek fears of serious Turkish challenges to the ownership of the islands.

But the greatest setback to the prospect of a Greek-Turkish settlement was dealt by Andreas Papandreou's PASOK government when it came to power in 1981. In opposition, Papandreou had made firmness in dealing with the Turkish threat a major element of his party's appeal. In office, he continued his strident anti-Turkish rhetoric for several years.

Van Coufoudakis described PASOK's view of Turkey and its alleged expansionist aims in the following terms:

> Turkey pursues these objectives with the tolerance and support of the United States, if not also the complicity of the U.S.S.R. And even though Turkey threatens to use force to achieve these objectives, Greece's allies are unwilling to protect it from these threats. Instead they issue consistent calls for Greek-Turkish negotiations and call on Greece to make concessions to Turkey. However, concessions by Greece will not contribute to peace. Compromise and concessions on Greek sovereign rights will indicate weakness and lack of resolve on the part of Greece, and will therefore increase Turkey's chauvinism and expansionism.[77]

Papandreou's emphasis on the "Turkish threat" struck a responsive chord at home. According to Mario Modiano, most Greeks "agree with him when he says that Turkey wants the dialogue in order to take, not to give."[78] But even before Papandreou, since Turkey's Cyprus intervention in 1974, a consensus emerged in Greece which portrayed Turkey as an expansionist power pursuing long-term goals to partition the Aegean. Most Greeks believe that Turkey has expansionist designs on Greece and that what happened in Cyprus might also happen in the Aegean.

Greek spokesmen have frequently cited the creation of Turkey's Army of the Aegean (the Fourth Army) and the stationing of landing craft in its Aegean ports as evidence of Turkish designs on Greek sovereign rights in the Aegean. Papandreou and other spokesmen of his government have repeatedly asserted that the threat to Greece's security no longer lies in the north but in the east; that is, from Turkey. Hence, the announcement of the new Greek defence doctrine in late 1984 which put major emphasis on the Turkish "threat" and thus reaffirmed previous statements.[79]

The Turks have dismissed Greek allegations regarding the "Turkish threat" as baseless. Turkish leaders believe that, apart from seeking to win electoral favour at home, Papandreou has used the allegations of a Turkish threat to help maintain the rationale for restricting United States aid to

Turkey. Furthermore, Turkish leaders have been aggravated by Greece's anti-Turkish campaign at the institutions of the European Community, NATO, and other international forums and have blamed Greece for seeking to isolate Turkey, particularly from the West.

In the Aegean itself, Turkey has been anxious to avert any unilateral extension of maritime jurisdiction by Greece, particularly a twelve-mile extension of territorial waters. The stationing of landing craft in its Aegean ports is a warning to Greece, as is the Army of the Aegean (the Fourth Army). Beyond such warnings, however, Turkish leaders have in recent years sought to assuage Greek fears. Thus, in contrast to the provocative statements made by Turkish Premier Demirel and other politicians, following the *Sizmik 1* crisis of 1976, President Evren and Prime Minister Özal have stated that Turkey has no claims on the eastern Aegean islands.

Actually, whether Greek leaders' actual perceptions of Turkey's threat fully correspond with their rhetorical claims may be arguable. In a conversation with an American official, Papandreou himself has reportedly underscored the importance of the Turkish threat in Greek perceptions. As he apparently stated:

> I may not believe in a Turkish threat, you may not believe in a Turkish threat, but the Greek public believes in it, and that makes it Greek reality and you have to deal with it in those terms.[80]

From virtually the start of the Aegean dispute, and particularly since Turkey's Cyprus operation in 1974, Greece has vigorously sought to improve both its diplomatic and military position vis-a-vis Turkey. Thus, Greece repeatedly appealed to the United States and NATO for guarantees against the Turkish "threat." These appeals were unsuccessful, although Greek leader Karamanlis managed to secure a pledge from Henry Kissinger, the American Secretary of State in 1976, that the "United States would actively and unequivocally oppose either side's seeking a military solution [of Aegean disputes] and will make a major effort to prevent such a course of action."[81]

More significantly, Greece has worked closely with the highly successful Greek lobby in the United States to curtail United States aid to Turkey and to maintain a balance which would not disadvantage Greece's efforts to build an effective military deterrence against Turkey. After the lifting of the embargo in 1978, Greek leaders called for parity in American aid programmes, notwithstanding the United States Executive's belief that Turkey needed much higher levels of aid.

In 1980, the American Congress allocated aid in the ratio of seven-to-ten for Greece and Turkey. This was clearly a pro-Greek formula, and since then the Greek government has attached a high priority for the maintenance of this ratio. The Turkish government has, equally vigorously, objected to the 7:10 ratio. Despite this objection, the Papandreou government has unsuccessfully sought to have it formalized. For example, after the 1983 Defence and Economic Cooperation Agreement (DECA) was initialled, Papandreou publicly asserted that the United States had "a contractual obligation" to preserve the military balance between Greece and Turkey and that Washington had committed itself "to maintain the 7 to 10 ratio."[82] However, the United States government rejected these interpretations and, indeed, the Reagan administration sought to alter the bases for the allocation of military aid to both countries. Nonetheless, Greek leaders have consistently argued that the ratio is necessary for Greece to maintain a military balance with Turkey. In recent years, Greece has received about $500,000,000 yearly, whereas Turkey's share has been determined by the customary 7:10 formula.

By contrast with Greek officials, Turkish leaders have lodged serious objections to the congressional 7:10 ratio. They have argued that Turkey's needs to modernize its armed forces far exceed those of Greece and are much higher than the level set by applying the arbitrary ratio. Officials in the Reagan administration acknowledged that most of Turkey's military hardware is outdated, and that it urgently requires higher levels of arms assistance than has been provided to fulfill its NATO responsibilities. Some of the deficiencies cited by Assistant Secretary of Defence Perle's testimony in February 1985 before the House subcommittee on Europe and the Middle East included the following:

Ninety seven percent of anti-tank weapons are of World War II and Korean War vintage; 89 percent of short-range air defense weapons were manufactured in 1940 or earlier; less than 1% are radar controlled; 75% of fighter aircraft are pre-1970 vintage, and there is virtually no modern air defense of air bases. These deficiencies extend to tactical communications and support equipment as well.[83]

According to Kuniholm,

a Department of Defense study that examined some of these deficiencies estimated that it would take military assistance funding levels of $1.2 billion over approximately ten to twelve years to make even 'reasonable progress' for Turkish military modernization.[84]

The level of assistance provided to Turkey by the United States has fallen short of such recommended levels. But the Turks have been especially irritated by the Congressional practice of cutting the administration's aid allocations. For example, Congress reduced the $739,000,000 aid bill set by the administration for fiscal-year 1987 to $490,000,000.[85] Nonetheless, the

Executive sometimes found ways of cushioning the blow by providing Turkey with additional aid; thus, an additional aid package of surplus military equipment worth $300,000,000 was offered to Turkey after the Congressional reduction of the administration allocation in 1986.[86]

Turkish officials have also contended that "the ratio... gives credence, intended or not, to the Greek allegation that Turkey poses a threat."[87] The Reagan administration was in agreement with Turkey that the 7:10 ratio is arbitrary and inappropriate in the allocation of aid to the two NATO allies. It is obvious that without the influence of the Greek lobby, the 7:10 ratio could not be sustained in the United States Congress. Still, even though it has proposed higher levels of aid to Turkey than would be provided by the Congressional ratio, the Reagan administration refrained from confronting Congress on the issue.

As leader of NATO, and as the major donor of aid and supplier of arms to both Greece and Turkey, the United States has been primarily concerned with saving the Alliance's southeastern flank from collapsing. By encouraging diplomatic ways of resolving their bilateral problems, the United States government has tried to place Greco-Turkish relations on a path of recovery. At the same time, the United States has acted as a balance against Greek vulnerability to Turkey. Thus, in spite of having been the object of Greek vilification for allegedly tilting towards Turkey, since 1974 the United States aid has helped bolster Greek military capabilities to the point where the Greek-Turkish military balance in the Aegean has appreciably improved in Greece's favour. Nonetheless, because of Washington's alleged acquiesence to Turkey's Cyprus intervention, and past toleration of the junta, the United States has received blame not credit for Greece's problems with Turkey.

According to observers well versed in the military capabilities of the two countries, in the Aegean itself Greece has maintained military advantage in the air and rough parity with Turkey in naval forces.[88] On the other hand, the Turkish land forces of 470,000 men is more than three times that of Greece and, on this score, Turkey has a substantial advantage. Accordingly, Turkey enjoys an overall military superiority over Greece. Turkey has a much larger population, 55,000,000, from which to recruit its armed forces than does Greece, whose population is 10,000,000. The Turkish military, which numbers 635,300 in total, is the second largest in NATO after that of the United States and compares with 214,000 for Greece.[89]

In the event of a war in the Aegean, it might appear that Greece's eastern Aegean islands would be vulnerable to the Turkish military. However, Greece has enhanced the defences of these islands "to the extent that foreign military experts now seem to agree that they may be impregnable short of a senseless sacrifice of power."[90] Nevertheless, Greece has to maintain the costly defence of all of its vulnerable islands without knowing which island or islands might be targeted by the Turkish military if large-scale hostilities broke out. Furthermore, there is another major concern with which Greece would have to wrestle in any crisis: the territory most vulnerable to the Turkish military is Greek Cypriot-ruled southern Cyprus and, in the event of an all-out war, Turkey using its military advantage in Cyprus by moving south cannot be ruled out.

That neither party has a decisive military advantage in the Aegean has helped reduce the possibilities of a flare-up. In the meantime, however, both countries have been involved in an expensive arms race since the outbreak of the Aegean and Cyprus crises in the mid-1970s. Greece, for example, has been spending 7 percent of its GNP, which represents one-fifth of its government spending, on defence.[91] Turkey's military expenditures represent close to 5 percent of its GNP, and its annual spending per soldier has been estimated at $4,216 as compared with $14, 628 per soldier spent by Greece.[92] Greece's capacity for such outlays are comparatively greater than Turkey's, given that at $4,200 per capita its income is more than three times the Turkish per capita GNP of $1,300.[93]

Although Papandreou's hard line on Turkey has provided a sense of psychological satisfaction and unity in Greece, it set back prospects for improving Greece's relations with Turkey. Soon after he became prime minister, Papandreou suspended the dialogue with Turkey, and his government declared that it would not abide by the Berne Declaration on the grounds that the bilateral talks conducted since 1976 had failed. The PASOK leader's basic position was that Greek sovereign rights in the Aegean (by which he meant Greece's claimed rights) were not negotiable and that Greece would not agree to any other avenue than to present the case to the World Court. Papandreou did not entirely rule out the resumption of a dialogue with Turkey but insisted on a condition which he knew the Turks would not meet: the withdrawal of Turkish troops from northern Cyprus prior to a settlement on the island.

Although there was a subsequent meeting of the Greek and Turkish foreign ministers at a NATO meeting in Montreal in October 1982, "partly in response to American prompting,"[94] it did not usher in more substantive discussions. Indeed, there was new friction when Turkey instantly recognized the Turkish Republic of Northern Cyprus that the Turkish-Cypriot leadership unilaterally set up in 1983.

However, rhetoric aside, on the *substance* of the Aegean issues Papandreou's position has been essentially the same as that of the previous governments led by Karamanlis. It is notable that despite fears his brinksmanship politics with Turkey might provoke a military confrontation, Papandreou stopped short of challenging the Aegean *status quo*. A crisis, which almost led to war, occurred during March 1987, when Greece appeared poised to drill for oil in a contested area (i.e., outside its territorial waters) off the island of Thassos. When Turkey threatened to send its research vessel, *Sizmik 1*, to the disputed waters, Greece threatened to confront it. The crisis was subsequently diffused when both countries agreed not to conduct any research or drilling activity outside their territorial waters. Thus, despite earlier claims by the Papandreou government that the Berne agreement was no longer in force, the post-March 1987 understanding has tacitly reaffirmed the validity of the Berne understanding.

The March 1987 crisis, like the confrontation in the Aegean eleven years earlier, demonstrated the potential dangers of an outbreak of violence in the Aegean. However, both Greece and Turkey's behaviour in diffusing the crisis is also noteworthy, notwithstanding the helping hand of NATO and the United States. Both countries have shown a marked disinclination to use force in obtaining their claimed rights, provided the existing *status quo* is preserved.

There is yet another disincentive for challenging existing Aegean arrangements: the expectations of the early 1970s concerning large oil and gas deposits have not materialized. Had they done so, it would have been much more difficult to postpone the settlement of the continental shelf issue. Thus, the lack of any discoveries since the modest Thassos find of 1973 may not be unwelcome in terms of preserving the peace between the Aegean neighbours.

Ironically, just as the 1976 confrontation was instrumental in helping reach an understanding for stability in the Aegean for just over a decade, the 1987 crisis may also have been a catalyst for improved Greco-Turkish relations. In the aftermath of their latest confrontation, Greek and Turkish prime ministers exchanged correspondence and proposals which led to their first high-level meeting at Davos, Switzerland in January 1988. At Davos, Greek Premier Papandreou and Turkish Premier Özal agreed to resume talks on their Aegean and other disputes; the two leaders agreed to meet at least once a year and to set up committees to foster economic cooperation and discuss mutual problems. The two leaders met again on the occasion of a NATO summit in March 1988, and in May 1988, Özal became the first Turkish Prime Minister to visit Greece in thirty-five years. Among the conciliatory gestures that have resulted from the rapprochement have been Turkey's repeal of a 1964 law, which released the properties of the Greek owners who had left Istanbul during the tense years of the Cyprus crisis. In its turn, Greece stopped delaying and finally signed the protocol that recognizes the association agreement between Turkey and the European Community.

Turkish membership in the EEC has opened a new opportunity for resolving Greek-Turkish disputes. Ever since Turkey formally applied for full membership in the Community in 1987, speculation has abounded about the potential of Greece vetoing Turkey's entry. The opposition parties in Turkey have warned Özal against making major concessions in Cyprus or the Aegean as a price to avert a Greek veto over Turkish entry into the Community.

It is premature to speculate on the impact which the conciliation process begun at Davos will have on the substance of Greek-Turkish issues on the Aegean and Cyprus. Some interesting ideas have already been broached that could help settle somewhat easier issues: joint air manoeuvres in "joint" airspace in the Aegean[95] is a good example of the kind of proposals that, if realized, could spur progress on other issues. In any case, the reversal of Papandreou's seven-year policy of no talks with Turkey and the emergence of the Greco-Turkish rapprochement augurs well for the future. At the very least, the new contacts and confidence building measures will help avoid the type of confrontation that nearly caused Aegean hostilities in March of 1987. A sensible step has already been taken with the setting up of a telephone hotline for instant personal communication between the Greek and Turkish leaders. In Cyprus itself, the Turkish-Cypriot and Greek-Cypriot leaders have taken a new initiative, partly influenced by the "Davos spirit," to discuss a settlement which would reunite the island within a bi-zonal federal state. Clearly, a Cyprus breakthrough, if realized, would create great expectations and encourage the solving of Greece and Turkey's Aegean problems as well. In any event, it is reasonable to expect that improved relations will help in the search for acceptable formulas for resolving the continental shelf and other issues.

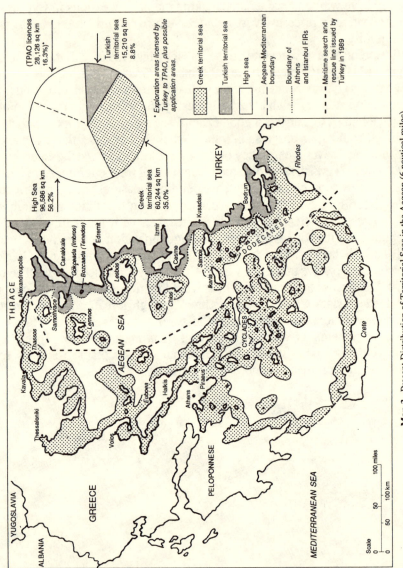

Map 3. Present Distribution of Territorial Seas in the Aegean (6 nautical miles)

Source: Andrew Wilson, The Aegean Dispute, Adelphi Paper No. 155, IISS. Reproduced with permission.

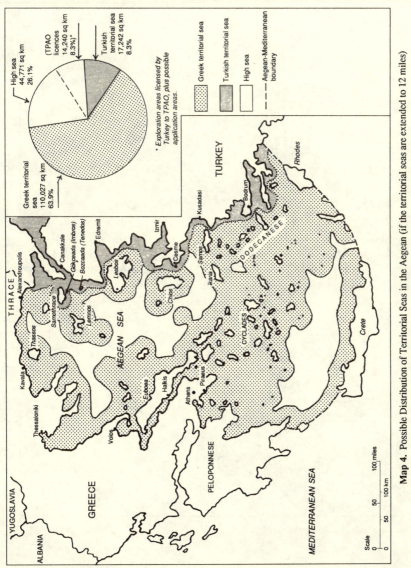

Map 4. Possible Distribution of Territorial Seas in the Aegean (if the territorial seas are extended to 12 miles)

Source: Andrew Wilson, *The Aegean Dispute*, Adelphi Paper No. 155, IISS. Reproduced with permission.

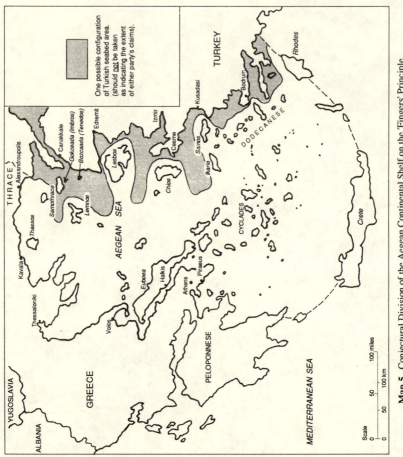
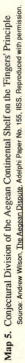

Map 5. Conjectural Division of the Aegean Continental Shelf on the 'Fingers' Principle

Source: Andrew Wilson, The Aegean Dispute, Adelphi Paper No. 155, IISS. Reproduced with permission.

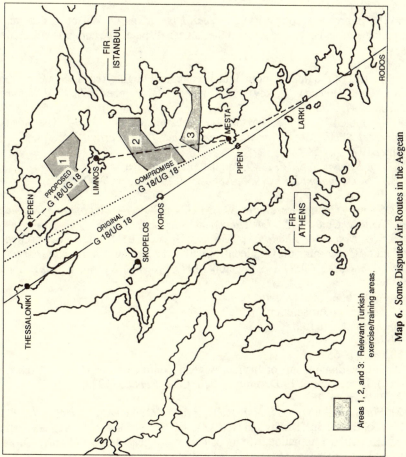

Map 6. Some Disputed Air Routes in the Aegean

Source: International Civil Aviation Organization.

Areas 1, 2, and 3: Relevant Turkish exercise/training areas.

Notes

1. See Maps 3 and 4.

2. See Article 76, *United Nations Convention on the Law of the Sea* [done at Montego Bay, December 10, 1982], *U.N. Document A/CONT. 62/122* of October 7, 1982.

3. *The Economist,* June 8, 1974.

4. For the Geneva Convention's provisions concerning the continental shelf, see Ian Brownlie, *Basic Documents in International Law,* Oxford: Oxford University Press, 1972, p. 107.

5. The figures are from Wilson, *Aegean Dispute,* p. 27. Wilson's is the most comprehensive and balanced study of the Aegean dispute. The author is indebted to this work.

6. *Ibid.,* p. 27.

7. The text of the final communique is contained in The Aegean Sea Continental Shelf Case (Greece v. Turkey), Judgement of 19 December 1978, *I.C.J. Reports,* 1978, para. 97.

8. As quoted in "Notes: Jurisdiction — Limits of Consent — The Aegean Continental Shelf Case," *Harvard International Law Journal,* Vol. 18, No. 3, Summer 1977, p. 654.

9. *U.N. Document S/PV. 1949,* August 12, 1976, p. 16.

10. *U.N. Document S/PV. 1950,* August 13, 1976, pp. 6, 7-10.

11. *Ibid.,* p. 17.

12. Security Council Resolution 395, 31 U.N. SCOR, *Resolutions and Decisions of the Security Council 15, U.N. Document. S/INF/ 32 (1976).*

13. See *"Notes: Jurisdiction,"* p. 656; Leo Gross, "The Dispute Between Greece and Turkey Concerning the Continental Shelf in the Aegean," *American Journal of International Law,* Vol. 71, No. 1, October 1977, pp. 37-9; Wilson, *Aegean Dispute,* p. 9.

14. Wilson, *Aegean Dispute,* p. 9.

15. "Notes — Jurisdiction," p. 657.

16. As quoted in *Ibid.*

17. *Ibid.*

18. *Ibid.,* p. 659.

19. International Court of Justice, Aegean Continental Shelf Case (Greece v. Turkey), Judgement of 19 December 1978, *I.C.J. Reports,* 1978, para. 78.

20. *Ibid.,* para. 78.

21. For the full text, see *U.N. Document A/CONT. 62/122* of October 7, 1982.

22. Joel E. Marsh, "Turkey and UNCLOS III: Reflections on the Aegean," paper presented at the International Symposium on Aegean Issues, Çesme, Turkey, October 15-17, 1987, p. 16.

23. *Ibid.*

24. *Ibid.,* pp. 16-17.

25. *Ibid.,* p. 18.

26. Jon M. Van Dyke, "The Role of Islands in Delimiting Maritime Zones: The Boundary Between Greece and Turkey," paper presented at the International Symposium on Aegean Issues, Çesme, Turkey, October 15-17, 1987, p. 19.

27. See Article 121 of the *Convention on the Law of the Sea.*

28. Marsh, "Turkey and UNCLOS," p. 18.

29. Van Dyke, "Role of Islands," p. 12.

30. *Ibid.*

31. See statement on Ambassador Kırca in *Official Records of the Third United Nations Conference on the Law of the Sea,* Vol. XVII, p. 77.

32. Marsh, "Turkey and UNCLOS," p. 19.

33. Van Dyke, "Role of Islands," p. 19.

34. Marsh, "Turkey and UNCLOS," p. 24.

35. Barbara Kwiatkowska, "Maritime Boundary Delimitation Between Opposite and Adjacent States in the New Law of the Sea — Some Implications for the Aegean," paper presented at the International Symposium on Aegean Issues, Çesme, Turkey, October 15-17, 1987, pp. 19-20.

36. Wilson, *Aegean Dispute,* p. 27.

37. Van Dyke, "Role of Islands," p. 16.

38. *Ibid.,* p. 17.

39. *Ibid.*

40. Wilson, *Aegean Dispute,* p. 27.

41. *Ibid.,* p. 23.

42. Gerald Blake, "Marine Policy Issues for Turkey," *Marine Policy Reports,* Vol. 7, No. 4, February 1985, p. 3.

43. In recent years, Turkish officials have avoided the use of the term *casus belli,* presumably because the threat does not permit a flexible response.

44. See Article 3 of the *Convention on the Law of the Sea.*

45. Official Records of the Security Council, Thirty-Eighth Year, Supplement of January, February, and March 1983, *U.N. Document S/15603,* p. 242.

46. *Ibid.*

47. Marsh, "Turkey and UNCLOS," p. 9.

48. *Ibid.,* p. 8.

49. Wilson, *Aegean Dispute,* p. 6.

50. This is based on confidential interviews with government officials.

51. Couloumbis wrote: "Should Greece extend its territorial waters to 12 miles, it is sometimes argued, in at least two places as they traverse the Aegean, U.S. and Soviet and other submarines would be required to surface and proceed under conditions of innocent passage." *Troubled Triangle,* p. 213.

52. Wilson, *Aegean Dispute,* p. 6.

53. *Ibid.*

54. *Ibid.,* p. 11.

55. International Civil Aviation Organization Council, *1855th Report to Council by the President of the Air Navigation Commission,* 114th Session, March 8, 1985, p. 2.

56. For the full text of the Lausanne Treaty, see Fred Israel, (ed.), *Major Peace Treaties of Modern History, 1648-1967,* Vol. IV, New York: Chelsea House, 1967, pp. 2301-68.

57. Foreign Policy Institute, "Views on the Questions Between Turkey and Greece," *Dış Politika (Foreign Policy),* Vol. X, Nos. 3 & 4, p. 10.

58. Ministry of Foreign Affairs, *Turkish Views on the Demilitarized Status of Lemnos and the Eastern Aegean Islands,* Ankara, n.d., pp. 9-10.

59. *Ibid.,* p. 10.

60. *Ibid.*

61. Couloumbis, *Troubled Triangle*, p. 122.

62. Quoted in The Journalists Union of Athens Daily Newspapers, *Threat in the Aegean*, Athens, n.d., p. 33.

63. "Turkish Views," p. 9.

64. Couloumbis, *Troubled Triangle*, p. 141.

65. *The Economist*, October 25, 1980.

66. *Ibid.*

67. This is based on interviews with officials of the Turkish Foreign Ministry in Ankara during November 1985.

68. *Wall Street Journal*, February 21, 1985.

69. Panayote Dimitras, "Greece: A New Danger," *Foreign Policy*, No. 58, Spring 1985, p. 143.

70. Bruce Kuniholm, "Rhetoric and Reality in the Aegean: U.S. Policy Options Towards Greece and Turkey," *SAIS Review*, Vol. 6, No. 1, Winter-Spring 1986, p. 148.

71. This is based on discussions with several officials of the United States government on the basis of non-attribution.

72. *New York Times*, August 14, 1988.

73. *The Christian Science Monitor*, September 17, 1985.

74. David Barchard, *Turkey and the West*, London: Routledge & Kegan Paul, 1985, p. 50.

75. See *The Globe and Mail*, March 31, 1987.

76. Wilson, *Aegean Dispute*, p. 26.

77. Coufoudakis, "Greek-Turkish Relations," p. 211.

78. Mario Modiano, "Domestic Factors That Influence Greek-Turkish Relations: The View From Athens," paper presented at the Lehrman Institute Conference on Greek-Turkish relations, May 17, 1986. (Mr. Modiano has been the long-time correspondent of *The Times*.)

79. Kuniholm, "Rhetoric and Reality," p. 148.

80. This is based on the author's conversations with two American officials in Washington, D.C. during March 1976 on the basis of non-attribution.

81. Quoted by Modiano, "Domestic Factors," p. 13.

82. Ellen Laipson, *The Seven-Ten Ratio in Military Aid to Greece and Turkey: A Congressional Tradition*, Congressional Research Service, The Library of Congress, Report No. 85-79, April 10, 1985, p. 11.

83. Quoted in Kuniholm, "Rhetoric and Reality," p. 153.

84. *Ibid.*

85. *Middle East Times*, November 30 - December 6, 1986.

86. *Ibid.*

87. Laipson, *The Seven-Ten Ratio*, p. 15.

88. Modiano, "Domestic Factors," p. 13.

89. The figures are from The International Institute of Strategic Studies, *The Military Balance, 1988-1989*, 1988, pp. 68, 79.

90. *The Times*, November 18, 1976.

91. The International Institute of International Affairs, *The Military Balance, 1986-87*, 1986, p. 212.

92. The figure representing Turkey's military expenditure is from *ibid*. The figures on annual spending per soldier are from Ruth L. Sivard, *World Military and*

Social Expenditures, Washington, D.C., 12th Edition, 1987, p. 46.

93. *Ibid.*

94. Kenneth Mackenzie, *Greece and Turkey: Disarray on NATO's Southern Flank,* The Institute for the Study of Conflict, London: Conflict Study No. 143, 1983, p. 6.

95. *The Middle East Times, March 13-19, 1988.*

6

Irritants over the
Treatment of Minorities

Although the most contentious issues between Greece and Turkey center on their interests in Cyprus and the Aegean, periodic accusations by Athens and Ankara regarding the treatment of their respective minorities have caused other irritations. Both the Turkish minority in Greece and the Greek minority in Turkey have experienced difficulties over their treatment and status for many years.

The Origins of the Minorities Problem

The issue over the treatment of minorities is actually older than the disputes over Cyprus and the maritime boundary disagreements in the Aegean and has caused occasional aggravations in Greek-Turkish relations since the Lausanne settlement of 1923.

Following the Turkish War of Independence (1919-1922), Turkey insisted on a compulsory exchange of population with Greece. The leaders of the new Turkish Republic wanted to create a nation-state with a homogeneous population in place of the multi-ethnic Ottoman Empire. In doing so, they were determined to avoid a repetition of the intervention of foreign powers in the internal affairs of the Ottoman Empire on the pretext of protecting Christian minorities. In addition, however, the Turks wanted to eliminate the basis for future Greek irredentist ambitions. Hence, their insistence that all Anatolian Greeks, most of whom had welcomed the invading Greek armies as liberators, be resettled in Greece.

Since the bulk of the Greek population had already left with the defeated Greek armies, Greece had no choice but to acquiesce in Turkey's demands. Greek leaders understood the reality of the accomplished facts, including the eclipse of the cherished *Megali Idea* policy, but they could not reconcile themselves to the total removal of the Greek presence from Istanbul, the city which Ioannis Kolettis referred to as "the dream and hope of all Greeks."[1] It was thus important for Greece that the historical link with the former

Byzantine capital be maintained. This is why Greek leader Venizelos made energetic efforts to exempt the Greeks of Istanbul and the Greek Orthodox Patriarchate from the compulsory exchange of populations.

It was ultimately agreed at Lausanne that all Greeks who were established in Istanbul before October 1918 be exempted from the population exchange. The number of Greeks who satisfied the "established" criterion was estimated in 1923 to be 110,000.[2] As part of the bargain, it was agreed that the Turkish community in Western Thrace, numbering 120,000, remain there under Greek rule. In addition, the chief Turkish delegate, Ismet Inönü, gave verbal assurances that the Patriarchate would be allowed to stay provided that it confined itself to purely spiritual matters. Finally, the Treaty of Lausanne (Article 14) decreed that Turkey provide a special administration and a locally recruited police force for the predominantly Greek inhabitants of the tiny islands of Gökçeada and Bozcaada, situated at the entrance to the Dardanelles.

The Lausanne Treaty used the criterion of religion to refer to the ethnic communities; hence, the reference to "Moslem" and "non-Moslem" minorities in the document. Although the terms "Greek" and "Turkish" were used in bilateral agreements in subsequent years, Greek government spokesmen have usually insisted that the basis of identification is religious and not national. Thus, Greek officials refer to the Muslim minority in Greece but deny the existence of a Turkish community.

As citizens of Greece, the Turks of Western Thrace were entitled to the rights of their fellow citizens, just as the Istanbul Greeks could enjoy the rights granted to all Turkish citizens. Beyond the rights enjoyed by all citizens, the Treaty of Lausanne conferred on these communities the right to run their religious, cultural, and educational institutions.

Both Turkey and Greece have asserted the right to monitor each other's treatment of their respective kinsmen under the terms of the Treaty of Lausanne various times since 1923 and have accused each other of discriminating against members of their respective communities and of pressuring them to emigrate. Although each country has usually denied the other's allegations, there is considerable evidence of officially sanctioned discrimination.

During the years immediately after the Lausanne Treaty, Greek and Turkish disagreements over the interpretation and implementation of the agreement concerning the population exchange were commonplace and kept tensions high among the two countries. Turkey was angered by Greece's expropriation of the Turkish community's land for the purpose of creating settlements for Greek refugees who settled in Western Thrace during 1922-1923. Since these acts were in violation of the Lausanne Treaty, Turkey demanded that the Greek government redress the situation. Further, the Turkish government retaliated by confiscating Greek properties in Istanbul[3], thus setting a pattern of tit for tat retaliation that often occurred. Ankara also appealed to the League of Nations, citing violations of the minority rights provided by the Lausanne Treaty.[4] Greece responded by making appeals of her own to the League, citing Turkey's violations vis-a-vis the Greeks of Istanbul, and defending its record.[5] In due course, Greek and Turkish governments were able to settle their differences, and some indemnities were provided to the Thracian Turks and Istanbul Greeks whose properties had been expropriated; some of the seized properties were also evacuated.

During periods of cooperative relations between Greece and Turkey, the Greeks of Istanbul and the Turks of Western Thrace were reasonably content with their status and treatment. This was the case for about one-quarter century during 1930-1955, with a few notable exceptions such as the emergency tax called *varlik vergisi* imposed in November 1942 which caused much distress for the Greek community in Turkey before its repeal a year later. Because of the Greek-Turkish rapprochement, the Patriarchate in Istanbul enjoyed an improvement in its status.[6] On the other hand, discriminatory acts and pressures by Athens and Ankara toward each other's minority community occurred during periods of strain following the emergence of the Cyprus issue in the mid-1950s.

Following the population exchange of 1923, the remaining minorities no longer posed a threat to the national majority. Nonetheless, many Greeks and Turks (and their officials) often doubted the loyalty of members of the minorities who lived in their midst, even though the bases for such doubts were not well-founded. Thus, for example, by encouraging Greek settlement in Western Thrace through a variety of incentives (such as concessionary loans for land purchase), Greek authorities have turned the Turkish community in that area (which borders on Turkey) from a majority into a minority status.[7] By the same token, when Cyprus emerged as a bone of contention between Greece and Turkey in the mid-1950s, ordinary Turks as well as officials suspected the Istanbul Greeks of taking the side of Greece and Greek-Cypriots against Turkey on the Enosis issue. These perceptions handicapped prospects for the successful integration of these culturally distinct communities within the larger "host" society.

Greek spokesmen and writers believe that the Turkish government's policy toward the Greek minority has been one of deliberate long-term pressure designed to force the community to leave. Thus, Alexandris has argued that

> the almost total disappearance of the Constantinopolitan [Istanbul], Imbriot and Tenediot Greeks is due above all to a well-planned and patiently executed Turkish foreign policy goal.[8]

Turkish writers have employed identical arguments concerning Greek policy toward the Turkish community in Greece. Thus in comparing Turkish and Greek policies concerning their minorities, Sezer has argued that

the Greek attitude has not been characterized by spectacular, sensational acts with the power to provoke adverse public opinion. It is a quieter, more systematic and apparently more carefully thought through [policy] with a long time perspective.[9]

While there is some validity to these allegations, the evidence concerning Greek and Turkish official policy and conduct vis-a-vis these particular minorities is not wholly justified. More often than not, the measures employed by Greek and Turkish governments toward the minorities under study were *ad hoc* and employed in retaliation for perceived adversarial acts by the other side. Yet, it is possible to ascribe to Athens and Ankara certain interests that affected their respective minorities and that they would have wished to pursue even without the hostilities created by the Cyprus dispute. Regardless of the Cyprus issue, the Greek government would have had a strategic interest in removing the bulk of the Turks from the Evros province on Greece's border with Turkey. In all probability, the pattern of retaliatory activity between Greece and Turkey after 1955 made it easier for the Greek government to attain the goal of reducing in a sensitive frontier area the presence of a community whose loyalties it suspected.

On the other hand, the Turkish authorities (like most ordinary Turks) resented the substantial economic presence of the wealthy Greek businessmen in Turkey's largest city. From the beginning, Turkish nationalists wanted to enhance the participation of the Turkish element in the country's commercial life and to reduce the economic influence of the minorities. Furthermore, Turks have suspected that Greek insistence on the continued presence of the Greek Orthodox Patriarchate has been motivated by a desire to keep the aspiration for *Megali Idea* alive. The restrictive measures which Ankara employed toward the Greek community in Istanbul helped to create an exodus of the Greek community even though the initiation of such measures were not part of a grand design to rid Turkey of the Greek minority.

The Fortunes of the Greek Minority and the Patriarchate

The anti-Greek riots of September 6-7, 1955 in Istanbul and Izmir had a major impact on the Greek community there. At the time, Turkish leaders and local party functionaries of the governing Democratic Party encouraged demonstrations to display the strength of Turkish feeling over the Cyprus issue. This was timed to coincide with the Tripartite Conference which began deliberations in London on August 29. The government did not anticipate, and was apparently shocked by, the violence and fury of the demonstrators who destroyed many churches, as well as Greek businesses and properties. The *New York Times* reported that "more than 4000 shops, mostly Greek and Armenian-owned, were totally wrecked by the rioters. Seven hundred homes were damaged as were a dozen churches."[10]

Most Turkish commentators have argued that the riots were not merely anti-Greek but also a protest by the poor elements of Turkish society against the wealthy. *The Economist* supported this interpretation as well in its report that "whatever the origins, the Istanbul riots last September would probably not have swollen into such an appalling orgy of destruction if the 'have-nots' had not seized the chance of aiming the blows at the 'haves'."[11]

Turkish leaders were embarrassed by the events. Nonetheless, although the Menderes government blamed the riots on Communists and other "foreign" agents, the government's culpability in the riots was suspected. It was widely reported that the police did not interfere with the rioters until the rampage had caused enormous damage. The fact that Turkish Prime Minister Menderes and Foreign Minister Zorlu were subsequently charged and found guilty of inciting the riots during the Yassiada trials of 1960-1961 may be viewed both as an acknowledgement of government responsibility and as a conciliatory gesture towards Greece.[12]

The Turkish leader (Menderes) apologized to the Greek government and offered compensation to those whose properties were destroyed and damaged.[13] However, the consequences of the riots were far greater than that which could be measured by the physical damage, and more difficult to repair because of the fear and insecurity they generated among the Greek population. Although precise numbers are not available, thousands of Greeks left Istanbul in the aftermath of the riots, and their departure represented the beginning of the exodus of the bulk of the Greeks of Istanbul.

In due course, the compromise reached by Greece and Turkey over Cyprus in 1959 that led to independence had a favourable effect on the status of the Greek community and the Patriarchate in Turkey, as it had on the conditions of the Turkish community in Greece. Concerning the Patriarchate, the Greek Foreign Minister of the time, Averoff, wrote later that:

> According to the assurances received from the Patriarchate and all our representatives in Istanbul — assurances which were repeated to me personally on my official visit of 3rd to 8th August, 1962 — their life had never been easier, their freedom of action never less restricted than at this time.[14]

However, the breakdown of the partnership government in Cyprus and the ensuing civil strife had (as in the mid-1950s) major repercussions for the

Greek community. Turkish leaders were particularly upset over the Greek government's decision to support the renewed Enosis campaign of the Greek-Cypriots in violation of the Zurich-London accords. In addition, given Athens' support for the Greek-Cypriot leadership, Turkey held Greece at least partly responsible for the Turkish-Cypriot losses and suffering in the civil strife on Cyprus.

In these circumstances, the minorities once again became pawns in the unending Greek and Turkish chess game. As punishment for the new Greek policy over Cyprus, the Turkish government took a series of restrictive measures that adversely affected the Greek minority in Istanbul and the Patriarchate. In March 1964, Turkey took advantage of a clause of the Convention of Establishment of 1930[15] which gave it the right to abrogate it at six months' notice and began to expel about 9,000 Greek citizens from Turkey over a period of months.[16] Unlike the majority of the Greek community who held Turkish citizenship and passports, these Greeks had not acquired Turkish nationality.[17] The expelled Greeks of Hellenic citizenship were prevented from selling their properties, which the Turkish government confiscated.[18]

In addition to these measures, Turkish authorities placed restrictions on Greek educational institutions. *The New York Times* reported that Greek teachers of the fifty-four elementary and secondary schools complained of frequent inspections by Turkish authorities who made enquiries "into matters of curriculum, texts, and especially the use of the Greek language in teaching."[19] The authorities banned morning prayers in Greek schools and prohibited Orthodox clergymen from entering Greek minority schools.[20]

In a statement made on April 20, 1988, Foreign Minister Hasan Esat Isık declared that

> there was no direct connection between the Cyprus problem and the Greek minority and patriarchate. But he added that if Athens refused to deal with Ankara over Cyprus this would have its effects on the Greek minority in Turkey.[21]

Turkish spokesmen tried to increase pressures on Greece over Cyprus by threatening that Turkey might demand a revision of the Lausanne Treaty. In addition, restrictions were placed on the Patriarchate and threats made about its possible removal from Turkey. At the time, the Turkish government was being urged by the press and parliamentarians to use the Greek citizens and the Patriarchate as "a weapon in the dispute on Cyprus."[22]

The Greek government issued protests and warnings to Ankara over the treatment of the Greek residents of Istanbul and the Patriarchate, but its leverage was undermined by the Greek-Cypriot harassment of the Turkish community in Cyprus and by charges of discrimination by the Turkish minority in Western Thrace. The expulsion of two senior churchmen of the Patriarchate, and the closing of its printing house by the authorities, raised fears that Turkey might seek to move the Patriarchate itself, but the Turkish government stopped short of taking such a step.

The removal of the Patriarchate would have been a heavy blow to Greece, and particularly the Greek community in Istanbul, whose religious life revolved around it and the seventy churches in the city. However, such a step would have had even wider international ramifications. There were fears that if the Patriarchate, as the center of Orthodox Christianity, was removed from Istanbul, the Soviets might use the Russian Orthodox Church to assume a position of leadership and larger influence among the Orthodox Christians. This may well have served as an added restraint to Turkey in its deliberations over the possible expulsion of the Patriarchate.

Most Turks view the presence of the Greek Orthodox Patriarchate in an overwhelmingly Muslim land as an anachronism. To Turkish leaders (and ordinary Turks), Greek insistence that this institution remain in Istanbul is a manifestation of the *Megali Idea*. As a *New York Times* report of March 1, 1976, on the Greek community of Istanbul concluded: "In their hearts, many Greeks have never completely abandoned the *Megali Idea*, the 'Great Idea' of recapturing Istanbul, and the Greek community here symbolizes that dream."

The relationship between Turkish leaders and the Patriarchate has not always been problematic, notwithstanding Turkish suspicions over what the institution represents in the minds of Greeks. Indeed, during periods of Greek-Turkish détente, Turkish authorities have been agreeable to improvements in the status and prestige of the Patriarchate. For example, in 1947, the Greek and Turkish governments were concerned that the initiative of the Russian Patriarchate to convene a Pan-Orthodox Conference in Moscow might "enable the Soviet-backed Russian Patriarchate to take over the spiritual supremacy of the Patriarchate of Constantinople."[23] As a result, the Greek and Turkish governments decided to bolster the position of the Istanbul Patriarchate. Rather than search for a local candidate, the Turkish government agreed to consider an Orthodox leader of international standing. These calculations led to the election of Archbishop Athenagoras of North America as Patriarch in Istanbul.[24]

Athenagoras, who served as Patriarch between 1949 to 1972, was a charismatic and politically astute leader who began his term by establishing excellent relations with Ankara and impressing upon many Turks that he was a loyal citizen of Turkey. But, like the Greek community, he could not escape suspicions of disloyalty as developments in Cyprus stimulated national passions; consequently, his role was diminished.

The much-less numerous Greeks of the islands of Gökçeada and Bozcaada were also adversely affected. The Lausanne Treaty had stipulated that a special administrative organization be provided for these two islands, most of whose people were Greek in 1923. The same treaty provided that the police force on these two islands be recruited from local (Greek) elements. The Turkish government did not fulfill these requirements. Nonetheless, during the period of Greek-Turkish détente, Greek cultural institutions enjoyed considerable latitude. According to Alexandris, between 1950 and 1963, the islands, with the encouragement of the Turkish government, enjoyed an unprecedented degree of development and were able not only to preserve their Greek identity but also to improve their lot economically and culturally.[25]

Following the outbreak of strife in Cyprus, however, the Turkish government imposed several restrictions on these islands. As from the 1964-1965 school year, the teaching of the Greek language was suspended, prompting many islanders to leave for Istanbul or Greece, where their children could receive a Greek education.[26] In addition, Turkish authorities nationalized land and expropriated several community buildings (including schools) for the benefit of Turks from the mainland. Furthermore, the establishment by the Turkish government of an open prison in Gökçeada, where convicts from the mainland could engage in farming represented another blow to the Greeks there and provided an additional reason for their emigration. The effect of the Turkish measures has been to de-Hellenize these islands. Whereas, the combined population of the islands consisted of over 9,000 Greeks in 1920, by the mid-1980s, their number had been reduced to 800.[27]

It is obvious that the Greeks of Istanbul and the Greek Orthodox Patriarchate became pawns in the adversarial Greek-Turkish relations as did their Turkish counterparts in Western Thrace. Large-scale emigration of Greeks from Turkey coincided with the most strained periods between Greece and Turkey. Thus, from a community of 100,000 in 1923, the number of Greeks in Istanbul has decreased to an estimated 5,000 in 1988. The Patriarchate itself has survived the vicissitudes of Greek-Turkish relations; but, with such a diminished flock, the justification for its continued presence in an overwhelmingly Muslim society has been weakened. As Alexandris has noted, "the Patriarchate of Constantinople is slowly but steadily dying from inanition."[28]

Turkish Grievances over the Treatment of Western Thrace Turks

There are an estimated 120,000 Turks in Greece, the great majority of whom live in Western Thrace which borders on Turkey. In 1923, this Turkish population constituted the majority in the region. This community includes about 30,000 Pomaks[29] (who speak a Bulgarian dialect with

Turkish as a second language) and some 5,000 Gypsies who speak Romany and Turkish.

Many of the grievances of the Turkish community have been identical to those of the Greeks in Turkey, but the fortunes of each of these communities have also been governed by important socioeconomic differences as well as patterns of settlement. For instance, as a community, the Greeks of Istanbul were much better off than their Turkish countrymen, and their grievances were political and social rather than economic. Their relative affluence helped them attain considerably higher educational levels than their Turkish counterparts. The Greeks of Turkey have been an urban and visible minority through their concentration in Istanbul.

By contrast, the Turks of Western Thrace have been a poor rural community of farmers concentrated in the least developed area of Greece. The mobility of members of this community has been sharply curtailed by high levels of illiteracy and the lack of skills other than farming. Consequently, in relative terms, emigration has not been as easy an option for them as for the Greeks of Istanbul. At the time of the Treaty of Lausanne in 1923, the population of Turks was an estimated 120,000 out of a total population in Western Thrace of about 190,000. [30] Given an average yearly birthrate of twenty-eight per thousand,[31] some sources estimate that the population of the community should have trebled by the mid-1980s.[32] However, due to a high rate of emigration, the number of Thracian Turks has remained virtually unchanged over the past sixty years.

In the early 1950s, conditions for the Thracian Turks were quite favourable because of the relatively smooth relations between Greece and Turkey, both of which applied and became members of NATO in 1952. However, as Greek-Turkish relations deteriorated over Cyprus, so did the conditions for the community; an estimated 20,000 emigrated to Turkey in the course of the 1950s.[33]

As the Cyprus dispute worsened in the 1960s, and Greece and Turkey became more bellicose towards each other, the pressures on the Western Thrace Turks intensified. This was especially the case after the 1967 coup which ushered in the military junta in Greece. When Turkey intervened in Cyprus by military force in 1974, in response to the Greek coup in the island, the conditions of the Turks became even more precarious. In referring to the post-1974 era, de Jong has stated that

> ...harassment, discrimination and administrative obstruction took place on a wider scale than ever before and seriously affected communal institutions and the well-being of the community's members.[34]

Although precise figures are not available, the number of Thracian Turks who have emigrated to Turkey now far exceed those currently living in

Greece.[35] Had the Turkish government encouraged or made it easier for them to emigrate, their numbers in Greece would have shrunk even more. Even though Turkish authorities discourage immigration of Turks from Greece, they provide special facilities for Thracian Turkish students wanting to pursue university education in Turkey. These students are given special admission consideration to selected university programmes, ostensibly to enhance their employment prospects in Greece upon graduation. However, the great majority of these students remain in Turkey and do not return to Greece, where their diplomas have not been recognized.[36]

Why do so many Turks from Western Thrace emigrate to Turkey? Wilson has stated that

> emigration... is not necessarily or simply the result of discrimination... Emigration to Turkey could be a natural outcome of ethnic and religious affiliation, or of a belief that Turkish cities provide more opportunities than Greek cities for Turkish-speaking Muslims."[37]

There is some basis to the contention that it is not always discrimination that prompts Turks to leave for Turkey. On the other hand, as members of a rural farming community, Thracian Turks do not possess the skills that would help them become employed in the Turkish cities to which they emigrate. (A small number of Thracian Turks have also emigrated to European cities for employment.) Moreover, living standards in Greece are higher than in Turkey; the per capita income in Greece is four times that of Turkey.[38] The field research conducted by a number of observers such as Oran and de Jong indicate that many Thracian Turks leave to escape the discriminatory and oppressive treatment they experience at the hands of Greek officials.

One of the major complaints of the Thracian Turkish community concerns the drastic shrinking of their ownership of land. According to Oran, Turks held 84 percent of the land in Western Thrace at the time of the Lausanne Treaty in 1923.[39] According to Turkish government figures presented at Lausanne, the Turkish community represented two-thirds of Western Thrace's population. The Turks now own only 20 percent of the land in Western Thrace and represent 34 percent of the population.[40]

Thracian Turks have complained that a variety of methods have been used by Greek authorities to reduce their land holdings. The Greek authorities have periodically expropriated land in Western Thrace, as elsewhere, in the public interest. In justifying the expropriations, the authorities have commonly cited the need to establish military bases, industrial sites, or universities.

In May 1978, 4,000 donums were expropriated in the Amaranda, Vakos, Triorion, and Pamforon villages of Komotini for use as industrial sites;

another 4,300 donums were also expropriated in northwest Komotini in the Yaka region, and 3,000 donums were expropriated in the same area to establish the proposed Dimokritos University.[41] This last expropriation, in particular, evoked bitter criticism from the Turks, who complained that the land earmarked for Dimokritos University consisted of prime irrigated farmland. A delegation of Turks submitted topographical plans and evidence to the Governor of Rodop Prefecture and asked that less productive land in the immediate vicinity be used instead for a university campus.[42] The Turks have also complained that the size of expropriated land far exceeded the need for the stated purpose; it was pointed out that the land area of the University of Thessaloniki is 640 donums as compared to the 3,000 donums for the proposed Dimokritos.[43] It has not helped matters that no building has occurred on the site since its acquisition in 1978.

The Turks in Thrace have also complained of discrimination in cases of government expropriations of land for other purposes to serve the public interest. For example, in accordance with a 1952 law, land holdings that exceeded the legally allowable 500 donums were expropriated for subsequent distribution to landless peasants.[44] Virtually no landless Turks have benefitted from such redistribution.

Another law, which originated in 1948, sought to combine small adjacent parcels of land in order to create larger, more economical, units; owners of such lands are entitled to be compensated by equivalent land elsewhere. Turks whose lands were "exchanged" in this manner have complained that they do not receive land of equivalent value in another area. As well, they are not represented on the Commissions that decide which parcels to expropriate and what land is to be offered as equivalent value. Furthermore, whereas the initiative to combine parcels of land once rested with a majority of the landowners in the area, since 1974 (the year of Turkey's military intervention in Cyprus) a change in the application in the law has empowered the governor to start the process. Both the change in the provisions of the law, and the manner of its application, have raised fears that the expropriations are politically motivated.[45]

The purchase of land by Turks is, with a few exceptions, made extremely difficult by Greek authorities.[46] An existing law has been used to deny Turkish applications for the purchase of land since 1965, when relations between Greece and Turkey reached a low ebb because of the Cyprus issue. On the other hand, Greek purchases of land (especially of Turkish land) are speedily processed.[47] Furthermore, Greek authorities have provided long-term loans at concessional rates for Greeks to buy land in Western Thrace.[48] These loans are readily available to Greeks but denied to Turks. According to Wilson, the use of this measure has been a major cause in the reduction of land ownership by Turks in Western Thrace.[49]

Members of the Turkish community have complained of other forms of discrimination that affect their material well-being. For example, Turks are rarely granted permits to repair their homes or build new ones. Moreover, they are seldom issued licences to operate motor vehicles, including tractors. In a community in which farming is the major source of income, the effect of these forms of discrimination has been to perpetuate primitive technology and poverty.

Although precise figures are not available, it is apparent that employment levels as well as income and other related indicators are much poorer for Western Thrace Turks than for the rest of the Greek population. Western Thrace is the least developed and poorest region in Greece, and this can be attributed largely to deliberate neglect by the Greek authorities. Visitors to Western Thrace can observe that Greek villages and settlements have better roads and facilities than adjacent Turkish ones. In theory, Turks can move to more prosperous Greek cities for a better life; in practice, this is not a credible option.

The education, language, and culture of the Turkish community are being threatened as a result of the policies pursued by the Greek authorities. Altogether, there are 241 primary schools, serving about 12,000 pupils. Most of these schools consist of dilapidated, one-room buildings, without adequate facilities or equipment. It is common to have one-classroom schools for the first to the sixth grades. Under these circumstances, the quality of the education received by the pupils is very poor. Those who finish primary school have great difficulties in gaining admission to one of the two high schools with a combined capacity of only 637.[50]

It is remarkable that there are only two secondary schools for a population of 120,000. Even more remarkable is the fact that, until 1952, there were no secondary schools at all for the Turkish community. According to Oran, only thirty-four students graduated from the two high schools during the 1982-1983 school year.[51] It is very rare to find any Turkish students enrolled in any one of the universities in Greece. In theory, there is nothing preventing Turkish students from entering Greek universities; in practice, however, the quality of education received by the Turkish students in Greece is below the level considered acceptable for university admission.

Most of the teachers at Turkish schools are appointed by the Greek authorities. Graduate teachers from Islamic institutions of higher learning are seldom appointed, and since the 1960s, graduates of teacher-training colleges in Turkey have not been allowed to teach in the community's schools.[52] These findings are borne out by other scholars like Oran who have conducted extensive research among the Turks in Greece. According to de Jong, the policies pursued by the Greek authorities represent "an effort to create an incompetent hellenised teachers' corps isolated from the main-stream of Turkish culture and civilization."[53]

Thracian Turks themselves believe that the Greek authorities deliberately appoint poorly qualified teachers especially in subjects taught in Turkish to prevent the acquisition of Turkish culture. Greek officials deny any respon-sibility for inadequate facilities and poor education of these Turks; however, the evidence of neglect and discrimination is substantial. It is no accident that the illiteracy rate among the Turks in Greece is an estimated 60 percent, compared with 14.24 percent for the total population of Greece.[54]

In addition to education, some of the most discriminatory acts of the Greek government have involved key communal Turkish institutions such as the *vakıf* (Islamic endowments) and the office of the *müfti* (Islamic leader), which are of fundamental importance to their existence as a community. For instance, the Greek government has sought to weaken and control the *vakıf*. Before the Greek junta came to power in 1967, the directors of the *vakıf* were elected by the community. The junta, however, altered this practice by taking over the power to nominate the directors. More recently, legislation passed in 1980 (Law No. 1091) has had the effect of seriously weakening the administrative and financial autonomy of the *vakıfs*. Among the most restrictive provisions is one calling for the administration of the *vakıf* by a board of five administrators, to be selected by the Greek governor of the province, who is also empowered to approve the *vakıfs'* budget.[55]

The new legislation provides that the schools of the Turkish community will receive funding not from the *vakıf*, as was previously the case, but from the Greek Ministry of Education. Another section of the law requires the *vakıfs* to prove their existence by applying to the Ministry of Finance with the original documents that set them up.[56]

The passage of this legislation provoked vigorous protests by the Turkish community, whose leaders appealed to the Greek government to rescind it. The Turkish government also objected on the grounds that the law violated the Lausanne Treaty and other agreements. As a result, the Greek govern-ment has deferred the application of the various provisions of this law.[57] However, members of the Turkish community take it for granted that the law will be fully applied in the future.

Another instance of government intervention involves the *müftis*, who are the supreme leaders of the Turkish community in Western Thrace. Until the military junta, *müftis* were elected by the community; since then, they have been appointed by Greece's Minister of Religious Affairs, despite repeated demands by the community for the restoration of the electoral process. The Greek government's appointments to the position of *müfti* have caused widespread discontent and anger within the Turkish community. As de Jong has stated:

the appointment of a Gypsy Muslim without any qualifications what-soever as mufti of Didymotichon (Evros province) in 1973, and the ap-pointment of the chairman of the council for the administration of pious foundations in Xanthi — who, as chairman of a Muslim body, openly declares that he is not a Muslim — are illustrative of Greek policy.[58]

For many years, the Greek authorities have refused the Turkish commu-nity permission to repair their mosques or to build new ones. Moreover, they have not exempted the real estate of the *vakıfs* from the general confiscation of Turkish land in Thrace. This has affected the financial basis of community life considerably and has caused serious problems for mosque personnel and for teachers in the community's schools, since the employees often receive part of their salary from revenues of the pious institutions.[59]

Among the various forms of discrimination employed by the Greek government, one of the most resented among the Turks relates to citizenship. According to Section 19 of Greek Nationality Law No. 3370, dated 1955, "a person of non-Greek origin who leaves Greece with the intention of not returning, may be declared as having lost Greek nationality."[60] This law has been applied by Greek authorities to deprive many Turks of Thrace of their Greek nationality when they travel to Turkey or to other countries.

There is a widespread Greek perception that there is little or no basis for Turkey's claims concerning the denial of rights of, and discrimination against, the Turks in Greece. Further, Greeks believe that Turkey has sought to strengthen the (Turkish) national character of the community and to support the nationalist groups over the religious ones in Western Thrace. Greek authorities claim that the real motive behind Turkey's policy is to use the Turkish community in Thrace to create difficulties for Greece.

In the aftermath of Turkey's military intervention in Cyprus in 1974, some Greeks have voiced concerns that Turkey might seek to exploit the presence of the Turkish community in Western Thrace in order to seize the area from Greece in the future. Since the 1960s, the outbreak of crises in Cyprus brought Greece and Turkey to the brink of war on several occasions. Although the two adversaries are most likely to fight over the Aegean or Cyprus, it is generally assumed that Western Thrace would become an area of engagement for Greece and Turkey.

Greek anxieties notwithstanding, Turkey has shown no interest in chal-lenging Greek sovereignty in Western Thrace. Moreover, despite the widespread abuses of the Turks' rights in Greece, especially since the mid-1950s, Turkish policy-makers have not assigned the issue as much impor-tance as the Cyprus and Aegean problems.

Turkey's usual response to new abuses or pressures on the Turks in Thrace has been to make periodic representations to the Greek government. However, it is obvious that because of the emigration of the bulk of the Istanbul Greeks from Turkey since the mid-1950s, largely as a result of official pressures, Turkey has lost an important leverage in pressuring Greece on the rights of the community in Thrace.

The emigration of Turks from Greece to Turkey continues. However, the Turkish government does not encourage such emigration, nor does it ordinarily grant citizenship to emigrants for fear that this would pave the way for the disappearance of the community in Greece.

Among the Turks in Thrace, there is a widely held belief that Turkey has not pressured Greece vigorously enough in defence of their rights. Accordingly, in recent years, the community has turned to other states, especially Muslim countries, and to international human rights institutions to publicize their case and to exert pressure on the Greek government. A highly publicized appeal was made to the ambassadors of the Islamic states in Greece in 1981 in response to the new law severely restricting the *wakf*. Apparently, Colonel Qaddafi of Libya brought up the issue of the Turkish community's grievances during a visit to Greece. The grievances of the community have periodically appeared on the agenda of the Islamic Conferences.

The development of ties between the Thracian Turks and Islamic institutions in the Middle East has coincided with the manifestation of greater Islamic identity and orientation within the community in Greece.[61] Actually, in recent years, Greece has made a special effort to cultivate closer ties with the Islamic countries of the Middle East in an effort to bolster its diplomatic position against Turkey. However, the interest shown in the plight of Turks in Thrace by various official organizations in such states as Saudi Arabia, Libya, and others does not appear to have made Greece any more sensitive to accusations of discrimination and oppression.

In the meantime, with Greece as a member of the European Community, the Turks of Thrace have recently been turning to European institutions, where there is considerable receptivity to human rights issues. Questions regarding discrimination against the community have been raised in the European Parliament, and appeals to the European Human Rights Commission are likely to be lodged.

The Promises of Détente

It is possible to view the problems presented by the minorities examined above as a carry-over of the circumstances that led to the massive Greek-Turkish population exchanges following the Greek invasion of Anatolia after the First World War. The Lausanne Treaty and both the Greek and Turkish constitutions provided these minorities with considerable legal protection. But as the sorry experience of many ethnic minorities elsewhere in the world demonstrates, the most effective protections are not those codified in constitutions and charters of rights. During periods of strain and confrontation between them, Greece and Turkey resorted to official discrimination and pressures leading to large-scale emigration of each other's minority groups.

At the same time, periods of détente were times of relative security for such communities and the best guarantee of their favourable treatment. The recent relaxation of Greek-Turkish tensions that accompanied the Davos meeting in January 1987 between Papandreou and Ozal has already paid noteworthy dividends. The Turkish government's decision to release the property assets of the nearly 12,000 Greek nationals seized in 1964 (estimated at $300,000,000 in value), to be invested in Turkey, [62] can contribute toward the creation of a climate of confidence. In such favourable circumstances, some Greeks who left Istanbul for Greece without the loss of their Turkish citizenship may take up Turkish Prime Minister Özal's invitation to return to their former city.[63] It is believed that many of the nearly 200,000 Greek tourists who have visited Turkey in recent years are former residents of Istanbul.

In view of the drastic reduction of the Greek community in Turkey (as compared with the Turkish community in Greece), Greek spokesmen have often complained of a lack of balance and the importance of reciprocity. But improvements in the climate of Greek-Turkish relations are bound to be reflected in the status of the Turkish community in Thrace as well, and hopeful signs have emerged since the initiation of the Davos process. According to a report which appeared soon after the January 1988 meeting between Papandreou and Özal,

> it is [for]... the first time that officials have — albeit privately — conceded that the Muslim minority in north-eastern Greece could have a few problems. Though Greece officially insists that its 100,000 Muslims have full and equal rights along with the Christian majority, an official conceded that a Muslim 'might have to wait a little longer for an official document' and allows there is room for some improvement.[64]

In recent decades, Greece and Turkey have been more concerned about their interests in Cyprus and the Aegean and have consequently treated the minority issues as secondary interests. Obviously, the security of the status of their respective minorities depends on how successfully they can deal with their disagreements in Cyprus and the Aegean. However, it is also conceivable that improvements made in the conditions of their minorities could have beneficial effects in their overall relationship. Furthermore, international public opinion may be increasingly sensitive to restrictions on the rights of ethnic and religious minorities. This, and the possibility of both nations becoming fellow members of the European community, will increase the incentives for improvements in the status of these communities.

Notes

1. Andrew Mango, "Remembering the Minorities," *Middle Eastern Studies*, Vol. 21, No. 4, 1985, p. 143.

2. The question of who qualified as an "established" Greek was disputed by Greece and Turkey; the issue was resolved to Greece's satisfaction in 1925.

3. Alexandris, *Greek Minority*, p. 124. See also Gönlübol et al., *Olaylarla*, p. 61.

4. Alexandris, *Greek Minority*, p. 124; See also Baskın Oran, *Turk-Yunan Iliskilerinde Batı Trakya Sorunu* (the Western Thrace Question in Greek-Turkish Relations), Ankara: Mulkiyeliler Birligi Vakfı Yayınları, 1986, p. 146.

5. Alexandris, *Greek Minority*, p. 124.

6. See chapter 7 in *ibid.*

7. F. De Jong, "The Muslim Minority in Western Thrace," in Georgia Ashworth, (ed.), *World Minorities*, Vol. 3, Sunbury, U.K.: Quatarmaine House Ltd., 1980, p. 96.

8. A. Alexandris, "The Minority Question: Greece and Turkey," paper presented at the Lehrman Institute Conference on Greek-Turkish relations, May 15, 1986, p. 45.

9. Duygu B. Sezer, "A Turkish Perspective on the Greek and Turkish Minorities," paper presented at the Lehrman Institute Conference on Greek-Turkish relations, May 15, 1986, p. 11.

10. September 7, 1955.

11. *The Economist*, December 24, 1955.

12. Menderes, Zorlu, and Hadımlı (the former governor of Izmir) were found guilty of inciting the riots by the court at Yassıada.

13. The amount of compensation fell short of the levels that the Greek community and the Patriarchate considered reasonable.

14. Averoff, *Lost Opportunities*, p. 418.

15. See *Observer News Service*, April 22, 1964 and *The Times*, August 13, 1964.

16. *New York Times*, April 20, 1965.

17. According to Alexandris, "they held Hellenic nationality because their ancestors had come from the provinces of the Ottoman Empire that were incorporated in the Greek kingdom in 1830 and later." "The Minority Question," p. 14.

18. *New York Times*, July 28, 1964.

19. *Ibid.*, April 24, 1964.

20. Alexandris, "The Minority Question," p. 16; See also E.I.A. Daes, "The Greek Orthodox Minority in Turkey," in Georgia Ashworth, (ed.), *World Minorities*, Vol. 2, Sunbury, U.K.: Quatarmaine House Ltd., 1978, p. 52.

21. *New York Times*, April 21, 1965.

22. *Ibid.*, April 23, 1964.

23. Alexandris, *Greek Minority*, p. 244.

24. *Ibid.*, pp. 244-5.

25. Alexandris, "The Minority Question," p. 23.

26. *Ibid.*

27. *Ibid.*, p. 25.

28. Alexandris, *Greek Minority*, p. 319.

29. Although Greek spokesmen claim that they are of Greek stock, Pomaks view themselves as Turks (as does the Turkish government).

30. Oran, *Turk-Yunan*, p. 15. Muslim population statistics of the 1923 era given in Greek official and secondary sources are somewhat lower than those in Turkish sources.

31. De Jong, "The Muslim Minority," p. 96.

32. Oran, *Turk-Yunan*, p. 8.

33. De Jong, "The Muslim Minority," p. 96.

34. Ibid.

35. Oran, *Turk-Yunan*, p. 8.

36. Recently, the Greek authorities reversed their long-standing policy and recognized the Turkish diploma of a Turkish dental surgeon, after a two-and-a-half year struggle. See *Newspot*, March 13, 1987. Although this decision is expected to help the case of other applicants, it is unlikely that the difficulties of recognition faced by graduates from Turkey will be relieved substantially.

37. Wilson, *Aegean Dispute*, p. 17.

38. Oran, *Turk-Yunan*, p. 162.

39. *Ibid.*, p. 120.

40. Wilson, *Aegean Dispute*, p. 17.

41. Oran, *Turk-Yunan*, p. 122.

42. *Ibid.*

43. *Ibid.*

44. *Ibid.*

45. *Ibid.*, p. 133.

46. De Jong, "The Muslim Minority," p. 96.

47. Oran, *Turk-Yunan*, p. 120.

48. Wilson, *Aegean Dispute*, p. 17.

49. *Ibid.*

50. Oran, *Turk-Yunan*, p. 92.

51. *Ibid.*

52. De Jong, "The Muslim Minority," p. 98.

53. Ibid.

54. Oran, *Turk-Yunan*, p. 95.

55. "The 'Gulag Archipelago' of Western Thrace," *Impact International*, August 13-26, 1981, published in *Newspot*, December 7, 1984.

56. *Ibid.*

57. Oran, *Turk-Yunan*, pp. 142-4.

58. De Jong, "The Muslim Minority," p. 97.

59. *Ibid.*

60. "The Gulag Archipelago."

61. F. De Jong, "Organizational Aspects of the Muslims in Western Thrace,"

paper presented at the Second International Turkic Conference in Bloomington, Indiana, May 16, 1987.

62. Robert McDonald, "Greece: The Search for a Balance," *The World Today,* June 1988, p. 101.

63. Interview with Professor Mümtaz Soysal, Ankara, October 5, 1985.

64. *Middle East Times,* March 20-26, 1988.

7
Prospects

The development of the disputes outlined in this study owe much to the long history of grievance and mistrust between the Greek and Turkish nations. Decision-makers, as well as their domestic constituencies at large, have a sense of the historical relationship with their adversaries when they are considering their problems. Thus, for example, in dealing with the Aegean maritime boundary issues, it would have been easier for the two neighbours to find mutually acceptable formulas for the resolution of conflicts if they had not been burdened by the historical baggage of animosity and suspicion. In the post-Second World War period, Greece and Turkey's rival claims in Cyprus and the Aegean were instrumental in nullifying the rapprochement of the previous quarter century, ushering in a period of estrangement and conflict.

Nonetheless, a history of conflict has not excluded periods of peace and reconciliation. Nor has it precluded the cultivation of co-operative and interdependent relations, particularly when external actors worked to support forces of conciliation and collaboration. The classic example of this has been the post-war Franco-German relationship. The entry of Greece and Turkey into the Western Alliance and the warming relationship they enjoyed before 1955 is another example, albeit one where the process of reconciliation eventually was reversed.

A return to the pattern of co-operative relations is bound to be a difficult task for Greeks and Turks, and the historical record may be discouraging. At the same time, one need not recall distant history to develop a more encouraging sense of future possibilities. In an article entitled "Sound Sense in the Near East" which appeared in *The Economist* on May 20, 1933, recent improvements in Greek-Turkish relations were described in these terms:

> ...the history of Turkish-Greek relations since 1930 ought to be read, marked and inwardly digested by all nations of Europe. For, if the hatchet can be buried by two peoples who have been burdened by the terrible Greek-Turkish heritage of mutual injury and mutual hatred, there is no excuse left for any of the rest of us to confess ourselves morally incapable of performing the same feat.

The Greek-Turkish reconciliation ushered in by Venizelos and Atatürk, which *The Economist* praised generously, was indeed of historic significance. It demonstrated that the burden of memories of grievance and mistrust could be circumvented if not entirely overcome. Obviously, the circumstances facing Greece and Turkey in the 1980s and 1990s differ markedly from those which the two neighbours faced in the late 1920s. But the potential rewards of a policy of accommodation and pragmatic problem-solving for Greece and Turkey are as high in our day as they were in the past.

For instance, one year after Greece and Turkey came to the brink of war during the March 1987 Aegean crisis, they initiated the Davos process of dialogue and adopted measures designed to prevent future confrontations. The Greek-Turkish detente initiated in early 1988 has already paid modest dividends in terms of lessening tensions and increasing contact between the two sides. More and more Greeks have visited Turkey during the late 1980s, encouraged by Turkey's abolition of visa requirements for Greek citizens and drawn by cheaper Turkish goods. Contacts between Greek and Turkish performers and intellectuals have become commonplace, and businessmen in both countries have been exploring avenues for increasing bilateral trade links. Ozal and Papandreou have even talked about examining Greek and Turkish history curricula in their schools in order to improve the unfavourable image of their respective nations. Since 1988, the range of confidence-building measures both countries have agreed to consider has been impressive, even though further means of building psychological bridges have yet to be considered. For example, student exchanges at all educational levels and the introduction of each other's language in Greek and Turkish universities are among a variety of measures that could contribute to a better mutual understanding.

While it is premature to speculate as to whether or not the 'Davos spirit' will yield a genuine reconciliation, we can be reasonably certain that the process of burying the hatchet will require a long period of time. It goes without saying that Cyprus and the Aegean are central to the future normalization of Greek-Turkish relations; their definitions of the issues and methods of resolving them remain difficult to reconcile. Thus it would be unrealistic to expect a total resolution of major disputes within a few years. Pramature efforts at resolving the major issues could discourage further settlements. Progress on these issues is bound to be incremental until such time as a comprehensive agreement on all outstanding issues becomes conceivable.

Since the 1950s, Cyprus has been the major issue driving a wedge between Greece and Turkey. Needless to say, Cyprus has been much more than a dispute between the two nations. Ankara and Athens have learned during the various phases of the Cyprus dispute, particularly after the advent of independence, that they could on occasion be swung by their tails by their respective communities. Both governments have been further restrained by other external actors, principally by the United States which has been a major donor of aid, but also to lesser extents by Britain, the Soviet Union and the United Nations.

It has been appropriate that the Cypriot communities, rather than Greece and Turkey, have been the principal negotiators for a settlement, particularly its internal aspects. Greece and Turkey may have the capacity to make a deal for Cyprus and pressure their respective communities to accept it. However, given the experience of the Zurich-London accords, the durability of any settlement requires that there be no hint of coercion of the Cypriot parties. For that matter, neither Greece nor Turkey should be pressured on the Cyprus issues; the Turkish resistance to the American arms embargo demonstrates the futility of such pressures.

At the same time, these two powers are in a position to encourage, even prod, their compatriots to adopt pragmatic positions that will help to reach a settlement on the island. For instance, Greece and Turkey could help alleviate the overriding security concerns of both Greek and Turkish-Cypriots. The problem has been more acute over a longer period of time for the smaller Turkish community. This has not been adequately appreciated by the Greek-Cypriots and Greece. For that matter, neither have the Turks and Turkish-Cypriots been sensitive enough to the fears Greek-Cypriots have of Turkey since their traumatic experience in 1974.

Ultimately, the best security for both Cypriot communities will emerge from their peaceful co-existence and ability to accommodate each other. Given their recent history, however, the need for external guarantees for the foreseeable future is apparent. Thus the retention of the previous Greek and Turkish guarantees (as advocated by Turkish-Cypriots) is justifiable, including increased troop levels for both Turkey and Greece beyond those allowed by the Treaty of Alliance. In any case, with or without legal sanction, Turkey would feel duty bound to intervene by force in any future contingency if the Turkish community was imperilled. In order to make such arrangements more palatable for the Greek-Cypriots, these troop levels could be subject to review in the future, say every ten years, with the objective of total withdrawal in the long run. In addition, Turkey could alleviate Greek-Cypriot security concerns in the short term by undertaking a substantial reduction of its forces on the island.

In addition to external guarantees, Greece and Turkey could lend their weight to the efforts of the United Nations (and other parties such as the United States and Britain) who have long encouraged the adoption of confidence-building measures on the island. They would be in a particularly credible position to do so if further progress is made with the measures adopted since the Özal-Papandreou meeting in Davos. Among the various steps that could be taken in Cyprus, the most urgent is probably the removal of the Greek-Cypriot economic embargo on the Turkish-Cypriot area. The indefinite maintenance of such sanctions has hurt northern Cyprus, contributed to widening the economic gap between the communities, and increased Turkish-Cypriot feelings of alienation. For their part, Turkish-Cypriot authorities could allay Greek-Cypriot fears regarding the total separation of the north by making it easier for people from both sides to move across the current boundary.

Just as the settlement of the Aegean issues has been rendered all the more difficult because of the Cyprus issue, any progress for a Cyprus settlement is bound to raise expectations and encourage negotiations of the Aegean issues. Here too, one should realistically expect modest confidence-building steps before all of the outstanding issues are resolved. The post-Davos measures such as the decision to install an Athens-Ankara telephone hotline, and avoiding military manouvres during the height of the tourist season are helpful ideas capable of reducing tensions as a prelude to coming to terms with the tougher issues, especially concerning the continental shelf.

Despite repeated crises over Cyprus and the Aegean, Greece and Turkey have avoided a direct military confrontation and, in effect, agreed to maintain the *status quo* for an indefinite period of time. Both states have lived up to the Berne Agreement of 1976, which prohibits any unilateral steps concerning the continental shelf. Given that Greek and Turkish positions on the territorial sea and continental shelf issues are far apart, a good case can be made for continuing to adhere to the *status quo* for the foreseeable future. That means retaining the territorial sea at six miles and limiting any exploration and research on the continental shelf to within the limits of their current (six-mile wide) sovereign waters.

At the same time, Greece and Turkey could avail themselves of various options to increase confidence and trust in the Aegean. Greece could begin a process of de-militarizing the eastern Aegean islands, and in particular, removing those weapons and aircraft that could be used against targets in the Turkish mainland. For its part, Turkey could disband the Fourth Army (popularly known as the Army of the Aegean), which after all is used only for training purposes, and redeploy the landing craft in the Aegean to the Sea of Marmara.

Ultimately, with the development of Greek-Turkish détente, the settlement of the territorial sea and continental shelf issues is possible. Given that an extension of the territorial sea to twelve miles would turn the Aegean into a virtual 'Greek lake' and unduly restrict Turkey, Greece would have to accept the retention of the six-mile territorial sea. In any case, the practice of maintaining six-mile seas for many years has strengthened the case against increasing Greek sovereignty in the Aegean waters.

Whatever formula is agreed upon concerning the apportionment of the continental shelf is bound to confer less to each state than if its individual case was to be fully vindicated. Greece will probably settle for much less than the nearly 97 percent of the shelf it has claimed. Similarly, Turkey will likely settle for less than the half it has claimed. Agreement to an allocation scheme would have to ensure the 'political continuity' of Greece's eastern Aegean islands with the mainland, perhaps by providing a variant of the 'fingers' principle (as shown in Map 5). Moreover, although the idea of a joint exploitation of the continental shelf has been impractical to date, a possible blossoming of Greek-Turkish détente could make that avenue quite feasible in the future.

Both Greece and Turkey will proceed with caution on the questions of sovereign rights in the Aegean and on the Cyprus issue. But on such secondary issues as the status of minorities, they are in a position to advance with greater dispatch at no cost. The Özal Government's encouragement to the Istanbul Greeks who left for Greece to return to Turkey is an encouraging gesture. So is the recent acknowledgement by Greek authorities that all is not well with the conditions of the Turks in Thrace. Improvements in the status of the minorities will reflect favourably the Greek-Turkish relationships.

As Andrew Mango and David Barchard have pointed out, the strategic balance between Turkey and Greece has gradually shifted in Turkey's favour since the days of the Lausanne Treaty.[1] In 1923, Turkey's population was less than 13 million as compared with 7 million for Greece. With a population of 55 million in 1988, Turks outnumber Greeks by more than five to one. Also, by the late 1980s, Turkey's gross national product had increased to twice that of Greece, even though per capita incomes for Greeks are considerably higher. In the future, Turkey is poised to become an important regional power.

"Will Greece work with or against"[2] a Turkey growing stronger with the passage of years? If the experiences of recent years, particularly in Cyprus, is considered, then the answer for Greeks should be emphatically in the affirmative. Whenever a sense of co-operation and compromise has prevailed, as for instance during 1930-1955, Greece and Turkey both were the beneficiaries. There are no abiding reasons why the same pragmatism could not be revived as Turkey gets ready to join Greece as a member of the European Community.

However intractable problems between Greece and Turkey seem to be, and however complex and multi-faceted the issues of dispute, there is no reason to assume that they are forever hostages to their own rivalries. On the contrary, there are sound reasons to believe in eventual means of resolution. It is this potential which which will challenge students of the subject and the parties themselves in the near future.

Notes

1. David Barchard, *Turkey and the West,* London: Routledge & Kegan Paul, 1985, pp. 48-9; Andrew Mango, "Greece and Turkey: Unfriendly Allies," *The World Today,* August/September 1987, p. 147.

2. Mango, "Unfriendly Allies," p. 147.

Appendixes

Appendix 1: The Berne Declaration

On the procedure to be followed for the delimitation of the continental shelf by Greece and Turkey.

(1) Both parties agree that negotiations be sincere, detailed and conducted in good faith with a view to reaching an agreement based on mutual consent regarding the delimitation of the continental shelf.

(2) Both parties agree that these negotiations should, due to their nature, be strictly confidential.

(3) Both parties reserve their respective positions regarding the delimitation of the continental shelf.

(4) Both parties undertake the obligation not to use the details of this agreement and the proposals that each will make during the negotiations in any circumstances outside the context of the negotiations.

(5) Both parties agree no statements or leaks to the press should be made referring to the content of the negotiations unless they commonly agree to do so.

(6) Both parties undertake to abstain from any initiative or act relating to the continental shelf of the Aegean Sea which might prejudice the negotiations.

(7) Both parties undertake, as far as their bilateral relations are concerned, to abstain from any initiative or act which would tend to discredit the other party.

(8) Both parties have agreed to study state practice and international rules on this subject with a view to educing certain principles and practical criteria which could be of use in the delimitation of the continental shelf between the two countries.

(9) A mixed commission will be set up to this end and will be composed of national representatives.

(10) Both parties agree to adopt a gradual approach in the course of the negotiations ahead after consulting each other.

Signed in Berne: 11th November 1976.
Released in Athens and Ankara: 20th November 1976.

Appendix 2

November 1984

AGENDA FOR THE THIRD ROUND OF THE SECRETARY-GENERAL'S PROXIMITY TALKS ON CYPRUS

(preliminary draft for a joint high-level agreement)
Held at United Nations Headquarters,
on   1984

The parties have agreed on the following matters which are to be viewed as an integrated whole:

The Parties:

a) Recommit themselves to the high-level agreements of 1977 and 1979;
b) Indicate their determination to proceed, at the date referred to in paragraph 14 below, to the establishment of a federal republic that will be independent and non-aligned, bi-communal as regards the federal constitutional aspect and bi-zonal as regards the territorial aspect;
c) Reaffirm their acceptance of those introductory constitutional provisions that were agreed upon at the intercommunal talks in 1981-82:
i) The Federal Republic of Cyprus shall have international personality; the federal government shall exercise sovereignty in respect of all the territory.
ii) The people of the Federal Republic shall comprise the Greek Cypriot community and the Turkish Cypriot community. There shall be a single citizenship of the Federal Republic of Cyprus regulated by federal law.

(Reference verbatim to the provisions agreed upon during the course of the intercommunal talks or to be annexed to this document. In both cases wording as reproduced in the revision dated 18.5.82 will be used and checked with both parties.)

1. Powers and functions to be vested in the federal government of the Federal Republic shall comprise:

a) Foreign affairs.
b) Federal financial affairs (including federal budget, taxation, customs and excise duties).
c) Monetary and banking affairs.
d) Federal economic affairs (including trade and tourism).
e) Posts and telecommunications.
f) International transport.
g) Natural resources (including water supply environment).
h) Federal health and veterinary affairs.
i) Standard setting: weights and measures, patents, trademarks, copyrights.
j) Federal judiciary.
k) Appointment of Federal officers.
l) Defence (to be discussed in connection with international guarantees); security (as it pertains to federal responsibility).

Additional powers and functions may be vested in the federal government by common agreement of both sides. Federal legislation may be executed either by authorities of the federal government or by way of coordination between the competent authorities of the federal government and the two (provinces or federated states).

2. The legislature of the federal republic is to be composed of two chambers, the lower chamber with a 70-30 representation and the upper chamber with a 50-50 representation. Federal legislation will be enacted with regard to the matters of federal competence referred to in 1 above. Appropriate constitutional safeguards will be incorporated in the federal constitution, including deadlock-resolving machinery and special provisions to facilitate action on matters necessary for the continued functioning of the federal government (for example, on budgetary questions), as follows:

_____

_____

_____

3. The president and the vice-president will symbolize the unity of the country and the equal political status of the two communities. In addition, the executive will reflect the functional requirements of an effective federal government. To this end, the following structure will be adopted:

_____

4. A tripartite body with one non-Cypriot member having a vote will have the responsibility of ruling on disputes relating to the distribution of powers

and functions between the federation and the (provinces or federated states) and on such other matters as may be assigned to it by the parties in accordance with the constitution.

5. As regards the freedom of movement, freedom of settlement and right to property, a working group will be established to discuss the exercise of these rights, including time frames, practical regulations and possible compensation arrangements, taking into account guideline 3 of the 1977 agreement.

6. Territorial adjustments in addition to the areas already referred to in the 5 August 1981 Turkish Cypriot proposals will be agreed upon at the high-level meeting, bearing in mind the criteria contained in the 1977 high-level agreement. The size of that adjustment will be expressed in the high-level agreement in a measurable form and will also be reflected in the number of Greek Cypriot displaced persons to be resettled. Those adjustments will correspond to _____

_____
_____
_____
_____

7. A timetable for the withdrawal of non-Cypriot military troops and elements, as well as adequate guarantees, will be agreed upon prior to the establishment of the transitional federal government. In the meantime, military deconfrontation measures will be pursued by both sides, using the good offices and assistance of UNFICYP.

8. A fund for Development of the Turkish Cypriot (province or federated state) shall be established with a view to achieving an economic equilibrium between the two (provinces or federated states). A fund will also be established to facilitate the resettlement of the Greek Cypriot displaced persons and for the Turkish Cypriot displaced persons as a consequence of the implementation of paragraph 6. The Federal Government shall contribute to these funds. Foreign governments and international organizations shall be invited to contribute to the funds.

9. The Varosha area and the six additional areas delineated in the Turkish Cypriot map of 5 August 1981 will be placed under United Nations interim administration by..........as part of the UNFICYP buffer zone, for resettlement.

10. Moratorium on actions tending to prejudice the process outlined in this agreement, both on the international scene and internally.

11. The Nicosia international airport to be reopened under interim United Nations administration with free access from both sides. United Nations arrangements to that effect will be concluded no later than_____months after the day of the high-level meeting.

12. Adequate machinery for the handling of allegations of non-implementation of confidence-building measures will be agreed upon.

13. Working Group(s) may be set up in light of the political decisions agreed upon at the high-level meeting to elaborate the details of the agreements involved.

14. The required working groups having completed their work, the parties agree that the transitional federal government of the Federal Republic of Cyprus will be set up on ....

ADDITIONAL POINTS

1. Executive (no rotation)
   A. Presidential system   1960 Constitution + weighted voting
       — VP veto   i.e. simple majority but with one
       Cabinet .... 7/3   Turkish Cypriot voting in favour.
   B. Safeguards/deadlock-resolving machinery:
       i) Constitutional court - referenda
       ii) President and vice president have right to send back for reconsideration both laws and cabinet decisions.

2. Legislative:
   A. Two chambers:
   Lower house   70/30   <u>On major matters, as for instance,</u>
   Upper house   50/50   <u>ten of paragraph 1 list)</u>
                   1   voting by separate majorities in both houses
                        On other matters:
                        Simple majority in both houses, but at
                        least 30% of Turkish Cypriots in upper house.

   B. Safeguards/deadlock-resolving machinery:
       i) Conciliation committee (3 Greek Cypriots and 2 Turkish Cypriots-weighted voting on Turkish Cypriot)

    ii) Constitutional court
    iii) Referenda

3. Three freedoms as per paragraph 5 without reference to articles 13 and 21.

4. Territory
    29+ (Twenty-nine plus).

5. Residual powers with provinces.

6. Both sides to <u>suggest special status area</u> adjacent to each other for the purpose of enhancing trust between sides (respective civilian jurisdiction to remain).

Selected Bibliography

Books and Dissertations

Adams, T.W. and Alvin J. Cottrell. *Cyprus Between East and West*. Baltimore: Johns Hopkins Press, 1968.

Adams, T. W. *Akel: The Communist Party of Cyprus*. Stanford: Hoover Institution Press, 1971.

Ahmad, Feroz. *The Turkish Experiment in Democracy, 1950-1975*. Boulder: Westview Press, 1977.

Alastos, Doros. *Cyprus in History: A Survey of 5,000 Years*. London: Zeno Publishers, 1955.

Alasya, Halil. *Kıbrıs ve Türkler (Cyprus and the Turks)*. Ankara: Ayyıldız, 1964.

Alexandris, Alexis. *The Greek Minority of Istanbul and Greek-Turkish Relations*. Athens: Center for Asia Minor Studies, 1983.

Alford, Jonathan (ed.). *Greece and Turkey: Adversity in Alliance*. New York: St. Martin's, 1984.

American Foreign Policy Institute. *NATO, Turkey and United States Interests*. Washington, D.C., 1978.

Andreades, K. G. *The Moslem Minority in Western Thrace*. Salonika: Institute for Balkan Studies, 1956.

Armaoglu, Fahir. *Kıbrıs Meselesi, 1954-59: Türk Hükümeti ve Kamu Oyunun Davranısları (The Reaction of the Turkish Government and Public Opinion in the Cyprus Dispute)*. Ankara: Sevinç Matbaası, 1963.

Arnold Percy. *Cyprus Challenge*. London: Hogarth Press, 1956.

Attalides, Michael. *Cyprus: Nationalism and International Politics*. New York: St. Martins, 1979.

Averoff-Tossizza, Evangelos. *Lost Opportunities: The Cyprus Question, 1950-1963*. New York: Aristide D. Caratzas, 1986.

Balfour, Patrick. *The Orphaned Realm*. London: Percival Marshall, 1951.

Ball, George. *The Past Has Another Pattern*. New York: W. W. Norton & Co., 1982.

Barchard, David. *Turkey and the West*. London: Routledge & Kegan Paul, 1985.

Barham, Richard, W. *Enosis: From Ethnic Communalism to Greek Nationalism in Cyprus, 1878-1955*. Ph.D. dissertation, Columbia University, 1982.

Birand, Mehmet Ali. *30 Sıcak Gün (30 Hot Days: An Account of Turkey's Intervention in Cyprus in 1974)*. Istanbul: Milliyet Publications, 1975.

_____. *Diyet: Turkiye ve Kıbrıs Üzerine Pazarlıklar, 1974-1979 (Bargaining Over Turkey and Cyprus)*. Istanbul: Milliyet Publications, 1979.

Bitsios, Dimitri. *Cyprus: The Vulnerable Republic*. Salonika: The Institute of Balkan Studies, 1975.

Borowiec, Andrew. *The Mediterranean Feud*. New York: Praeger, 1983.

Bowett, Derek W. *The Legal Regime of Islands in International Law*. New York: Oceana Publications Inc., 1978.

Brownlie, Ian. *Basic Documents in International Law*. Oxford: Oxford University Press, 1972.

Callaghan, James. *Time and Chance*. London: Collins, 1987.

Campbell, John and Philip Sherrard. *Modern Greece*. London: Ernest Benn, 1968.

Carey, J. P. C. and A. G. Carey. *The Web of Modern Greek Politics*. London and New York: Columbia University Press, 1968.

Çelik, Edip. *Türkiyenin Dıs Politika Tarihi (A History of Turkish Foreign Policy)*. Istanbul: Gerçek Yayınevi, 1969.

Centre for International Development and Conflict Management. *U.S. Security Concerns in the North-Eastern Mediterranean*. University of Maryland, 1987.

Clerides, Glafcos. *My Deposition*. Vol. 1. Nicosia: Alithia Publishing, 1979.

Clogg, Richard (ed.). *Greece in the 1980s*. London: Macmillan, 1983.

_____. *A Short History of Modern Greece*. Cambridge: Cambridge University Press, 1986.

Clogg, Richard and George Yannopoulos (eds.). *Greece Under Military Rule*. London: Secker & Warburg, 1972.

Couloumbis, Theodore A. *The U.S. and Greece and Turkey: The Troubled Triangle*. New York: Praeger, 1983.

Couloumbis, Theodore A., J. A. Petropoulos and H. J. Psomiades (eds.). *Foreign Interference in Greek Politics: An Historical Perspective*. New York: Pella Publishing Co., 1976.

Crawshaw, Nancy. *The Cyprus Revolt: An Account of the Struggle for Union with Greece*. London: George Allen & Unwin, 1978.

Danopoulos, Constantine P. *Warriors and Politicians in Modern Greece*. Chapel Hill: Documentary Publications, 1984.

De Jong, F. *Names, Religious Denomination and Ethnicity of Settlements in Western Thrace*. Leiden: E. J. Brill, 1980.

Denktash, Rauf R. *12' ye Bes Kala Kıbrıs (Moment of Decision in Cyprus)*. Ankara, 1966.

_____. *The Cyprus Triangle*. London: George Allen & Unwin, 1982.

Dicks, Brian. *Greece*. London: David & Charles, 1980.

Dodd, C. H. *Politics and Government in Turkey*. Berkeley: University of California Press, 1969.

Doumas, Christos L. *The Problem of Cyprus*. Ph.D. dissertation, University of California (Los Angeles), 1963.

Durrell, Lawrence. *Bitter Lemons*. New York: Dutton, 1957.

Eden, Anthony. *Full Circle*. Boston: Houghton Mifflin Co., 1960.

Ehrlich, Thomas. *International Crises and the Rule of Law: Cyprus 1958-67*. Oxford: Oxford University Press, 1974.

Erim, Nihat. *Bildigim ve Gördügüm Ölçüler Içinde Kıbrıs (The Cyprus Issue As I Have Known It)*. Ankara: Ajans-Turk Matbaacılık Sanayii, 1976.

Ertekün, Necati M. *The Cyprus Dispute and the Birth of the Turkish Republic of Northern Cyprus*. London: K. Rustem, 1981.

Fallaci, Oriana. *Interview With History*. London: Michael Joseph, 1974.

Foley, Charles (ed.). *The Memoirs of General Grivas*. New York: Frederick A. Praeger, 1964.

Foley, Charles and W.I. Scobie. *The Struggle for Cyprus*. Stanford: Hoover Institution Press, 1975.

Foot, Hugh. *A Start in Freedom*. New York: Harper & Row, 1964.

Gönlübol, Mehmet, Cem Sar et al. *Olaylarla Turk Dış Politikası (A Survey of Turkish Foreign Policy)*. Ankara: Turkish Foreign Ministry Press, 1968.

Günver, Semih. *Fatin Rüstü Zorlu' nun Öyküsü (The Story of Fatin Rüstü)*. Ankara: Bilgi Yayınevi, 1985.

Harbottle, Michael. *The Impartial Soldier*. London: Oxford University Press, 1970.

Harris, George S. *Troubled Alliance: Turkish-American Relations in Historical Perpective, 1945-1971*. AEI Hoover Policy Studies, 1972.

_____. *Turkey: Coping With Crisis*. Boulder: Westview Press, 1985.

Hill, George (Sir). *A History of Cyprus*. 4 Vols. Cambridge: Cambridge University Press, 1952.

Hitchens, Christopher. *Cyprus*. London: Quartet Books, 1984.

Holden, David. *Greece Without Columns: The Making of the Modern Greeks*. New York: J. B. Lippincott Co., 1982.

Hotham, David. *The Turks*. London: John Murray, 1972.

Ierodiakonou, Leontios. *The Cyprus Question*. Stockholm: Almqvist & Wiskell, 1971.

Institute for the Study of Turkish Culture. Proceedings of the First International Congress of Cypriot Studies. Ankara: Ayyıldız Matbaası, 1971.

Israel, Fred (ed.). *Major Peace Treaties of Modern History, 1648-1967*. Vol. IV, New York: Chelsea House, 1967.

Jelavich, Barbara. *History of the Balkans* (Vol. 2). Cambridge: Cambridge University Press, 1983.

Karpat, Kemal (ed.). *Turkey' s Foreign Policy in Transition, 1950-1975*. Leiden: E. J. Brill, 1975.

Kinross, Lord. *Atatürk: The Rebirth of a Nation*. London: Weidenfeld and Nicolson, 1964.

_____. *The Ottoman Centuries*. London: Jonathan Cape, 1977.

Kitsikis, Dimitri. *Yunan Propagandası (Greek Propaganda)*. Istanbul: Kaynak Kitaplar, 1974.

_____. *Sugkritiki Istoria Ellados Kai Turkias ston 20 Aiona (A Comparative History of Greece and Turkey in the 20th Century)*. Athens: Estia Publishers, 1978.

Koslin, Adamantia P. *The Megali Idea: A Study of Greek Nationalism*. Ph.D. dissertation, The Johns Hopkins University, 1958.

Koumoulides, J.T.A. *Cyprus and the Greek War of Independence, 1821-1829*. London: Zeno Publishers, 1974.

_____. (ed.). *Greece and Cyprus in History*. Amsterdam: Adolf M. Hakkert Publishers, 1985.

_____. (ed.). *Cyprus in Transition, 1960-1985*. London: Trigraph, 1986.

Kousoulas, D.G. *Power and Influence: An Introduction to International Relations*. Monterey: Brooks/Cole Publishing Co., 1985.

Kyle, Keith. *Cyprus*. London: Minority Rights Group Report No. 30, 1984.

Kyriakides, Stanley. *Cyprus: Constitutionalism and Crisis Government*. Philadelphia: University of Pennsylvania Press, 1968.

Kyrris, Costas D. *History of Cyprus*. Nicosia: Nicocles Publishing, 1985.

Lanitis, Nicos. *Our Destiny*. Nicosia: 1963.

Laponce, J. A. *The Protection of Minorities*. Berkeley and Los Angeles: University of California Press, 1960.

Lewis, Bernard. *The Emergence of Modern Turkey*. London: Oxford University Press, 1961.

Lewis, Geoffrey L. *Turkey*. London: Ernest Benn, 1965.

Lijphart, Arend. T*he Politics of Accommodation*. Berkeley and Los Angeles: University of California Press, 1968.

Loizos, Peter. *The Heart Grown Bitter: A Chronicle of Cypriot War Refugees*. Cambridge: Cambridge University Press.

Luke, Harry. *Cyprus Under the Turks, 1571-1878*. London: Oxford University Press, 1921.

_____. *Cyprus: A Portrait and An Appreciation*. London: George G. Harrap & Co. Ltd., 1957.

MacHenry, J.A., Jr. *The Uneasy Partnership on Cyprus, 1919-1939: The Political and Diplomatic Interaction Between Great Britain, Turkey, and the Turkish-Cypriot Community*. Ph.D. dissertation, University of Kansas, 1981.

Macmillan, Harold. *Tides of Fortune, 1945-1955*. London: Macmillan, 1969.

_____. *Riding the Storm, 1956-1959*. London: Macmillan, 1969.

Mango, Andrew. *Turkey*. London: Thames and Hudson, 1968.

_____. *Turkey: A Delicately Poised Ally*. Washington Paper Series, No. 28, London: Sage Publications, 1975.

Markides, Kyriacos. *The Rise and Fall of the Cyprus Republic*. New Haven: Yale University Press, 1977.

Mayes, Stanley. *Makarios: A Biography*. London: Putnam Press, 1981.

McCarthy, Justin. *Muslims and Minorities: The Population of Ottoman Anatolia and the End of Empire*. New York and London: New York University Press, 1983.

McDonald, Robert. *Cyprus*. London: International Institute of Strategic Studies, Adelphi Paper No. 234, 1988/89.

Necatigil, Zaim M. *Our Republic in Perspective*. Nicosia: Tezel Printing, 1985.

Newman, Philip. *A Short History of Cyprus*. London: Robert Scott, 1953.

Oberling, Pierre. *The Road to Bellapais: The Turkish Cypriot Exodus to Northern Cyprus*. Boulder: Social Science Monographs distributed by Columbia University Press, 1982.

Oran, Baskın. *Turk Yunan Iliskilerinde Batı Trakya Sorunu (The Western Thrace Question in Greek-Turkish Relations)*. Ankara: Mülkiyeliler Birligi Vakfi Yayınları, 1986.

Orr, C. W. J. *Cyprus Under British Rule*. London: Robert Scott, 1918.

Panteli, Stavros. *A New History of Cyprus: From the Earliest Times to the Present Day*. London: East-West Publications, 1984.

Papandreou, Andreas G. *Democracy at Gunpoint: The Greek Front*. New York: Garden City, 1970.

Patrick, Richard A. *Political Geography and the Cyprus Conflict, 1963-1971*.

Waterloo: Department of Geography Publications Series, No. 4, 1976.

Pazarcı, Hüseyin. *Dogu Ege Adalarinin Askerden Arındırılmış Statüsü (The De-militarized Status of the Eastern Aegean Islands)*. Ankara: Publications of the Political Science Faculty, 1986.

Pentzopoulos, Dimitri. *The Balkan Exchange of Minorities and Its Impact Upon Greece*. Paris, 1962.

Polyviou, Polyvios G. *Cyprus: Conflict and Negotiation, 1960-1980*. London: Duckworth, 1980.

Prescott, J.R.V. *The Maritime Political Boundaries of the World*. London: Methuen, 1985.

Psomiades, Harry J. *The Eastern Question: The Last Phase — A Study in Greek-Turkish Diplomacy*. Salonika: Institute for Balkan Studies, 1968.

Purcell, H. D. *Cyprus*. London: Ernest Benn, 1969.

Reddaway, John. *Burdened with Cyprus*. London: Weidenfeld & Nicholson, 1986.

Royal Institute of International Affairs. *Cyprus: Background to Enosis*. London: Chatham House, 1958.

_____. *Cyprus: The Dispute and the Settlement*. London: Chatham House, 1959.

Rustow, Dankwart A. *Turkey: America's Forgotten Ally*. New York: Council on Foreign Relations, 1987.

Salih, H. Ibrahim. *Cyprus: An Analysis of Political Discord*. New York: Theo Gaus Sons, 1968.

_____. *Cyprus: The Impact of Diverse Nationalism on a State*. Alabama: The University of Alabama Press, 1978.

Sezer, Duygu B. *Turkey's Security Policies*. London: International Institute for Strategic Studies, Adelphi Paper No. 164, 1981.

Shaw, Stanford. *History of the Ottoman Empire and Modern Turkey*, Vol. 1. Cambridge: Cambridge University Press, 1976.

Shaw, Stanford and Ezel Kural Shaw. *History of the Ottoman Empire and Modern Turkey* Vol. II. New York: Cambridge University Press, 1977.

Simsir, Bilal. *Aegean Question (1912-1913)*, Vol. I. Ankara: Publications of the Turkish Historical Society, 1976.

_____. *Aegean Question (1913-1914)*, Vol. 2. Ankara: Publications of the Turkish Historical Society, 1982.

Smith, Michael Llewelyn. *Ionian Vision: Greece in Asia Minor, 1919-1922*. London: Allen Lane, 1973.

Spain, James W. *American Diplomacy in Turkey*. New York: Praeger, 1984.

Stavrianos, L. S. *The Balkans Since 1453*. New York: Rinehart, 1958.

Stavrinides, Zenon. *The Cyprus Conflict: National Identity and Statehood*. Nicosia: Stavrinides Press, 1976.

Stegenga, James A. *The United Nations Force in Cyprus*. Columbus: Ohio State University Press, 1968.

Stephens, Robert H. *Cyprus: A Place of Arms*. London: Pall Mall Press, 1966.

Stern, Laurence. *The Wrong Horse: The Politics of Intervention and the Failure of American Diplomacy*. New York: Times Books, 1977.

Tamkoç, Metin. *The Turkish-Cypriot State: The Embodiment of the Right of Self-Determination*. London: K. Rustem, 1988.

Toker, Metin. *Ismet Pasayla 10 Yıl, 1961-1964 (10 Years with Ismet Inönü)*.

Istanbul: Burçak Yayınları, 1969.

Tsoucalas, Constantine. *The Greek Tragedy.* London: Penguin, 1969.

Urquhart, Brian. *A Life in Peace and War.* London: Weidenfeld & Nicholson, 1987.

Vali, Ferenc A. *Bridge Across the Bosporus: The Foreign Policy of Turkey.* Baltimore: The Johns Hopkins Press, 1971.

Vanezis, P. N. *Makarios: Pragmatism Versus Idealism.* London: Abelard-Schuman, 1974.

Veremis, Thanos. *Greek Security: Issues and Politics.* London: International Institute of Strategic Studies, Adelphi Paper No. 179, 1982.

Volkan, Vamık D. *Cyprus: War and Adaptation: A Psychoanalytic History of Two Ethnic Groups in Conflict.* Charlottesville: University Press of Virginia, 1979.

Volkan, Vamık D. and Norman D. Itzkowitz. *The Immortal Atatürk.* Chicago: The University of Chicago Press, 1984.

Waldheim, Kurt. *In the Eye of the Storm.* London: Weidenfeld & Nicholson, 1985.

Watanabe, Paul. *Ethnic Groups, Congress, and American Foreign Policy: The Politics of the Turkish Arms Embargo,* Westport and London: Greenwood Press, 1984.

Weiker, Walter. *The Turkish Revolution, 1960-1961.* Washington, D.C.: The Brookings Institution, 1963.

Wiener, Sharon A. *Turkish Foreign Policy Decision Making on the Cyprus Issue.* Ph.D. dissertation, Duke University, 1980.

Wilson, Andrew. *The Aegean Dispute.* London: International Institute of Strategic Studies, Adelphi Paper No. 155, 1980.

Windsor, Philip. *NATO and the Cyprus Crisis.* London: International Institute of Strategic Studies, Adelphi Paper No. 14, 1964.

Woodhouse, C. M. *Modern Greece: A Short History.* London and Boston: Faber and Faber, 1968.

_____. *Karamanlis: The Restorer of Greek Democracy.* Oxford: The University Press, 1982.

_____. *The Rise and Fall of the Greek Colonels.* New York: Franklin Watts, 1985.

Worsley, Peter and Paschalis Kitromilides (eds.). *Small States in the Modern World: The Conditions of Survival.* Nicosia: Zavallis Press, 1979.

Wosgian, Daniel S. *Turks and British Rule in Cyprus.* Ph.D. dissertation, Columbia University, 1963.

Xydis, Stephen. *Cyprus: Conflict and Conciliation, 1954-1958.* Columbus: Ohio State University Press, 1967.

Young, Kenneth. *The Greek Passion: A Study in People and Politics.* London: J.M. Dent & Sons Ltd., 1969.

Articles, Pamphlets, and Unpublished Papers

Ahmad, Feroz. "Domestic Factors in Greek-Turkish Relations: The View from Ankara," paper presented at the Lehrman Institute Conference on Greek-Turkish relations, May 15, 1986.

Alexandris, Alexis. "Turkish Policy Towards Greece During the Second World War and its Impact on Greek-Turkish Détente," *Balkan Studies,* Vol. 23, No. 1, 1982.

_____. "The Minority Question," paper presented at the Lehrman Institute Conference on Greek-Turkish relations, May 15, 1986.

Angelopoulos, Ath. "Population Distribution of Greece Today According to Language, National Consciousness, and Religion," *Balkan Studies*, Vol. 20, No. 1, 1979.

Bahcheli, Tozun. "Turkey and the E.C.: The Strains of Association," *Journal of European Integration*, Vol. 3, No. 2, 1980.

_____. "The Muslim-Turkish Community in Greece: Problems and Prospects," *Journal: Institute of Muslim Minority Affairs*, Vol. 8, No. 1, January 1987.

Bayulken, U. Haluk. "Turkish Minorities in Greece," *Turkish Yearbook of International Relations*, No. 4, 1965.

Beckingham, C. F. "The Cypriot Turks," *Royal Central Asian Journal*, Vol. XLIII, Part II, April 1956.

_____. "Islam and Turkish Nationalism in Cyprus," *Die Welt des Islam*, Vols. No. 1-2, 1957.

Blake, Gerald. "Marine Policy Issues for Turkey," *Marine Policy Reports*, Vol. 7, No. 4, February 1985.

Brands, H.W., Jr. "America Enters the Cyprus Tangle, 1964," *Middle Eastern Studies*, Vol. 23, No. 3, July 1987.

Bruce, Leigh H. "Cyprus: A Last Chance," *Foreign Policy*, No. 58, Spring 1985.

Camp, Glen D. "Greek-Turkish Conflict over Cyprus," *Political Science Quarterly*, Vol. 95, No. 1, 1980.

Cassia, Paul Sant. "Religion, Politics and Ethnicity in Cyprus during the Turkocratia (1571-1878)," *Archives: European Journal of Sociology*, Vol. XXVII, No. 1, 1986.

Charney, Jonathan. "Ocean Boundaries in the Aegean Sea," paper delivered at the symposium on Aegean issues in Çesme, Turkey, October 14, 1987.

Connor, Walker. "Self-determination — the New Phase," *World Politics*, Vol. XX, No. 1, October 1967.

Coufoudakis, Van. "Greek-Turkish Relations," *International Security*, Vol. 9, No. 4, 1985.

Daes, E.I.A. "The Greek Orthodox Minority in Turkey," in Georgia Ashworth (ed.), *World Minorities*, Vol. 2. Sunbury, U.K.: Quatarmaine House Ltd., 1980.

De Jong, F. "The Muslim Minority in Western Thrace," in Georgia Ashworth (ed.), *World Minorities*, Vol. 3. Sunbury, U.K.: Quatarmaine House Ltd., 1980.

Dimitras, Panayote. "Greece: A New Danger," *Foreign Policy*, No. 58, Spring 1985.

"Document: Correspondence Between President Johnson and Prime Minister Inönü, June 1964, as Released by the White House, January 15, 1966," *The Middle East Journal*, Vol. XX, No. 3, Summer 1966.

Doob, Leonard. "Cypriot Patriotism and Nationalism," *Journal of Conflict Resolution*, Vol. 30, No. 2, 1986.

"Enosis and its Background: Race and Religion in Cyprus," *Round Table*, Vol. 47, No. 186, March, 1957.

Ergin, Feridun. "The History of Cyprus and the Turks on the Island," *Turkish Economic Review*, Vol. IV, No. 10, January 1964.

Evriviades, Marios L. "The Problem of Cyprus," *Current History*, January 1976.

Georghallides, G. "Turkish and British Reactions to the Emigration of the Cypriot

Turks to Anatolia, 1924-7," *Balkan Studies,* Vol. 18, No. 1, 1977.

Groom, A.J.R. "Cyprus: Light at the End of the Tunnel ?" *Millennium: Journal of International Studies,* Vol. 9, No. 3, Winter 1980-81.

_____. "Cyprus: Back in the Doldrums," *The Round Table,* Vol. 300, October 1986.

Gross, Leo. "The Dispute Between Greece and Turkey Concerning the Continental Shelf in the Aegean," *American Journal of International Law,* Vol. 71, No. 1, October 1977.

Gurkan, Ihsan. "Realities and Dreams in Greek-Turkish Relations: A Turkish Perspective," *Dıs Politika (Foreign Policy),* Vol. X, Nos. 1 & 2.

Haass, Richard N. "Managing NATO's Weakest Flank — The United States, Greece, and Turkey," *Orbis,* Vol. 30, No. 3, 1986.

_____. "Cyprus: Moving Beyond Solution?" *The Washington Quarterly,* Spring 1987.

Henze, Paul. "Turkey, the Alliance and the Middle East: Problems and Opportunities in Historical Perspective," paper presented at the Wilson Center on January 19, 1982.

Hodge, Barbara and C. L. Lewis. *Cyprus School History Textbooks.* London: Education Advisory Committee of the Parliamentary Group for World Government, n.d.

Hughes, James. "Cypriot Labyrinth," *New Left Review,* No. 29, January-February 1965.

Kitromilides, Paschalis. "From Co-Existence to Confrontation: The Dynamics of Ethnic Conflict in Cyprus," chapter in Michael Attalides (ed.), *Cyprus Reviewed.* Nicosia: Zavallis Press,1977.

Kohlhase, Norbert. "The Greco-Turkish Conflict from a Community Perspective," *The World Today,* April 1981.

Kuniholm, Bruce R. "Rhetoric and Reality in the Aegean: U.S. Policy Options Toward Greece and Turkey," *SAIS Review,* Vol. 6, No. 1, 1986.

Kwiatkowska, Barbara. "Maritime Boundary Delimitation Between Opposite and Adjacent States in the New Law of the Sea: Some Implications for the Aegean," paper delivered at the symposium on Aegean issues in Çesme, Turkey, October 15, 1987.

Loizos, Peter. "Cyprus: Exclusion and the Ethnic Factor," *New Society,* December 2, 1971.

_____. "An Alternative Analysis," *Cyprus.* London: Minority Rights Group Report No. 30, 1976.

Mackenzie, Kenneth. *Greece and Turkey: Disarray on NATO's Southern Flank.* London: The Institute for the Study of Conflict, Study No. 154, 1983.

_____. *Turkey in Transition: The West's Neglected Ally,* Institute for European Defence and Strategic Studies, 1984.

Mango, Andrew. "Remembering the Minorities," *Middle Eastern Studies,* Vol. 21, No. 4, 1985.

_____. "Greece and Turkey: Unfriendly Allies," *World Today,* August/September 1987.

Marsh, Joel E. "Turkey and UNCLOS III: Reflections on the Aegean," paper presented at the symposium on Aegean issues in Çesme, Turkey on October 15, 1987.

McDonald, Robert. "Cyprus: The Gulf Widens," *The World Today*, November 1986.

Modiano, Mario. "Domestic Factors That Influence Greek-Turkish Relations: The View from Athens," paper presented at the Lehrman Institute Conference on Greek-Turkish relations, May 17, 1986.

Nikolayev, G. "Soviet-Turkish Relations," *International Affairs* (Moscow), November 1968.

"Notes: Jurisdiction — Limits of Consent — The Aegean Continental Shelf Case," *Harvard International Law Journal*, Vol. 18, No. 3, Summer 1977.

Oran, Baskin. "The Inhanli Land Dispute and the Status of the Turks in Western Thrace," *Journal: Institute of Muslim Minority Affairs*, Vol. 5, No. 2, 1984.

Pipinelis, Panayotis. "The Greco-Turkish Feud Revived," *Foreign Affairs*, Vol. 37, No. 2, January 1959.

Popper, David. "Cyprus in Greek-Turkish Relations," paper presented at the Lehrman Institute Conference on Greek-Turkish relations, May 16, 1986.

Samyanov, N. "Cyprus Yesterday and Today," *International Affairs* (Moscow), March 1969.

Sezer, Duygu B. "A Turkish Perspective on the Greek and Turkish Minorities," paper presented at the Lehrman Institute Conference on Greek-Turkish relations, May 15, 1986.

Sulzberger, C. L. "Greece Under the Colonels," *Foreign Affairs*, Vol. 48, No. 2 January 1970.

Tachau, F. "Face of Turkish Nationalism as Reflected in the Cyprus Dispute," *Middle East Journal*, Vol. 13 , Summer 1959.

Tsoukalis, Loukas. "Greece in Europe: the Tenth Member," *The World Today*, April, 1981.

Ulman, Haluk. "Turk Dıs Politikasına Yön Veren Etkenler, 1923-1968," (Influences on Turkish Foreign Policy). *Styasal Bilgiler Fakultesi Dergisi*, Vol. XXIII, No. 3, 1968.

Van Dyke, J.M. "The Role of Islands in Delimiting Maritime Zones: The Boundary Between Turkey and Greece," paper presented at the symposium on Aegean issues in Çesme, Turkey, October 15, 1987.

Official, Parliamentary, and Congressional Publications

Association of Journalists. *The Aegean Realities*. Istanbul, n.d.

The Journalists Union of Athens Daily Newspapers. *Threat in the Aegean*. Athens: n.d.

Laipson, Ellen B. *U.S. Interests in the Eastern Mediterranean: Turkey, Greece and Cyprus*. Washington: Congressional Research Service, The Library of Congress, Report No. 83-73, April 19, 1983.

———. *Cyprus: Turkish Cypriot "Statehood" and Prospects for Settlement*. Washington: Congressional Research Service, The Library of Congress, February 7, 1985.

———. *The Seven-Ten Ratio in Military Aid to Greece and Turkey: A Congressional Tradition*, Washington: Congressional Research Service, The Library of

Congress, Report No. 85-79, April 10, 1985.

_____. *Greek-Turkish Relations: Beginning of a New Era?* Washington: Congressional Research Service, The Library of Congress, Report No. 88-724 F, December 1, 1988.

Ministry of Foreign Affairs. *Turkish Views on the Demilitarized Status of Lemnos and the Eastern Aegean Islands.* Istanbul, n.d.

Turkish Republic of Northern Cyprus. *Economic and Social Developments in the Turkish Republic of Northern Cyprus.* Nicosia: January 1987.

United Kingdom, *Cyprus.* London: HMSO, Cmnd. 1093, 1960.

United Kingdom (House of Commons). *Report from the Select Committee on Cyprus Session 1975-1976,* London:HMSO, 1976.

_____. *Foreign Affairs Committee Report on Cyprus.* London: HMSO, May 1987.

United Nations. *United Nations Convention on the Law of the Sea.* U.N. Document A/CONT. 62/122, October 7, 1982.

United States Senate, Committee on Foreign Relations. *Greece and Cyprus, 1975.* Washington: U.S. Government Printing Office, 1975.

Index